SOUL
WITHOUT
SHAME

SOUL
WITHOUT
SHAME

*A Guide to Liberating Yourself
from the Judge Within*

BYRON BROWN

SHAMBHALA
Boston & London
1999

In loving memory of my father-in-law,
Monroe (Jim) Friedman

Shambhala Publications, Inc.
Horticultural Hall
300 Massachusetts Avenue
Boston, Massachusetts 02115
www.shambhala.com
© 1999 by Byron Brown

The Diamond Approach is a registered service mark of the Ridhwan Foundation.

Questions or comments about *Soul without Shame* may be e-mailed to:
bybrown@earthlink.net

9 8 7 6 5

Printed in the United States of America
⊗ This edition is printed on acid-free paper that meets the American National Standards Institute Z39.48 Standard.

Distributed in the United States by Random House, Inc.,
and in Canada by Random House of Canada Ltd

Library of Congress Cataloging-in-Publication Data

Brown, Byron, 1952–
Soul without shame: a guide to liberating yourself from the judge within/Byron Brown.—1st ed.
p.   cm.
ISBN 1-57062-383-X (pbk.: alk. paper)
1. Criticism, Personal.   2. Self-acceptance.   3. Happiness.
I. Title.
BF637.C74B76   1999   98-23402
158.1—dc21   CIP

The problem is not that we want to be happy, but that we are going about it in the wrong way. When we really see that we are going about it in the wrong way, we quit. And then life can unfold on its own. We cannot make it unfold. We can quit our rejection, our judgment, our intolerance, but we will quit these patterns only when we completely and totally see what they are doing — that they are hurting us.

—A. H. Almaas,
Diamond Heart,
Book 2, *The Freedom to Be*

CONTENTS

Contents

FOREWORD

WE ALL WANT TO be free and happy. Many of us believe that we can attain these qualities through external success, and so we tend to see our obstacles as out there in the world, in people and situations. When we recognize that the promise of fulfillment and what stands in its way are both within us, we begin the inner journey. It is a journey into our own consciousness and experience, a path of discovery and realization of the inner riches of human potentiality. Even though it is a thrilling adventure, the inner journey, as with any real adventure, is not an easy one, for it is full of challenges and difficulties, obstacles and barriers.

The inner obstacles have been known and discussed for thousands of years by many of the wisdom teachings and teachers. However, some of these primary obstacles could not be understood in a precise and detailed manner until the development of modern depth psychology. Now with this understanding the inner journey is assisted in ways not possible in previous times. One of these obstacles to inner work and spiritual realization is the painful and difficult one of the inner critic, the coercive agency within us that criticizes, judges, compares, condemns, blames, and attacks us and others mercilessly and constantly.

Depth psychology has demonstrated that we always develop a part of our selves to take the role of inner conscience, traditionally referred to as the superego. But this ego structure of conscience is built mostly through identification with the judging, critical, blaming, and punishing attitudes in the environment we grow up in. It becomes a harsh judge and a cruel source of punishment, instead of being the light of true conscience. It tends to develop into a rigid part of our mind that embodies inflexible rules and commandments, impermeable to understanding and deaf to reality. The superego becomes one of the main sources of inner suffering, through low self-esteem, guilt, shame, devaluation, and self-recrimination. It acts whenever it recognizes in our experience of ourselves, or in the perception of others, something of which it does not approve. Besides the pervasive suffering it causes in our experience, the rigidity and judgment of the inner critic make it difficult for us to go deeply into ourselves. This is because we are attacked by it every time we uncover something of which it disapproves. So in the inner journey, we either unnecessarily suffer, or to avoid this suffering we veer away from parts of our own experience. In both cases, our inner work becomes difficult and limited, and frequently comes to a halt.

Because of the greater understanding of the genesis and structure of the inner critic available in modern depth psychology, we can now deal with it more effectively than ever before. We can recognize it for what it is, address it in ways that liberate us from its cruel inner attacks, and henceforth journey inwards with greater freedom and more enjoyment of the thrill of discovery.

This book is unique in providing the reader with the understanding and methodology to do just that. In very clear and available language, it details how to recognize the inner critic and how to effectively deal with it. Byron Brown's presentation is useful for any individual who wishes to be free from the inner suffering and coercion of this ancient foe of our humanity, but it is specifically directed to those individuals interested and engaged in the inner journey toward realization and enlightenment.

Byron has been a student of mine for many years, and a teacher with considerable experience in the Diamond Approach to the inner journey. He has expressed his own understanding of how to work with the judge, culled from many years of his own inner work, and his work with students and groups, in a way that reveals its roots in the actual essential states of inner realization. As a result, this book is not only a study of the inner critic and how to deal with it, but a clear presentation of how this work can be done in a way that actually helps reveal our true and spiritual nature. In other words, it demonstrates how the work on the inner critic can become a path toward realizing true conscience—the essential conscience of which the inner critic is merely a limited imitation. Byron has also succeeded in demonstrating how the work with the inner critic and the arising of inner spiritual states are related, and how they contribute to and support each other. His extensive understanding of the subject matter derives not only from his own inner work and work with students in the Ridhwan School, but also from the many classes he developed and taught, devoted specifically to working with the inner critic.

I believe the reader will find this book a unique opportunity to deal with an age-old problem, with intelligence and efficiency. The application of its knowledge will contribute significantly to one's inner development.

A. H. Almaas
Berkeley, California
February 1998

ACKNOWLEDGMENTS

I WOULD LIKE TO express special thanks to Hameed Ali (A. H. Almaas), with whom I have studied and trained as a teacher during the last sixteen years. He is the founder of the Diamond Approach, a modern spiritual path based on self-understanding. Through the work of his Ridhwan School, I have learned this approach to the judge, or superego. I am completely indebted to Hameed for the profound teaching of Essence and its aspects, and for illuminating the ways in which the superego hinders us from knowing our true nature. Learning to disengage from the attacks of the superego is a fundamental step in early stages of the Diamond Approach. I hope this book may be of some assistance in supporting students involved in the Ridhwan School, as well as interested people everywhere. My heartfelt appreciation also goes to Karen Johnson, Hameed's colleague and my individual teacher, who has so patiently guided me through the maze of my own psychic reality for many years.

I am grateful to Michael Torresan, former teacher in the Ridhwan School, for first organizing this material and presenting it as a body of teaching in workshop format. He was an inspiring and provocative model for assisting others in confronting their judges. I have found his work an important starting point for much of what I have developed in this book.

Throughout my years of teaching the Diamond Approach, and this material in particular, I have worked with many students. I am grateful to each one for what he or she has taught me. Many of them appear directly and indirectly in the pages of this book.

Much of the writing of this book was made possible by the solitude and quiet of the Vedanta Retreat in Marin, California, and I am appreciative of the welcome offered me to have quiet time and to write. I would also like to thank Deborah Meyer for her belief in the profound value of this work for her psychotherapy clients as well as her encouragement and feedback in an initial reading of the manuscript. Special thanks to my father, Quentin, for a patient and detailed editing of my rough grammar and questioning of my unfamiliar concepts. He has always supported me in my pursuit of writing and has set a high standard for an appreciative use of the English language. And thanks to Alia Johnson and Sara Hurley, who have given me feedback and cheered me on during the four years it has taken to complete this book. Many people encouraged me as they read through the initial drafts, including Loie Rosenkrantz, Ward Stoneman, Sherry Anderson, Robert Birnbaum, Barry Rothman, Pam Weiss, Jessica Britt, Karen Johnson, and Hameed Ali.

After writing four drafts on my own, I made a New Year's resolution in 1997 to find an editor to work with me. I am deeply indebted to my father-in-law, Jim Friedman, and my father for helping to make this step possible. As a result, the book took a great leap forward into its final form through the invaluable attention of The Writer's Midwife, Elianne Obadia. We established a wonderful partnership as she helped me realize the energy and clarity needed to make the material speak most effectively. Thank you, Elianne, for your enthusiasm, appreciation, and critical consideration of my writing.

I offer many thanks to the staff of Shambhala Publications, particularly my editor, Emily Hilburn Sell, for believing in this book and helping birth it into the world.

Last, I am forever grateful to my wife, Ellen Friedman, for her ongoing support, interest, and energy, which have sustained me throughout the process of bringing this project to completion. My life with her has provided the ultimate laboratory and testing ground for the success of the principles described in this book.

PREFACE

DURING THE MANY YEARS I have been teaching people how to work with self-criticism, I have witnessed a great deal of suffering resulting directly from the negative ways people treat themselves. I have also seen their surprise and concern as they come to recognize how serious this situation is. Perhaps most important, I see their hunger for a sense of personal integrity based on compassion and understanding rather than a belief in deficiency based on self-blame.

There is nothing more poignant and heart-wrenching than to witness a friend treat himself badly out of a well-intentioned desire to do the best thing. It is painful to see his self-punishment, to recognize its inappropriateness, and to know you are helpless to stop it. You are helpless because the friend sees his actions as the logical and necessary outcome of who he is. Even when he recognizes the pain and struggle caused by the self-blame, he is not necessarily any closer to stopping it from happening. You might see that he believes he is responsible for something he is not and want him to recognize that. You may try to talk to this friend about it or give him books to read. But these things will have little lasting impact on his internal world unless they awaken his hunger to know himself beyond his hopes and fears.

To challenge your *own* patterns of self-judgment is an equally difficult task. Simply to recognize how harsh and intolerant you can be toward yourself is uncomfortable enough. But to expose and explore this part of yourself also means questioning basic assumptions about your upbringing and the society in which you live. This may mean setting personal priorities counter to those held by friends, family, and colleagues—something that is hard to do alone.

For this reason, you can benefit greatly from doing inner critic work with like-minded souls in workshops or ongoing groups. You see that you are not alone in your patterns of self-blame, and you receive external support for challenging these patterns. Working with others can counteract the isolation that you fear will come as you begin questioning the standards of those around you as well as your own expectations.

For those who do not have the opportunity to be in a group that supports this focus, working with the inner critic can be a lonely and often discouraging process. A book can give some background, suggest ways of working, and offer some guidelines, but it cannot replace the personal contact of other people or the feedback of a teacher or therapist. This book presents a perspective that frees you from the pervasive orientation of self-improvement, an approach that often reinforces rather than liberates you from the suffering of self-blame. I hope it will offer support for your own growth by validating the importance of challenging self-judgment on the path to self-understanding.

Byron Brown
Albany, California
November 1997

INTRODUCTION

THIS BOOK INTRODUCES YOU to the lifelong process of disengaging from self-judgment and, through and beyond that work, to knowing yourself as a living soul. Specifically, it will lead you on an experiential process of unraveling the judgment in your inner life. The abundant information here is not arranged as a theoretical treatise but as an interactive process and a practical guide to help free you from self-attack. Throughout the book, personal examples from individuals and from my work with students are included to illustrate the principles presented, as well as exercises and practices to encourage discovery of your own understanding of the material. The knowledge offered will have little impact unless you actively explore its relevance to your own experience.

Working with the judge and discovering the truth is a journey of liberation. As you come to recognize that you are in a prison guarded by the judge, you appreciate the soul's powerful longing for freedom. Every external form of bondage in human history reflects the psychic confinement of the soul resulting from ignorance and unquestioned beliefs. You are a slave to your own ideas of who you are and how you need to be.

The ability to defend against the judge's attacks and disengage from its activity offers you the possibility of discovering who you are independent of ideas. Actively standing up for the truth of your experience breaks the habitual patterns of your familiar identity. Where expectations and standards ruled, there can be openness and allowing. Fear of retribution can give way to self-trust and curiosity. From hopelessness and defeat can arise acceptance and confidence. And confinement and tension can be transformed into spaciousness and ease.

A Journey of Truth

And truth guides the journey. In combination with the grounding and practicality of your personal will, truth acts as an objective conscience for action in the world. One of the original functions of the judge was to act as your conscience. The judge learned standards of right and wrong from parents and society. Then, by using guilt and shame, it helped you as a child to behave and act appropriately according to that moral code. Unfortunately, this process suppressed your spontaneity, aliveness, and instinctual power in order to make you socialized and acceptable. You needed the judge's firm support and direction as you developed your own ability to perceive, evaluate, and understand. However, the outcome of that development was not grounded in your true nature. As an adult, you have continued to rely on the judge's internalized standards of right and wrong. Only true maturation can replace the judge with a living conscience. This capacity of the soul depends on the recognition of your essential nature and the development of your ability to be authentically yourself.

Disengaging from the judge thus serves two functions: to free you from the confinement of old, limiting patterns and beliefs and, at the same time, to demand that you actively practice living in a way that eliminates the need for the judge. You cannot simply throw off a structure that has defined and supported you unless you have something more effective with which to replace it. You must learn to function, interact, and make choices freed from the standards of the judge, which means living in alignment with the truth and reality of your own life at the present time. This creates a living conscience that is not based on rules. Such a conscience allows the fullness of your living soul to express itself. This happens when you have transformed the self-centeredness of instinctual impulses, the self-destruction of compulsive patterns, and the rigidity of internalized authority. This is not a small task. It is the work of learning to be a responsible, mature human being. You cannot plan how to do it, you cannot only read about how to do it, you cannot simply follow someone else's instructions. You must learn how to live spontaneously by recognizing and following the guidance of what you know to be true.

A Journey of Recovery

Working with the judge is a journey of recovery. Disengaging helps free you from the harsh oppression of the judge and also accelerates your movement into experiencing the aliveness of the soul. This is the doorway to recovery of your soul nature. You have the opportunity to recover a fresh and dynamic aliveness at the heart of your life. And aliveness means the presence of passion and spontaneity, two qualities noticeably absent in the world of judgment. It also means the experience of yourself as a life source. Life flows from and through you, taking on both familiar and unfamiliar forms. The soul's aliveness is the sense of something conscious and unpredictable, awake and mysterious.

My desire is to support you to be directly in contact with your own lived experience without the judge as intermediary. The central practice in this process is to return to *your* experience of *yourself* in this moment. As you learn to know yourself each moment with curiosity and openness, you allow the process of self-discovery to open new doors. You find your own natural resources that have gone unrecognized because of the judge's controlling influence. When you actively disengage, you begin to recognize what is called *presence* as a ground of support for being who you are from moment to moment. You are offered tastes of being a soul that is alive, dynamic, and immediate—a soul that is open, changing, and responding, but also a soul that is rooted in the reality of the truth.

The various flavors of presence arise to enrich your experience: *Awareness* wakes you up to the ever-changing elements of each day, and *personal will* brings you back to your direct experience of what is true at the present time. *Acceptance* encourages vulnerability to the ups and downs of your inner world, and *strength* gives you the courage to expand your boundaries and go beyond what you think is possible. *Joy* and *curiosity* help you appreciate and celebrate the mystery of you and your world, while *compassion* tenderizes you as it allows contact with the fullness of your heart, including its pain, grief, and longing. *Spaciousness* transforms the anxiety about lack into the allowing of openness, and *value* offers sweetness and satisfaction to your soul as you learn to appreciate your true nature. *Peace* stills the inner activity that undermines the quietness and simplicity of being yourself, allowing the *truth* of you and your life to be more apparent.

The soul's journey does not take you away from the physical, emotional, and social realities of your life. It is not about otherworldly experiences. Recovery of the soul enriches the life you have by bringing in the dimension of presence and its qualities, the invisible essence of what it means to be alive. Spirituality is the heart of human life, the subtle dimension of being a soul. It gives your experience fullness and immediacy so that you feel more in contact with each moment as you live each day.

How This Book Is Structured

This book addresses the human dilemma of the soul through answering two questions: what is this soul that you have lost touch with, and what prevents you from recognizing it? These two questions are basic to all spiritual work, and answering them can be approached in many ways. Here, we look at the barrier by working with self-judgment and how it blocks you from knowing yourself as soul. We explore the soul itself by focusing on some of its essential aspects that have largely been disowned or forgotten.

The following pages present a step-by-step method for confronting self-judgment. You will learn to recognize the presence of the judge, notice its effect on you, discover how it functions, explore how you support its activity, uncover its motivation, and most important, find ways to free yourself from its influence. This process is necessary for you to have the freedom to discover who you are beneath the myriad beliefs you have accumulated about yourself over the years. The information in the book is presented in an order most useful for working on your own: gradually developing the awareness and skills to support a true and effective defense against self-judgment. If you were working with the ongoing support of a teacher or group, the presentation of the material might have a different emphasis.

The first half of the book focuses on understanding judgment and how it affects you. The second half moves you into taking steps to defend against the activity of self-judgment. Twelve chapters address the judge process, each one concluding with a summary of its significant points and one or more exercises for supporting you in pursuing the work on your own.

The second focus of this book is the reconnection with your soul, the forgotten potential of who you truly are. Complementary to the work on the judge is the process of rediscovering inherent qualities of your true nature that you lost touch with as you grew up, in particular those relevant to freeing you from self-judgment.

Traditional spiritual work tends to focus on aspects of your nature considered spiritual (meaning beyond worldly life), such as universal love, self-realization, transcendent unity, ultimate empti-ness, or spiritual insight. These are important for knowing the deeper dimensions of human experience. However, you have other essential qualities, often overlooked, that are more relevant for life in the world.

Working with the judge is a particularly down-to-earth affair and needs the support of more basic, familiar soul qualities, freed from beliefs and personal history. In the soul chapters, you are invited to contact the clear simplicity of awareness, the energetic expansion of strength, the solid reliability of will, and the gentle warmth of compassion. These qualities and others provide a con-trast to the experience of yourself supported by the inner critic and at the same time give you access to inner resources for challenging its power. Each quality presented has a particular relevance for an aspect of your work with the judge. The soul quality chapters alter-nate with the judge chapters, and each contains a practice to help you reconnect with that quality.

These two dimensions, dealing with the judge and contacting soul qualities, mutually support and reinforce each other. Seeing through the judge's attitudes and beliefs allows you to observe your-self and your experience with fresh eyes and begin to recognize your deeper soul nature. You make space to know yourself in a different way. At the same time, directly sensing an aspect of your true nature provides a vivid and definite alternative to the reactive nature of self-judgment.

In addition, a story that follows a young couple, Frank and Sue, as they live through one Saturday together threads through the book. Their day is told in short episodes on the page facing the opening of each successive chapter. Every episode touches on the material in that chapter and helps place the subject matter of the book in the context of real life. When a judgment is arising in the characters' minds or in their own words, it is generally preceded by the symbol ❁ to help you learn to recognize the prevalence and variation of this element of both inner and outer activity. When Frank or Sue is engaged in inner dialogue, whether a judgment or not, the words are in italics. You may find it useful to reread an episode after you finish reading the chapter it precedes.

The Beginning of a Process

This is a lifelong journey of discovering the truth in your life as you liberate your soul. Recognizing, appreciating, and disengaging from your judge is a vital way of ensuring that it becomes *your* journey. This book is only a beginning, but it will provide a useful foundation for opening the prison door and stepping into the heart of life.

NOTE TO THE READER

THIS BOOK SPEAKS TO more than just your mind. It is addressed to your soul. At different times, the material will resonate in your body or your heart or in your very being. The chapters are packed with information, insights, and inquiries. It is not light reading. This is a book to work through slowly, allowing it to stimulate you, unsettle you, move you. Take it in small bites so you can absorb the tastes and textures. Go away and come back. Stop and reread.

As you read, you will find yourself responding to the ideas that are relevant to where you are in your own journey. You will draw from what is presented the nourishment you need at the moment for your own development. This means that much of what you read will pass into your mind and out again without any significant impact. This is natural. However, it also means that you can come back to any part of this book in one month, six months, or a year and you will resonate with material that was not important for you the first time.

I particularly recommend that as you read, you pay attention to your body and your energy. Notice how they are affected by your reading. If you become aware of having a hard time concentrating or feeling restless, stop and take a break. Perhaps something has struck home and stirred a physical or an emotional response. When one part of you is strongly affected, it can prevent you from taking in any more. The focus of this book on connecting with your experience in the moment makes it ideal for learning to track yourself in this way. Making space for your responses to the process of reading will create a greater impact and also allow the material to nourish and awaken more aspects of your soul.

Do not expect instantaneous change or development; be patient with yourself as you respect your soul's need to go at its own pace. Integrating into your life the various elements of this self-discovery process can take many years. The exercises and practices in this book are designed to expose you to different dimensions of inner experience in a gradual way. The resulting effect is cumulative: each facet of the work is reinforced by all the others.

SOUL
WITHOUT
SHAME

A Day with Frank and Sue

Sue was awoken by Frank returning to bed from the bathroom. It took quite a while before she finally acknowledged that she couldn't go back to sleep. He, meanwhile, seemed to have fallen asleep right away. The clock radio was glowing 3:30 when Sue twisted her head to the left and opened her eyes. She remembered too late what she had heard on the radio from some sleep expert: you should never look at the time when you wake up in the middle of the night because that seems to make it harder to go back to sleep. This reminded her of how often recently she had been waking up in the middle of the night. Fortunately, this time it was Saturday and she didn't have to get up early, but she was frustrated with herself and dreaded lying awake for the rest of the night.

♲ *So what has been your problem lately anyway, Sue? You didn't used to have difficulty sleeping. Something's wrong here. You know you are eating too late, and you are getting into that bad habit of black tea after dinner.*
   I think it must have something to do with either lack of exercise or being anxious about my work. I will have to get some of that melatonin at the vitamin store tomorrow . . .

As her mind continued working, Sue was getting more and more unsettled in her body. She could feel the heaviness of sleep still in her system, and her eyes were aching. A sense of low-grade agitation was developing in her limbs, as though a subtle current of energy had been turned on and she could no longer relax. She desperately longed to shut it off and drop back into sleep.

With some effort, Sue stopped her mental obsessing and focused her attention on her arms and legs and began controlled breathing to try to relax. At first, she felt more tension than relaxation from trying to concentrate. Then, as she continued, the outline of her body slowly transformed into a vivid presence charged with a slightly prickly energy. This shifted into a pulsing flow moving through her; it was both soothing and enlivening. And then for a moment, Sue experienced herself floating in the middle of a dark, spacious field with a vibrant perimeter. She was feeling herself in an immediate and unfamiliar way, when suddenly a familiar voice broke in: ♲ *But you're supposed to be going to sleep!*

The internal voice brought her back to being Sue lying in bed not sleeping. Where had she been? Not asleep but not anyplace familiar. She found herself yawning as she puzzled over what had just happened. Sue turned over, pulled up the covers, and was soon fast asleep.

1

THE SOUL PERSPECTIVE

YOU ARE A SOUL. And if you allow it, your life can become a journey of unfolding for your soul. The fact is, you do not recognize yourself as soul. You do not know the source of your own aliveness. You are not aware of the potential for freedom and responsiveness that is your true nature. In order to see your inner critic in a proper perspective, in relation to the totality of who you are, you must have some sense of being a soul. What does that mean?

What Is the Soul?

Whenever people say the word *I*, they generally are referring to a person who was born of certain parents, has a certain history, and acts and behaves in certain familiar ways. This is often referred to as the ego or personality. The soul, in fact, is the true "I." It is the present-moment experience of yourself as the agent in your life, the sense of a livingness that is here now. Can you say what you are if you don't refer to who you have been?

The soul is the you who experiences your life—the one who perceives, acts, learns, and changes. It is not the body that was born many years ago; it is not the self-image of a person who has particular skills and capacities; and it is not the mind that thinks and worries about everything that happens. The soul includes all of these, but as the experiencer, it is more fundamental and less defined than any of them. Who is it that experiences being an ego, being a body, or being a mind? Who at *this* very minute is reading these words? Can you define who or what that is? This I call the soul.

All aspects of your experience emerge out of your soul. Not only is the soul the experiencer, it is also *what* is experienced and the *locus* of your experience. In other words, your soul is what underlies and unifies every part of you and your experience. The deep longing to be whole, to feel integrated, to be yourself without division, is a longing to experience the soul.

The closer you are to sensing your own immediate aliveness, the closer you are to soul. The soul is the substance of living consciousness. To feel it is to recognize the miraculous and mysterious quality of what you are—a flowing presence, dynamic, alive, and ever-changing. To feel you are a soul is to know the unboundedness of life. The soul extends beyond the usual boundaries and categories of the human mind, beyond the familiar notion of a human life. It is not limited by history, concepts, or the physical body. It defies exact definition or analysis. As such, the soul is better felt, sensed, and known in the heart than it is through the structures and perceptions of the mind. Have you ever wished for ease and spontaneity in your heart? Have you ever felt limited by the idea of having to be or act a particular way? If so, imagine what sense of yourself would allow spontaneity, ease, and freedom. Who would you be, and how would you feel? You are imagining a fundamental quality of your soul nature.

The nature of the soul is pure consciousness, experienced as a field of awareness in relation to physical reality. This field of awareness contains your mind and your body without being bounded by either. Normally, you experience yourself as a physical body that has a mind with awareness as one of its capacities. But your soul is more like an expanse of awareness particles condensed in your location into a solid physical presence known as a body. And these awareness particles permeate every cell, sensation, and thought you have. The most external expression of your consciousness or soul *is* your body, which brings your awareness into intimate contact with the physical world as you know it. How different it would be to experience your whole body made out of this consciousness—with your awareness consciously inhabiting and living through every cell in your body!

The Presence of the Soul

To be in touch with your actual consciousness, which is the substance of your soul, is to be aware of your existence in each moment—to be aware of presence. Presence means the sense of immediate existence or being. And presence is a primary quality of the soul. You cannot be aware of your own soul nature unless you are present to your own experience, unless you know your reality as it exists right now. Presence is your direct knowingness of being alive in the present moment. That knowingness is not an idea or a thought but an actual felt awareness. It is what gives your body its felt sense. The soul's presence is substantial without being physical, and that substance gives the physical body a sense of living fullness.

Presence is to the soul what wetness is to water: one is an inseparable quality of the other. However, if you only look at water or only touch it with rubber gloves, you may not know that water is wet. Similarly, the presence of the soul cannot be erased or separated out, but it can go unrecognized if you are not in touch with it. Ignorance of the presence of your own soul is a deep and painful loss that stirs the longing to know yourself more intimately. This longing may be expressed as the search for meaning and truth, the desire for self-realization, or the pursuit of freedom and liberation. All are fulfilled through experiencing the living presence of the soul—the true nature of who you are.

The soul's presence comes in many subtle but distinct flavors that underlie the richness of life. These are the basic elements of human existence, such as strength, clarity, compassion, joy, love, intelligence, value, will, acceptance, and vulnerability. These essential aspects make up your true nature, that in you which is innate or God-given and not dependent on your parents, your appearance, your behavior, or your achievements.

Soul Qualities

The soul is also the source of qualities that inform physical existence: life, growth, dynamism, and flow. The physical body is alive because of the soul's presence: the body is experienced as dead when the life, or soul, has gone out of it. Your own sense of aliveness is only partially due to physical factors; more fundamentally, it derives from your openness to the soul. Similarly, your body has a physiological pattern of growth, but *your* growth is more than physical. You develop and transform, learn and mature in ways related to, but not caused by, the biological growth of the body.

You as a soul have dynamism, experienced as vitality, inherent movement, and transformation. Objects remain at rest unless acted upon; your soul has action, change, and continual revelation implicit in its very nature. And that dynamism flows: it is not static, rigid, or mechanical. Your soul is an unending movement in space and time, a literal stream of consciousness rather than an object that stops and starts, reacts and resists. When you feel lifeless, unchanging, and at the mercy of external forces, you are no longer aware of your soul nature. If ever you have longed to experience yourself as a dynamic source of vitality and transformation, then the aliveness of the soul is your birthright waiting to be discovered.

Beyond these qualities, however, are two unique attributes of the human soul. First is the soul's extraordinary potential to experience anything that can be experienced. In other words, as a field of consciousness, the soul has an unlimited malleability. In its pure form, it has no resistance to being formed by any impulse arising within it. It is shaped and transformed in a dynamic flow of consciousness that you know as the experiences of your life. You know this potential for experience as the profoundly human capacity to respond to the world with feeling, curiosity, and insight. At more subtle levels, you can empathize with others and imagine unfamiliar ways of being, and even enter directly into the experience of different forms of life. Such is the true freedom of the soul—not to be defined or limited by external form. This is not only freedom from the limitations of being something in particular, but it is also the freedom to be anything. Your body is limited, but your soul is not because it is pure consciousness.

The second attribute is the soul's capacity to identify. Not only can you experience anything, you can believe that you *are* anything that you experience. This is related to the human capacity for self-reflection: you have consciousness of your own existence; therefore, you can know yourself. However, because the soul takes on many forms through the impact of experience, you can know yourself in many ways. You as soul are not limited to knowing yourself as soul. In fact, you long ago stopped recognizing yourself as soul. Instead, you identify with emotions, thoughts, beliefs, physical sensations, images in your mind, relationships with other souls, memories of previous experience, or states of consciousness, to name a few possibilities. These forms in which the soul appears are much more familiar to you than the soul itself, even though it is the common substance of all the forms. Consequently, you as soul tend to know yourself through your forms rather than as a presence of pure consciousness.

The soul's identification can shift in a fluid way as part of its growth and unfolding, or it can become fixed on particular forms. When identifying becomes fixed on some *part* of your consciousness, some particular form, you easily lose sight of the *whole*—yourself as a soul. You may never have known yourself as anything but forms of the soul (your body, your history, your thoughts, your emotions). Or you may remember beginning your life with some awareness of the soul and later losing touch with it when you became identified with one or more of its forms. Either way, you do not now recognize your true nature as presence, transformation, unfolding experience, and aliveness.

This soul loss is often not noticed until you begin to feel your experience pervaded by a lack of substance or inner meaning. When this happens, you have come to a point where your identity is so much about familiar forms that you have lost all contact with the living, dynamic substance of who you are. There's no juice left in your life. You find yourself saying, "This can't be all that I am. There must be more to life than this." Many people consider this indicative of a midlife crisis. In fact, it is the cry of your soul reminding you of your soul nature.

Losing Touch with Your Soul Nature

The fact that you identify and then are not aware that you have identified is the reason you do not experience yourself as a soul. You have become deeply grounded in the belief that you are one part of the soul, so you experience your life through that part. For example, you believe that your fundamental nature is physical. Even if you would like to believe otherwise, you continually act from a profound conviction that your ultimate nature is a physical body. This belief, which was established in the first two years of life, forced upon you many other beliefs necessary for that body's survival. At that time, your body was small, undeveloped, and defenseless, so being in that body meant you were helpless and totally dependent on your parents. This, in turn, meant you had to accept their beliefs about life in order to survive. And so the experience of being a soul became increasingly faint.

As you grew up, you added more beliefs about who you were to those learned earlier. Perhaps, when you were little, you saw that your father knew how to do things. This naturally sparked your own curiosity about how things work. Because he answered your questions, you came to believe he was the source of intelligence. Perhaps he did not appreciate your intelligence, so you tried to be like him in order to "gain" intelligence. You came to believe you had no innate intelligence, only what you learned by imitating him. Now you constantly relate your sense of intelligence to the standards he taught you. You believe that others assess your intelligence in the same way. Furthermore, if you find yourself knowing something in a different way from your father, you doubt the usefulness or veracity of your own intelligence. Consequently, your sense of who you are in relation to intelligence is completely colored by these beliefs. You are cut off from any sense that intelligence is implicit in your true nature, your soul potential.

In this way, by the time you are an adult, you have moved very far from the experience of yourself as a soul. You are now well defined by your physical, emotional, and personal history. Your sense of yourself is not fluid, changing, dynamic, and unfolding. You do not have the sense of impressionability of the soul in which every experience touches and affects your presence. You tend to believe, on the contrary, that your independence, integrity, and capacities are based on your ability to hold on to a definite idea of who you are and not be easily influenced or swayed by the experiences in your life. This is a common result of life in modern society. There is nothing wrong with it. However, it does mean you are not aware of the actual depths of who you are—your soul nature and its potential. It is from here that the journey of soul recovery begins.

Practice: Sensing Aliveness

This practice is a support for being more in touch with the living quality that exists in you at each moment. It is not designed to create or encourage any particular energetic state.

Step 1. Choose a household task such as washing the dishes, sweeping the floor, cleaning up your desk, or weeding the garden. Before you begin, notice how your body feels (tense, tired, energetic, slow, numb . . .). Feel your feet on the floor or ground, stretch your fingers, rub your hands together, and take a few deep breaths. As you begin your task, be aware of how the object you are working with feels in your hands. Notice its texture, weight, and shape. Allow yourself to experience how you feel about it: Do you like the dish you are washing? Does holding the broom remind you of mother? Are you angry at not having the right places to put all your papers? In the garden, would you rather wear gloves, or do you like the feel of earth on your skin?

Step 2. Periodically during the task, stop and notice what the energy is like in your body. What is your breathing like: shallow, held, relaxed, expanded? How is your concentration: is it easy to stay focused, or does your mind wander and you find yourself easily distracted? Are you aware of feeling any particular emotion as you work: anxious, sad, hopeful, excited, peaceful, scared, guilty? How do you feel your own aliveness or lack of it at this moment?

Step 3. Take whatever sense you now have of yourself, both physically and emotionally, back into your task. Continue to
work while being aware of your energetic state. Does this
awareness make it easier or harder to do what you need to
do? A good practice to support being with your own aliveness as you function is to follow your breath. Actively
attending to your inhalation and exhalation will keep your
attention and your energy from becoming fixed, shut
down, or frozen.

When the soul is caught up in rigid identifications with others and the world, it is not satisfied. In every soul there is an inherent drive toward truth, an inherent desire to feel fulfilled, real and free. Although many people are not able to pursue this desire effectively, the impetus toward the realization of the self is in all of us; it begins with the first stirrings of consciousness and continues throughout life whether or not we are directly aware of it. This impetus spontaneously emerges in consciousness as an important task for the psychologically and spiritually maturing human being. As maturity grows into wisdom in an optimally developing person, this task gains precedence over other tasks in life, progressively becoming the center that orients, supports and gives meaning to one's life, ultimately encompassing all of one's experience.

— A. H. Almaas, *The Point of Existence*, p. 16

Frank rolled over in bed and opened his eyes. The sunlight was streaming in through the window, and the air felt clear and fresh. He remembered that it was Saturday and he had no obligations this morning. He was smiling when he turned his head to look at his wife, Sue, beside him. That's when he felt the pain in his neck. The smile disappeared, and the voices in his head started up:

❧ *Now you did it. This is what happens when you read in bed until midnight with your neck all cramped up. You just went to the chiropractor yesterday and can't go again until Monday, so you're going to have a sore neck all weekend. When will you ever learn?*

Well, it's not all my fault. That guy just can't get my neck right. I think he's lost his touch. I've read in bed for years and didn't put my neck out. Besides, I wasn't reading last night; I watched TV. Damn!

It's your own fault because you never get enough exercise. You just sit all day.

You're right; I am lazy.

Frank took a deep breath and sighed. Time to get up. Sue was still asleep. He felt an impulse to lean over and give her a kiss.

❧ *Better not do that or you'll wake her up. You know how little sleep she got last night with her insomnia. She'll be in a really bad mood if you wake her up now.*

Maybe, but what about later, when she asks how come I didn't hang around in bed with her on our one free morning? If I don't at least kiss her or hug her, she will be resenting me all day long.

Boy, you have a problem, Frank. All you do is try to figure out how to avoid aggravating her. You don't really love her or you wouldn't be so concerned about being a nice guy.

Frank sat up on the edge of the bed and straightened his back, feeling the soreness in his neck, and wondered what he could look forward to today. He felt deflated and restless already. The morning that had felt so fresh and bright moments ago now felt all too familiar and depressing. *Oh well, let's eat.* He always liked breakfast. He stood up and, pulling on his robe, quietly slipped out of the room, drawing the door closed behind him.

2
WHAT IS THE JUDGE?

Welcome to the Courtroom of Life

You wake up in the morning, and before you know it, you feel anxious about getting out of bed and facing your day. . . . You feel guilty when you heap jam on your toast, then congratulate yourself for having only one cup of coffee. . . . When you arrive at your job, your boss says he loves your work and he can't believe he made such a good choice in hiring you. You feel your stomach tighten: you're scared you'll disappoint him. . . . You walk into your office and pick up your voice mail; your best friend has left an enthusiastic message that she got the job you had just applied for, and you collapse inside. . . . You don't want to call her back because you are afraid to tell her how envious you are. . . . You realize how all of your relationships are shaped by your childhood need for approval, and you can't imagine talking to anyone. . . . Later, you want to shake off the nagging uneasiness that has been building all morning, so you decide to buy flowers for your lover but then change your mind because she might not like the kind you get. . . . You are reminded that she can't understand why, if you really love her, you withdraw all the time, and you can't understand either. . . . You try to work but can't concentrate on the report that's due tomorrow. As you get a candy bar from the machine, you tell yourself to snap out of it and stop being so self-indulgent. . . .

You can't relax and enjoy your own life.

The common theme in this scenario is a particular kind of

relationship between you and your experience. This relationship involves expectations, standards, evaluations, judgments, and consequences. How much is your response to your experience—and your experience itself—determined by what you expect to happen? How much time do you spend evaluating your performance, your appearance, your capacity, your history? How difficult is it to live up to the standards you use to judge yourself? How often is your underlying sense of self determined by your notions of right and wrong?

This is the courtroom of life. And you are the one who is on trial.

Sometimes, you feel accused of doing something wrong or unthinkable; at other times, you feel you have been caught red-handed. Sometimes, you present a case for your own guilt and corruption; at other times, you argue hard to justify your innocence. Sometimes, you threaten and warn yourself of dire consequences for disobeying; at other times, you confess your sins in a plea for a reduced sentence. Sometimes, you weigh the evidence on each side to reach a verdict; and at other times, you simply pass sentence without hesitation or consideration.

These activities make up *the judgment process,* this courtroom of life that is presided over by *the judge.* The judge is a part of your mind. It is embedded in ideas, thoughts, beliefs, images, and internal voices. At the same time, it also lives through your body and your energy. The judge is a master of words, and yet you can feel it in your belly, your shoulders, and your jaw without any awareness of words. The judge is both pervasive and invisible. It speaks to you from commercials on TV, magazine ads, and movies, as well as from the expression on your partner's face, the dirty dishes in the sink, and the tone in your supervisor's voice.

It has access to a storehouse of learned information. This is the accumulation of all the knowledge you believe you need to be successful, safe, supported, recognized, and loved in the world. The judge sets the standards for what will make you a good, acceptable, and happy person. Of course, it also has standards for everybody else. Its voice guides your external life, consciously and unconsciously, through opinions, advice, warnings, suggestions, beliefs, evaluations, and admonishments about all aspects of your behavior. And as though this weren't enough, the judge directs nearly all aspects of your inner life as well.

Comparison and Judgment

In addition to setting standards, another activity integral to the judgment process is comparison. Your judge doesn't only evaluate you according to its standards, it also constantly compares you with other people to evaluate your worth. Comparison is a very close cousin of self-judgment. In fact, you can be sure that if you are engaged in comparison, judgment is going on. The judge uses both of them interchangeably to achieve its desired effect. Even when you are doing well according to one standard, you can always be compared to someone else who is doing better. And when you are doing better than those around you, you can still be judged against a standard of greater perfection. Some people feel more at the mercy of comparison, and others are more subject to internal standards, but everyone deals with both.

Living in modern society means constantly being subjected to comparison through commercial advertising, social intercourse, popular entertainment, and the pressure to succeed in your work. It is hard to imagine engaging in any activity without some experience of comparison. It is the basis of the competition that is integral to Western life. No one would deny its usefulness in driving down prices, inspiring great athletic achievements, stimulating scientific discoveries, and improving many aspects of our world. However, comparison becomes self-destructive when it becomes the lens through which you experience yourself. In this realm, it becomes a tool of the judge. The result is constant self-assessment relative to the behavior and appearance of others at the expense of aligning with the truth of your own experience.

Viewing your life through the lens of comparison orients you away from your soul nature. With the judge in control, comparison is always oriented toward determining worth or value—that is, who is "better." This means that if you are different from someone in some respect, then one of you must be better than the other. This is the insidious nature of judgmental comparison, in which difference is always an indication of relative value. The judge wants to know who is right, who is better, and why. It is not interested in understanding the complexities or subtleties of why things are the way they are. In particular, judgmental comparison never takes into account the soul, which by its nature has implicit value unrelated to any other soul. Souls cannot be compared in value or goodness, no matter how one may differ from another.

Even in self-exploration, the tendency is for the judge to use comparison to devalue and trivialize your present experience by criticizing you for being or acting the same as you always have. Or it will say you are doing worse or better than before, as if the value of your present experience could be measured by its relationship to what happened in the past. Judgmental comparison kills any possibility of freshness and spontaneity when it is continually applied to feelings, actions, and interactions. The soul cannot bring forth aliveness and openness in an atmosphere of comparison and judgment. Understanding how these related processes maintain a grip on your life and imprison you in the world of the past is an important step in freeing yourself of self-judgment.

Life Lessons

Carol was in her thirties and had no partner to share her life with. No matter how much she believed in the value of her career as a university professor, it did not offset the deficiency she felt about her inability to be in a successful intimate relationship. Whenever she was about to date someone new, she felt excited and optimistic. But as soon as the connection began, she became plagued with doubts and questions: Does he like me? How did I appear to him? Was I too interested and asking too many questions? What if he doesn't call me again? Should I call him? How come he didn't ask me about my life? Maybe I seem too boring. And so on.

When she recognized that she had become obsessed with the relationship after only one date, she would decide that it had become too important and that her neediness would surely wreck any possibility of the man's liking her. She would determine not to let her needs show. This meant that Carol had to act aloof and unemotional in subsequent encounters, and the man would find her controlled and rather dull. As a result, her connections with men never seemed to last more than three or four dates, and she could never understand how to change this outcome. Carol felt caught in a painful cycle. She could see no way out and felt worthless. She often sank into periods of depression and hopelessness during which she avoided all social contact except with a few close women friends.

Self-blame can be transformed only by coming to understand how your sense of who you are and the options open to you is determined by your past experiences and beliefs. In order to do this, you will need to explore some important questions. Can you recognize how you define yourself through a familiar pattern of feelings, conflicts, behaviors, and assumptions? How did you learn to know yourself this way? Will you always fight the same battles to prove your worth, gain others' love, and feel deserving of rest and relaxation? Is there any part of you that is not subject to critique by inner voices? Relief from your suffering is not a matter of getting better at what you think you need to do. It is about finding out how you ended up where you are in the first place.

Inner Work

Everyone tries to live a fulfilling and rewarding life. This means taking care of the physical necessities of surviving and prospering: earning a living, maintaining shelter and clothing, buying and cooking food, getting enough sleep and exercise, and so on. In addition, human beings naturally seek a sense of ease and enjoyment in their life alone and with others.

For some, this means pursuing active and dedicated inner work—such as understanding motivations and longings, developing awareness and sensitivity, and exploring memories and imagination—to understand and enrich what it means to live a human life. The fact that you are reading this book indicates you are one of these people. Your inner work may take the form of psychotherapy, a self-help group, journaling, personal exploration, or some kind of spiritual practice, such as meditation. Whatever the form, attention to your personal inner process—how you think and feel about yourself and your life—makes you aware of forces that shape that process. The judge is one of the most powerful of these forces. If you pursue inner work, you can only go so far without coming to terms with this ever-present companion, also referred to as the superego, the inner critic, or top dog.

Often, the voice of the judge appears as your own voice: you are the one who has these notions about what is necessary, what is right, or what things mean. However, by paying attention to your self-judgment, you will recognize that your standards are learned from others, and they can run counter to what you yourself want, feel, or know to be true. If you see this, you will realize that the voice you hear is not yours. It belongs to a familiar companion who lives inside you, someone you have brought along on this journey of life.

And yet even when you realize the voice is not yours, you can't separate from it. It seems to live under your skin, in your joints, behind your eyes. You watch yourself mercilessly keeping track of the pluses and minuses in your daily behavior. You watch others as well. Sometimes, *you* feel watched by those around you—friends, family, or strangers—and you fear their disapproval, rejection, or indifference. You withdraw. Then you realize you are seeing your own judge outside in others as well as hearing it inside. You begin to recognize how little control you have over this judgment process. Whether you are the watcher or the watched, you are at the mercy of a critical, punitive attitude, for this kind of watching is inherently a manifestation of self-distrust and self-hatred.

The Judge Runs the Show

The judge overrides your inherent intelligence and your direct response to life by superimposing its beliefs about what is real. It is a warped lens that distorts reality. Because of this distorted perception, you have come to distrust your intuitive contact with life. In fact, you have lost any sense of what direct contact with living means. You have become dependent on the judge (and those for whom it speaks: parents, society, God) to give your life meaning, significance, and direction. It tells you what to experience, how to experience it, why you experience it, what the experience means, and what you need to do about it. Most of this process is invisible to you, or unconscious, and the result seems perfectly normal. Even in reading these words, the way you are taking them in—whether they touch you or not, and how you are responding to them—is affected by your judge.

Though it acts as if it were helping you get what you want in life, the judge actually resists your movement toward growth and development. Its function is to maintain the status quo in two ways: It keeps you away from what it considers to be dangerous or unmanageable parts of yourself. And it directs you toward whatever ideals it feels will make you an acceptable, successful person. It constantly admonishes you, "Don't do that; do this!" Yet because its demands are never-ending, the actual feeling you are left with is "I am not good enough, and I never will be."

But the judge's impact on change is even more insidious and undermining. It tells you, "Change. You're not enough. You need to get better for people to like, accept, and love you"—while also saying, "You will never succeed at changing. You're deficient. You haven't got what it takes." However, should you actually come to a place where real change is possible and you could choose to act differently, the judge will scare you by taunting, "People won't like you or support you if you change; they'll turn their backs on you, and you will be all alone." You're damned if you do and damned if you don't.

The more you recognize and feel trapped by this situation, the more a natural response arises: "I want out. I want space from this taskmaster I carry around inside." And even as you suffer and crave relief, you find it hard not to believe what it is telling you.

The Judge Has Many Faces

One reason you continue to believe what the judge says is that it takes on many important roles for you. These roles clothe its judgmental attitude in attractive guises. Self-discovery requires disrobing the judge and exposing the truth about how it affects your life.

You must begin by seeing its apparel—the roles within which it hides.

The judge is a conscience that helps you distinguish right from wrong. It is a motivator to push and persuade you to act in your life. It is a guard that stops inappropriate feelings and behavior. It is a counselor for support in making decisions. It is a guide that provides direction as you make your way. It is an authority figure offering recognition and approval. It is a yardstick for measuring your progress. And last, it is a mirror that reflects back to you who you think you are.

Each person needs help in these ways. What you were not taught while growing up was how to discover the true source of these functions in your own soul. Your true nature has the potential to meet all these needs, but only if the qualities necessary to do that are recognized as existing in you. When you were a young child, it was important that parents or responsible adults were there to fulfill these roles. As you grew up and became responsible for yourself, you had to find ways to meet these needs on your own. Unfortunately, you got little if any support in recognizing and developing your own inherent capacities. You had little choice but to internalize your parental role models in the form of the judge. You may not be happy with the way it performs these important functions, but you are familiar with your judge, and you know that it is dependable and will always be there for you.

Lest we forget, the judge is not bad or evil, or even useless. None of us would have survived into adulthood without a judge; our society would not be as civilized as it is without the judge's constant presence. Each of us will need a judge until we find a source of effortless functioning, direct knowing, and objective conscience inside ourselves. In the meantime, the judge is all most people have to get the job done. However, it is also mechanical, restrictive, inefficient, and insensitive; it does a poor job of supporting the life of the soul.

Though the judge has no sense of you as a living soul, it does have much information about your life in the world: your habits, behaviors, preferences, weaknesses, strengths, friends, and enemies. Not much slips past its watchful eye. This fact makes it very powerful. In fact, the judge often makes accurate observations about what you have and haven't done. You need that kind of knowledge to grow and mature. However, the judge's observations always come at a price. They are not freely given so you can learn the truth. They are thrust upon you to convince you that you don't measure up.

The trap is, unless you learn to disengage from the judge, there is no way to take in the observations without the judgmental packaging. If you see that you have behaved in such and such a way, then you accept that you are this or that kind of person. The assessment of your value is always embedded in the external facts of your life. You can't separate one from the other. You don't even want to separate them because you are afraid that you would have no value at all!

For this reason, recognizing that it hinders, limits, and even hurts you generally has little effect on the habitual activity of the judge: recognition just makes you more aware of your own helplessness. One of the greatest dangers of becoming aware of self-judgment and its negative effects is that that awareness will become the basis of more self-judgment. You will judge yourself for having a judge!

Nevertheless, in spite of the hopelessness or self-criticism that may come with it, awareness of the reality of your experience with the judge is vital. For most of your life, you have lived with the judge, and in many cases, you have felt motivated, protected, disciplined, and guided by its presence. This situation has been maintained by an unconsciousness about what was occurring. For the self-judgment dynamic to change, the first step must be awareness.

So we begin with a definition:

> The judge is the force in you that constantly evaluates and assesses your worth as a human being and thus limits your capacity to be fully alive in the present moment.

Awareness begins the process of disentangling your worth from the facts of your life. It is true that you have skills and capacities to develop as you grow and that you must learn from your experience in order to make sensible and informed choices. But your value is not dependent on achievement or approval. The judge leads you to believe that you are subject to evaluation and improvement rather than having inherent value and worth. Implicit in this belief is the judge's assumption that your value is conditional, that you are worthless on your own: you need to accomplish, you need to change, you need correction, you need to be watched, you need direction, you need a kick in the butt!

The Judge Doesn't Tell the Whole Truth

The more you know about the judge, the more you realize it is central to your definition of yourself. You measure your own worth and substance by evaluating yourself against its standards. The more you know yourself, the more you see that this kind of evaluation has major negative consequences. You are used to thinking of yourself in disparaging terms—including put-downs you would scarcely allow someone else to say to you or would never say to others because they are too unkind. Furthermore, your attempts to avoid disparagement inevitably compel you to strive to improve yourself so you can measure up to those same standards.

What can one do to counteract the effects of such negative conditioning? Most people are convinced that you need large and continuing doses of positive reinforcement and affirming judgments to offset such a negative self-image. Parents focus on being positive and complimentary about everything a child does. Friends try hard to say positive things to those who berate themselves. People with low self-esteem practice affirmations daily to try to reprogram their beliefs. The attempt is to internalize a judge that will give you approval and recognition instead of disapproval and rejection. If you are truthful, you will see that you fervently hope the positive regard of the judge will eventually replace its negative attention.

The problem with this approach is that it simply substitutes a good judgment for a bad one. It is not focused on affirming or even recognizing what is true but simply counteracting or overcoming a negative assessment. The fact of judgment remains unchanged. In other words, you are still basing your self-worth on external or internalized standards. You are seeking approval rather than criticism. What is missing is the direct experience in you of your own worth. Positive judgment can expose the unconscious acceptance of inner devaluation. It can make you feel better, providing temporary relief from the berating of your judge. It can also reflect what you have at some time experienced to be true (such as a deep insight, a moment of bliss, or an openness from meditation). All of these are important and useful at times.

But even powerful experiences of truth don't change long-held beliefs about the self unless they are taken into the soul and understood. Simply using the insight as a new standard or belief does not accomplish this. Understanding and integrating an experience means recognizing the implications that this new awareness has on your experience of your life as you learn to live in accordance with it.

Positive judgment only superimposes a new belief about yourself on top of an old one. It tries to assert something that is not an expression of what you experience as truth. It can never root out the original conviction of your own lack of worth. This is why you will often find yourself distrusting the praise of others, making inner comments like, "The fact that they say that shows they don't know me very well!" The fact is, positive judgment is like makeup: it must always be reapplied, and a good hard rain will wash it away.

The only real alternative to self-judgment is knowing the truth about who you are. If you have a deep belief that you are worthless, you must discover where that belief came from and why you believe that it is true. Until you understand that, nothing fundamentally will change. Once you know deep inside you, with a direct and felt sense, that you have inherent value and are fully acceptable to yourself, then you will begin to free yourself from the need for positive judgment and approval, from others or from your own judge.

The path to truly knowing who you are requires challenging the presence of the judge. You must find the courage and wisdom, the determination and clarity, the compassion and desire to see what the truth is and stay with the process of supporting that truth. All these qualities are needed to make space for your own experience, regardless of whether you consider it good or bad, right or wrong, joyous or painful. Otherwise, your feelings of shame, guilt, wrongness, and selfishness provoked by your judge will make it impossible to stay with the richness, challenge, and mystery of what you find.

The process you are setting in motion in the first few chapters of this book will bring you into more awareness of and contact with your judge, which means you will be more vulnerable to the feeling of being attacked. This is not enjoyable or comfortable. Your judge will say that it is bad and must be avoided. But if you are willing to bring the judgment experience into consciousness and be compassionate and strong in supporting your growing openness and vulnerability, you can undertake this work in a meaningful way. This inner work is what will reconnect you with your soul nature; through it, you will discover a true guide for living and understanding your life, one that can replace the judge you have grown up with.

Your true guide arises spontaneously through your contact with and awareness of your own life; this guide responds to the truth of who you are and what is needed. The practice of working with your judge is thus simultaneously immediate and long-term. You must confront the judge as you live your life now; otherwise, judge work will remain a good idea saved for some future time. On the other hand, the process is never finished; it will continue throughout your life, for the judge's influence runs deep in your soul and impacts you with amazing subtlety. The journey is not easy, but few others are more rewarding in expanding your sense of who you are and in allowing you to live a full and meaningful life.

POINTS TO REMEMBER

- The judge is the force in you that constantly evaluates and assesses your worth as a human being and thus limits your capacity to be fully alive in the present moment.
- The judge's voice guides your life, consciously and unconsciously, through opinions, advice, warnings, suggestions, beliefs, evaluations, and admonishments about all aspects of your behavior and your inner life.
- The judge's function is to maintain the status quo in two ways: It

keeps you away from what it considers to be dangerous or unmanageable parts of yourself. And it directs you toward whatever ideals it feels will make you an acceptable, successful person. Self-judgment is based on the accumulation of all the knowledge you believe you need to be successful, safe, supported, recognized, and loved in the world.

- Comparison is a very close cousin of self-judgment. It is useful for improving many aspects of our world. However, comparison becomes self-destructive when it becomes constant self-assessment relative to the behavior and appearance of others at the expense of aligning with the truth of your own experience.

- The judge overrides your inherent intelligence and your direct response to life by superimposing its beliefs about what is meaningful and real. Its standards are learned from others, and they can run counter to what you yourself want, feel, or know to be true.

- One of the greatest dangers of becoming aware of self-judgment and its negative effects is that that awareness will become the basis of more self-judgment.

- Positive judgment can expose the unconscious acceptance of inner devaluation, but it can never root out the original conviction of your own lack of worth.

- Judgment, comparison, and self-blame can be transformed only by coming to understand how your sense of who you are and the options open to you is determined by your past experiences and beliefs.

- Once you know deep inside you, with a direct and felt sense, that you have inherent value and are fully acceptable to yourself, then you will begin to free yourself from the need for positive judgment and approval, from others or from your own judge.

- Your true guide arises spontaneously through your contact with and awareness of your own life; this guide responds to the truth of who you are and what is needed.

EXERCISE: OBSERVING YOUR MOTIVATIONS

Step 1. Choose one day to focus on what motivates your various activities and behaviors. In particular, you want to observe how you tend to navigate between criticism and the need for approval.

Step 2. At the end of the day, make two lists. One consists of all activities motivated by the desire to avoid criticism. Separate those activities aimed at avoiding the criticism of others from those aimed at avoiding self-criticism. The second list consists of actions motivated by the desire to gain approval. Separate it the same way between the desire for others' approval and the desire for self-approval.

Step 3. Compare the two parts of each list to see which activities are directed toward others and which are directed toward your own judge. Do they overlap? Is your avoidance-of-criticism list longer than your desire-for-approval list, or vice versa? Why?

The superego is a structure that forms the apex of the psychic structure and includes the ideals of the personality and the principles of judgment. It is the seat of what is customarily called the conscience. It develops mainly by internalizing and identifying with the prohibitions, rules, values, and preferences of the parents and society at large. . . .

From our perspective, the superego is the inner coercive agency that stands against the expansion of awareness and inner development, regardless of how mild or reasonable it becomes. It is a substitute, and a cruel one, for direct perception and knowledge. Inner development requires that in time there be no internal coercive agencies. There will be instead inner regulation based on objective perception, understanding, and love.

The best approach is to decrease the power and influence of the superego and to replace it with awareness as much as possible, all the way to the final and complete dethronement of the superego.

— A. H. Almaas, *Essence,* pp. 134, 137

Frank washed the sleep from his eyes and gazed at his reflection in the bathroom mirror. His hair sticking up in all directions reminded him of his father's saying he looked like a rooster in the morning. As he leaned closer, he was aware of all the familiar aspects of his face: his broken nose bent slightly to the right, which always bothered him when he looked in the mirror; the dusting of freckles on his cheeks and the dimples framing his mouth—those "boyish" qualities he had mixed feelings about; his hazel eyes set back deep in his face, overhung by sparse, lengthy eyebrows that curled down and caught on his eyelashes in a way that often annoyed him; the lines across his forehead by now permanently etched, though he would often rub his fingers over them, attempting with determined pressure to erase them. His hairline had receded about an inch, and the territory of his scalp was infiltrated with white settlers equal in number to the original dark inhabitants.

❧ *You look a lot older than you used to. In fact, you look a lot like your father now, you realize that? Even the way you run your hands through your hair and rub your chin. The worst thing, though, is how you pick your nose like him. I can't believe you have never learned to stop doing that. It's so disgusting!*

Frank observed the hairs sticking out of his nostrils and wished his fingers didn't enjoy scraping the inside of his nose so much. He reached down and picked up his electric razor, flicked it on, and carefully trimmed his nose hairs and then his eyebrow hairs. He pondered the state of his unshaved chin and decided to stay with the Indiana Jones look today.

❧ *Go ahead, be a slob. After all, it's Saturday, and no one will care. Besides, you love any excuse to be lazy.*

Frank was used to trying to ignore his judge, pretending what it said didn't matter. Today, he realized that feigned indifference never worked; he was just feeling withdrawn and hollow inside. Looking at himself in the mirror, he began to wonder what he was looking at besides the body he knew so well with all the stories and judgments associated with it. Was there anything else there? Frank looked into his eyes and wondered what he was seeing. Was it just the analytic gaze of his own judge? Or was he seeing sadness and fear? Perhaps there was nothing there but emptiness. Slowly, it became clear that Frank was seeing curiosity in the eyes watching him—a curious being clothed in a familiar body. He felt as if that curiosity were him.

3

TRUE NATURE
AND REALITY

TWO CONCEPTS REFERRED TO throughout this book that are fundamental to the perspective of the soul are *true nature* (with its related essential qualities) and *reality*. They are not specifically defined because they are more directions for exploration and revelation than terms with a single definition. By the time you have finished reading and working with this book, you will have experienced each of these concepts for yourself. For now, I will say a few things to orient your consideration.

True Nature

True nature refers to the essence of you as a human being. It is the experience of who you are that is not related to your physical dimensions or characteristics, not defined by your emotional propensities or personality type, not a result of your particular history and conditioning, and not affected by your beliefs or opinions. It is the ground of the soul, the heart of your own living consciousness. When you meet someone and you don't know a name or anything about the person, what is it that you are meeting? You see a body and hear a voice, listen to stories and watch behavior patterns. But is there something more fundamental and common to all human beings that you can be aware of in this person? When someone says, "After all, we are all human beings," what does that mean?

We all share something that allows us to respond to a story from a primitive tribe in Africa or a myth arising out of ancient Japan. We are all linked by these experiences of being human, no matter what our family, racial, or religious background; physical characteristics; psychological development; or education. Some spiritual traditions refer to true nature as Being or Essence—the essence of what we are beneath our individual histories.

True nature also refers to the part of you that is most permanent, unchanging, and central in defining who you are. In general, you consider your body, your personal history, and your emotional makeup to be the most distinctive and unchanging aspects of your experience of yourself. These aspects in one way or another seem to define who you are, distinguishing you from other people and setting limits on how much you can change. Furthermore, they are so familiar you can't imagine experiencing yourself without them. But are they who you are? Or are you something more fundamental known through or beyond these traits?

"I am a forty-five-year-old man, curly haired, slender of build, fair-skinned, and flat-footed. I am intelligent, even-tempered, and slow to express emotions. I was born in Canada to parents of Scottish and German heritage. I have been a dancer and a typesetter, and now I am a spiritual teacher." I can be defined by any or all of these descriptive elements, which, except for my age, will not likely change. Though I may think of myself in these ways, these facts define only the outer layer of me. They are not what I know as me. I know myself most intimately through an immediate awareness of my own presence—a core sense that "I am here now." This inner sense also contains the feeling of self-recognition: "This is me." Ultimately, you know yourself through this inner sense or perception of your own existence. That never changes; as long as you are alive, you can sense your existence and your "youness." And whatever arises in you can be felt as an expression of your presence in your own life. This is your true nature, that which makes you unique *and* gives you kinship with all other human beings.

Because the soul is pure consciousness, its true nature, its defining and unchanging core, is beyond the physical body, with its intellect and emotions, and beyond your accumulated history. The soul's true nature exists most fundamentally as a nowness; it is a nature that does not depend on the past or the future, nor does it depend on the experience of being a physical body. The more you have a sense of yourself as soul, the more you are aware that who you truly are is not really defined by your body. Neither is it defined by what you have learned or known in the past. Who you are is something much more intimate and immediate and something much more mysterious and harder to define. To be aware of this is to begin to open to the true nature of the soul, your own beingness *now* in your life.

Though it is a common birthright of all people, true nature manifests uniquely in each person through the soul. Furthermore, that uniqueness of the soul is inherent in who you are at birth: it is not achieved, nor can it be destroyed, and it is not dependent on your appearance or anything you do. You can, however, lose touch with your true nature—or even forget that it exists.

Do you believe in such a thing as the soul's true nature? This book assumes that it exists—that as a human being you did not begin life as the proverbial blank slate ready to be written on or lump of clay ready to be shaped by your upbringing. The existence of true nature means you have implicit qualities or capacities beyond those learned or instilled in you as you grow. True nature is the spiritual foundation of the soul, and thus it underlies your psychic reality, and the judge in particular. However, you need not believe in true nature to find this book of use; just take it as an interesting hypothesis and see what happens. I encourage you to be open to this perspective and observe how it affects you and relates to your own experience.

Essential qualities are elements of your true nature—attributes *essential* to what is most true in the experience of being human. These qualities include truth, joy, compassion, will, strength, and peace, to name only a few. They are not mental descriptions of experience but actual substantial forms of presence. Always existing as potentials in the soul, essential qualities manifest individually in consciousness in response to the needs of the situation. Each is a distinct manifestation of true nature, having its own flavor, texture, feeling tone, and effect on the soul. For example, compassion is warm, soft, expansive, gentle, and provides appreciative support for being with hurt, while personal will is solid, definite, confident, and a source of firm support for persisting on a difficult path.

True nature includes all these qualities and many more as well. It is a many-faceted diamond of priceless value buried in the unconscious depths of each person. The exploration of your personal relationship to your own true nature is a major element in self-understanding. Do you experience your true nature? Do you recognize it in yourself and in others? Does it play a part in your life? What gets in the way of it? Can you allow it to shine through you? How does self-judgment affect your appreciation of your true nature?

Reality

While true nature is something inside you—part of your inner experience rather than your outer or physical life—*reality* includes both internal and external. It is perhaps even more difficult to define than true nature. In simplest terms, reality refers to how things are, what the facts are about a situation, the actual elements that make up what is occurring at any given place and time.

One of the greatest challenges in self-understanding and, specifically, confronting your inner critic is learning to attend to what feels most true in each moment and thus orient to reality. The degree to which you are in contact with reality will depend on the extent of your awareness at any moment. Let me give you an example.

I am sitting at my desk mulling over my unfinished book. What is the reality of my situation? My reality includes what is happening with me, so we begin with the fact that my attention is focused on my book. My book is the physical product of my writing, but it is more than that: it is the entire psychic composite of what the book represents: the ideas, the history of writing it, my feelings about being an author and claiming to be an authority, my hopes for its success, and so on. Since "my book" could refer to many things, we will have to be more specific in order to be clear about present reality. To be more precise, the reality of my inner state is worry and concern about being able to complete the book: Will I do it? When will I do it? Will I be satisfied with it? What is stopping me from finishing? Do I really want to finish? Do I need to be more disciplined about working on it?

Behind these questions, I begin to recognize my judge saying to me, "You are so slow getting this done. You keep distracting yourself with other things. You'd better watch out or you will give up and stop altogether." I feel evaluated, criticized, and motivated. This is familiar.

My awareness is focused now on the content of my intense thinking. I can easily become lost in my thoughts and self-judgments. But that is not all of my reality. If I expand my awareness a bit, I realize my reality is that I am sitting at my desk while worrying about my book. This puts me in touch with more of my reality: not only my psychic process but also the physical experience of being engaged in that process. My head feels thick with the psychic busyness of planning my book. Then I notice how my body feels: tension contracts my arms and legs, my breathing is shallow, my stomach muscles are a little knotted, and my brow is furrowed.

As I pay attention to my physical sensations, I discover a new element in my reality: I am feeling afraid. When this recognition comes together with what my judge has been saying, I am immediately aware of the source of the fear: I am afraid I won't finish my book. This brings a new insight: the fear connects me with my belief that I am someone who has great ideas but often fails to bring them into existence. I realize I am afraid this book will be another example of such a great idea. The judge is now telling me that my slowness means I will most likely not finish, which will be more proof of my lack of will.

So now I don't just have a tense body with a head full of worries and plans, I have the body and mind of a particular someone who doesn't complete things and is afraid of being considered a failure if that happens again. More precisely, I am someone who believes he *is* a failure and must struggle to prove that it's not true. The judge is telling me what my experience means and who I am as a person. So now the larger reality is that I am someone with a history of believing certain things about himself, who has self-judgments that cause him to feel and behave in certain ways.

I feel a strong tendency to want to argue with my judge, to

explain myself and justify my actions. I want to convince it that I am not a failure. Shame begins to arise in me. This is territory I know well. At this moment, the judge is a major factor in shaping my reality. Part of me wants to distract myself so I don't have to feel all these uncomfortable emotions, and another part is determined to know my reality fully. I feel a certain solid energy filling my belly and legs; it seems to provide me with the will to continue being aware without engaging the judge in argument. My judge, however, is not easily discouraged: "You can't ignore me because you know that what I am saying is true." I find I must be more forceful in supporting myself to keep it from taking over. I imagine turning toward the judge and using all the energy in my belly to yell "Shut up!" That aggressive mental action clears my head and allows me to come back to my self-awareness.

Now what arises is the recognition that taking myself to be someone struggling against failure has been around a long time. This sense of myself has been a recurring theme throughout my life. I can feel that it stems from a childhood belief that if I didn't follow through on my potential to achieve, my parents would be disappointed and I would lose their love. I am now seeing a deeper level of my present reality. Who I am and what I'm experiencing in the moment is rooted in the child who wants his parents' love and is afraid of losing it. This child's feelings underlie the self-judgments that drive my concern about completing my book. At this point, I find I am no longer caught up in the worrying and self-judgment; instead, I am experiencing the sense of being an unloved child. I feel small, alone, and afraid of a world that seems much bigger than me. I am sad and long for my parents' love. I am aware of the way the tension in my body reflects these feelings.

Usually, I hate feeling like a small, helpless child. I don't want reality to be this way, so whenever I feel like this, I react and tell myself (as my judge), "You don't need your parents' love anymore; you're an adult. Grow up and stop worrying." From there, I put my attention back on some activity and ignore my emotions. Unfortunately, adopting this attitude has never changed reality; it has only cut me off from the truth of my reality in the moment.

This time, however, I am touched by this young sense of myself. I begin to experience a gentle warmth in my chest and a feeling of appreciation and caring for the scared child. This compassion for myself in my present situation relaxes me and quiets my mind. I breathe more fully and am able to allow the small-child feelings while being aware of myself as much more than those feelings. The unconscious link between the child and my book has been broken. The self-judgment that was affecting my writing is now gone, and I can proceed with my work feeling more grounded in an expanded sense of reality.

You can always increase your awareness of reality by recognizing more of the truth of what you are experiencing. Or you can choose to deny, avoid, or only selectively be in contact with reality by focusing on what you believe or prefer rather than on what you actually experience. The judge is an active participant in all of these activities, as in the example above. Denial, avoidance, and selective contact all go on without choice when you are unconscious of the role your judge plays in your experience and your motivations.

For growth and change to occur, it is important that you recognize your experiential reality in each situation of your life because that reality determines the limits and potential of what is possible at any given time. The work on my book was plagued by self-judgment and fear of failure. Without seeing the deeper aspects of my reality, I would never have been free of the need to prove that I could succeed. Once I recognized my identification as someone who had to struggle against failure and the underlying fear of losing my parents' love, a shift occurred. The self-judgment stopped. Reality felt less limited, more open. The more I was aware of the truth, the more my true nature began to arise in the form of personal will, strength, and compassion. These, in turn, supported a fuller contact with reality.

The key ingredient in being in contact with reality is attention to what feels most true at the present moment. However, being in touch with a truth in your experience does not mean you are aware of all of your reality. Each moment of truth, when allowed without judgment, will become a door to a deeper experience of reality and what is true.

My awareness of reality moved through many steps:

The book
The worry and self-judgment
My physical sensations while worrying
My fear of failure
My judgment about failing
The determination not to justify myself
Standing up to the judge
The recognition of my history around failure
Anticipated parental disappointment
Me as an unloved child with his painful feelings
The awareness of and compassion for that child
An ease once again with my book

This is an example of inquiring into reality in the moment, a process that can reveal the unfolding depths of one's present experience. Inquiry of this kind is a profound practice requiring many years to become skillful at allowing. Do not expect that your own awareness of reality will reveal itself as simply or directly as I have described. However, my process captures many elements that you will be working with throughout this book. You may choose to refer back to it after you have read further.

The Judge Avoids Reality

Listening to your judge orients you *away* from reality. The judge believes that reality is not safe, is problematic, and will get you into trouble. Many times in your childhood, you endured situations that were painful, scary, overwhelming, and frustrating. Such feelings were hard to tolerate, and their impact on you had to be controlled for you to feel safe. The judge's job was to protect you from being overwhelmed or threatened by these experiences. It used denial, avoidance, and selective awareness as basic defenses. Now it continues to believe that you must be protected from the reality of your life; in fact, you must be protected from almost any direct experience of reality. The judge defines the way you experience reality by telling you what to pay attention to and what is important. It will constantly steer you away from paying attention to your full experience in the moment. It does not trust that there is any value or benefit in being more real with yourself.

The judge generally recognizes the importance of essential human qualities such as value, strength, peace, compassion, and will. However, it does not believe that you have them innately; it tells you that you must acquire them from the outside through accomplishments and good behavior: "If you are an unselfish, giving person, then perhaps you have some value." The judge believes that you can only claim these qualities when you prove that you have earned them, you can control them, and you can live up to them through meeting its standards. If you can't, then it tells you, "You must be faking the experience; these qualities are only a temporary occurrence, and they will be taken away from you at any moment because they don't belong to you anyway."

This perspective gives the judge the important job of preparing, instructing, and warning you about what you must do to have access to these basic elements of human experience. For the judge, these soul qualities are more like rewards or achievements that are desirable but not necessary. The judge believes true nature is an illusion or a myth when it refers to anything other than your body, your personality, and your history.

In order to confront the judge's dominance in guiding and controlling your experience, you must first recognize true nature does exist in you and that it is not the result of your accomplishments or effect on others. It is and has always been part of you. You also must see how your judge continually undermines such an awareness. Then you must call upon specific qualities of your true nature to challenge the way the judge operates. In the example above, awareness, will, strength, and compassion each played a part in breaking the control of the judge on my experience. As you recognize and develop your contact with these aspects of your humanness that lie deeper than habit, preference, and early conditioning, you will discover an alternative guidance and support system that is grounded in a more fundamental sense of reality.

With each of the aspects of true nature presented in this book, you will see that the judge has common and familiar ways of trying to minimize, undermine, or attack that quality. The degree to which it has succeeded in cutting you off from your true nature is the degree to which you are dependent on it as a substitute for those lost qualities. So with each quality, we will look at common ways your judge attacks you for activating that capacity and, in contrast, specific ways that capacity helps you eliminate the need for the judge.

PRACTICE: THE REALITY OF DRIVING

This practice encourages recognizing some of the different facets of reality in the experience of traveling in a car. It can be done anytime you are driving or riding in a car and are not fully occupied with the driving or in some other way. It is good practice for deepening your contact with reality.

Step 1. Put your attention on the external physical reality of the car, the road, and the larger environment (weather, landscape, other cars, and so forth). Notice the familiar elements, new objects, and ones you had not noticed before even though they have been there.

Step 2. Tune in to your own physical sensations as you sit in the car. How does your body feel—comfortable, relaxed, tense, headache, shallow breathing? Is your physical state related to the driving or to something else (such as a previous physical condition or something that happened earlier in the day)?

Step 3. Now notice what you are feeling emotionally. Are you anxious, worried, excited, joyful, scared, angry, sad, numb, pressured? Is this a continuation of an emotional state you were in before getting in the car or a reaction to your experience of driving?

Step 4. Let yourself focus on the content of your mind. You may have noticed this content coming in as you paid attention to the three previous facets of your reality, or you may have noticed your mind (judge) explaining what you were experiencing, what it means, or what to do about it. What are you thinking about? Are you preoccupied with something as you drive? Does your thinking stop your awareness of the other facets of the reality of driving?

Step 5. Having checked in with these four dimensions of your personal reality, take a look at how your experience of driving changes, if at all. Is it possible to hold all the dimensions in your awareness at once? What happens then? Do you feel more (or less) comfortable, expanded, in control, overwhelmed, tense, relaxed, open, awake?

Entering the kitchen, Frank noticed the dirty dishes from yesterday on the counter and in the sink.

❧ *Why didn't she clean up last night? I hate having to walk into a dirty kitchen.*

Well, she did make dinner for us, you know. I think it was your turn to clean up. It's your own fault you were up till one in the morning watching TV and were too tired to do anything after that except go to bed. You waste so much time in front of that tube.

Frank turned on the hot water and began rinsing the dishes, using his hands to make sure all the food was wiped off and then stacking them in the dish rack.

❧ *You know you're supposed to use soap and a sponge. Someday, you're going to get sick . . .*

Oh, shut up, you old turdface. I'll do what I want to do.

As he cleaned, Frank could feel the tension in his jaw that seemed to add to the pain in his neck. His chest felt constricted, and he was tight in the shoulders. As his inner agitation increased, he began to worry about breaking a dish.

❧ *Hey, what are you so uptight about? Get a grip on yourself and relax.*

At that, Frank stopped, putting both hands on the edge of the sink with the water still running, and took a deep breath. He moaned to himself as he exhaled. He couldn't seem to focus his thoughts or clear his head. Finally, he straightened up, shut off the water, and walked to the kitchen door. He opened it and stepped out into the sun on the porch, letting his robe fall open and the warm air touch the skin all over his body. He shivered as the warmth clashed with his jangled nerve endings. Slowly, he began to relax as his body bathed in the sunshine, his closed eyes gazing upward.

❧ *You know, some neighbor is going to see you out here naked. It's your exhibitionism again. You just want someone to see you.*

Frank had to open his eyes and check to make sure that the bushes and the fence blocked him from the neighbors' view. They did, but now it was hard to relax. He wrapped his robe around him and stood surrounded by the trees in the sunlight, the movement and singing of small birds, and the bright magenta color of the bougainvillea growing up the side of the porch.

4

RECOGNIZING JUDGMENT

JUDGMENT IS A WAY OF describing part of the terrain of your inner world. If you pictured the world inside your mind as a landscape, different kinds of mental activity would appear as different kinds of terrain. For instance, there might be the lush jungles of fantasy, the geometrical cities of financial calculation, the flowing rivers of dreams, and the silent, expansive deserts of simple awareness. In this inner world, judgment would appear in various forms, such as the old, familiar neighborhood of your childhood, unchanged and lifeless. Or the surrealistic freeways that move you quickly from one place to another but never let you get off except for gas and food, because all exits are permanently under construction. Or the set of a Hollywood movie where the surroundings appear impressive and desirable but have no substance or reality.

Judgment is a central element of your inner dialogue, the way you talk to yourself. From that point of view, it is second nature to you, so close to you that it is hard even to become aware of its existence. "So I talk to myself—I rationalize, explain, justify, question, doubt, evaluate, scold, gossip, confess—all kinds of things. Why should I make a big deal about judgment?" It seems natural, and even when someone else judges you, if it is in the familiar terms you use with yourself, you assume that it is part of life, to be expected.

However, there is good reason to isolate this part of your inner process. Self-judgment is perhaps the greatest source of inner suffering and discontent. More than that—or because of that—it is one of the major barriers to change, growth, expansion, and transformation. In particular, it prevents you from simply resting in yourself from moment to moment. Presumably, you have picked up this book because you have recognized that judgment has a negative impact on you. We will see much more about what this means as we go along. This chapter will focus on recognizing the activity of judgment and seeing how it works in your inner life.

First, a preliminary definition: *A judgment is a statement of evaluation that implies an assessment of one's value or worth and is felt as a rejection of one's present state.* Here, *present state* can refer to an emotion or feeling, a particular behavior, a bodily experience, a self-image, or an idea about yourself—whatever the central elements are of your immediate experience.

The work begins with learning to recognize when you are experiencing a judgment. This may seem simple, but it is not. Certain judgments you are aware of and can describe. Most of your experiences of judgment, however, are unconscious. Your judgments of yourself are generally more visible to those close to you than they are to you. Generally, you don't want to see your self-criticisms; you feel your badness will be exposed. That fear is natural and to be respected. As you learn about yourself, you will become more compassionate and grounded and thus able to see more of what creates this fear. The process of self-acceptance takes time. Just be aware that any feelings or reactions you have now are part of the first steps in that process.

So the first task is to learn to recognize what a judgment is. A judgment may be felt as any of the following: criticism, condemnation, guideline, motivator, accusation, advice, rejection, suggestion, question, or praise. It may come from another person or from inside your own mind. However you interpret its intention and whatever its source, you are affected by it in a particular way that makes it fall under the heading "judgment." To see this more clearly, it helps to reduce the implied content of the statement or question to a single declarative sentence.

What Judgment Says

Step one of recognition is: Identify the judgmental statement. If it wasn't explicit, you need to make it explicit. Sometimes, someone will talk to you for five minutes and only if you boil it all down to one statement will you realize that you felt judged by her words. Similarly, you can tell yourself all kinds of stories in your head, but if the net result is that you feel bad about yourself, then you have been engaged in self-judgment. So if someone says to you when you are ten minutes late for an appointment, "Look what time it is! My four-year-old could have ridden his tricycle here by now. I hope you feel good about making me miss morning coffee," you can boil that down to "You are a jerk for being late." You begin to confront the judge by making it visible or, in this case, audible.

I recommend the following practice for verbalizing judgments: Put the judgment statement in the second person. Word the statement as if you were the judge talking to someone else. In other words, make "you" statements rather than "I" statements. This helps distinguish the judge from the one being judged, even if both parts are inside you. So instead of saying "I really screwed up," the judgment is "You really screwed up."

Note: On the surface, this seems to go against the current recommendation for self-expression, which is to make "I" statements. However, the purpose here is not to have you take responsibility for your own feelings, as it is when "I" statements are encouraged in interpersonal communication. The purpose is to clarify the fact that there are two different parts inside of you in dialogue. When you say, "I really screwed up," you are taking responsibility for something as if it were a fact, without acknowledging that there is a judgment involved and critical energy is being directed at you.

Let's look at some examples of judge statements. Notice that the judgmental quality derives from how they make you feel and is unrelated to whether or not the statements are true. Let's begin with obvious ones:

You shouldn't have done that.

You are such a weakling.

I can't believe you made such a stupid comment.

You'd better not let that happen again.

If you don't get started now, you'll never amount to anything.

Now you really blew it.

You are so fat no one will ever be interested in you.

You will never be a success, so forget it.

I told you you didn't have a chance.

It's about time you got that right.

What makes you think anyone cares about you at all?

No one will ever take you seriously.

You think you're so smart, don't you?

Some less obvious but no less devastating ones:

If only you weren't so slow, you could probably amount to something.

How come you don't really care about me?

You should be making more money at your age.

I knew you could do better if you really tried.

You have such incredible potential.

Only really lazy people sleep in until 9:00 AM.

How come you can't understand that I'm just trying to help you?

You shouldn't be so hard on yourself.

You really have a hard time accepting criticism, don't you?

Notice that many of these statements could be distilled even further to get a clearer judgment out of them. For instance, "How come you can't understand that I'm just trying to help you?" is more simply stated as "You are an ungrateful slob." Or "How come you don't really care about me?" boils down to "You are uncaring and selfish."

When you add the tone of voice of the one making the statement and your own history around being judged, all kinds of other seemingly innocuous statements can be felt as judgments. Ones like:

You look tired. (Heard as: What's wrong with you?)

I hate it when you talk like that. (Heard as: There's something wrong with you.)

How old are you? (Heard as: You are over the hill.)

You made a mistake. (Heard as: You're useless!)

One question often arises at this point: What about positive judgments? Should you only be concerned about statements with a negative content? This is a good question. The statements that cause the most difficulty are clearly the negative ones; in fact, if your own self-judgments were always positive, you would be unlikely to care about challenging the judge. Perhaps you are actually seeking a way to turn your negative judgmental statements into positive ones. That would undoubtedly make you feel better, but it would not change the underlying dynamic of engaging in self-judgment in the first place.

Life Lessons

Michael had worked hard on his dance piece for two months, and in the days before he was to perform, he became very anxious. However, when the night of the performance arrived, he was surprised to find himself calm and confident. Spurred on by the lights and the energy of the audience, he danced better than he ever had. As he left the stage, his judge was there to provide comment: "You showed them; man, you are great. I bet they were secretly hoping you'd fail, but you are the number one top dog! Now don't say anything, though, because you don't want anyone thinking you got a swelled head."

At the reception, he grinned when his girlfriend, Carla, came up to congratulate him. "You were so beautiful up there. I couldn't believe how perfectly you danced. You are so inspiring to me. Oh, I wish I could dance like that. I didn't see one mistake. And what was that wild music you used?" Michael just kept smiling, but his

judge was talking again:"What did she mean she didn't see one mistake? This could be trouble. What if you blow it next time? After all,
dude, you may have been good, but you weren't perfect. Who does
she think you are anyway, Baryshnikov?"

A positive or negative judgment is different from a positive or negative feeling. A feeling is an emotional state arising in response to
something. In contrast, a judgment is an evaluation of yourself as
good or bad, right or wrong. Judgments and feelings are closely associated, as we shall see. However, you can like or dislike something
without having a judgment about it.

When you say something like "I like the job I did, and I feel
really good that I completed it," it might seem that the first part is
a statement of feeling and the second is a positive self-judgment.
Let's look more closely. If it is a self-judgment, you are saying: "I
really am a good person because I completed it." This is clearly a
defense against a judgment that you are not a good person. There is
nothing wrong with this; recognizing you have value that is reflected in functioning is an important element in building self-
esteem. However, it is not the same as knowing that your own value
is completely separate from the results of what you do. In the preceding example, Michael's judge is clearly passing judgment on him,
saying how great he is because he did so well and countering an
implicit evaluation of inferiority.

On the other hand,"I feel really good that I completed it" might
not be judgmental but instead descriptive of how you feel in a non-
specific way. It could then be restated as:"Having completed the job,
I feel happy [satisfied, expansive, excited, appreciative]." No judgment of self is involved here.

Negative judgments stimulate feelings of rejection, guilt, doubt,
shame, and self-hatred, while positive judgments tend to arouse feelings of self-esteem, pride, excitement, self-righteousness, and superiority. Either way, these results are conditional, and you are left
dependent on the judge to reject or approve of you. In this book, I
am encouraging you to go beyond turning rejection into approval
and to question the very assumptions underlying self-judgment.

There is no quick route to undoing this mental activity, which serves as glue for our psychic structure. The process is gradual and requires patience and commitment. Positive self-judgments are an important support and guide for life in the world and cannot be put aside until you discover and integrate the self-knowing for which they are a substitute. Negative self-judgments are generally less functional, as well as more painful and debilitating, so we put our attention on them first. For that reason, most of the examples used here are negative, but the principles of self-judgment apply to positive content as well. Learning to stop the effects of negative self-judgment will create a ground for considering the limitations in giving and receiving positive self-judgment.

How Judgment Feels Energetically

Whatever the content of the statement or question, judgments always have an energetic effect on the one feeling judged. Besides recognizing the actual content that contains the judgment, it is equally important to notice how the statement affects you. If it doesn't have an effect, there would be no reason to be concerned about judgments. Fortunately, it is not too difficult to begin to recognize the effects of being judged as you develop somatic (body) self-awareness. This means sensing your own energetic state, your bodily sensations, and your capacity to function physically. The more you can distinguish among various states such as being numb, spaced out, distracted, aroused, tense, agitated, alert, anxious, calm, relaxed, protective, or vigilant, the more you will be able to carry out step two of judgment recognition: Learn to recognize the experience of judgment through the way it changes your energetic and somatic state. Becoming familiar with your own particular energetic symptoms will help you to know when you are feeling judged, even if you don't recognize in your mind that a judgment has taken place.

- Robert is talking to his girlfriend, and she says, "You never buy me flowers. I don't think you really care about me." What happens to his energy? His gut tightens up, his face stiffens, his breath becomes shallow, his center of gravity feels up in his throat, and he is no longer aware of the rest of the room.

- Lois spends all afternoon shopping and making a special dinner for her partner and a couple of friends, only to realize she forgot to get dessert and has no time now to go get it. Her judge speaks up, "Wow, you really blew this one." How is she doing now? Her face flushes, her shoulders tighten up, and it is harder to concentrate on what she has left to do. She can no longer feel the rest of her body, and she begins rushing.

- Marie is thirty-seven years old and overweight. While working out in a Jazzercise class one day, she finds herself fixated on the eighteen-year-old girl in the front who is lean and trim. Her judge whispers, "Why don't you look like her, dear?" Her stomach is tied in a knot, her feet and legs feel as if they were made out of lead, her palms are sweaty, and she can't make her body coordinate to the music anymore.

- Ralph gets a notice from the IRS that he is going to be audited. He spends the rest of the day dazed and out of his body. Twice his business partner has to shake him to get his attention. Later he runs into a door and knocks over a can of Pepsi.

Common physical experiences of judgment include loss of energy, agitation, tension, depression, anxiety, heat, weakness, restlessness, deadness, spaciness, tunnel vision, and numbness. Notice that these responses occur regardless of the judgment's content. They indicate that a judgment affects you through its form as well as its content. When a judgment is directed at you—whether you are conscious of it or not—you tend to experience the world closing in on you. Your functioning becomes impaired due to this narrowing of attention and loss of flexibility and aliveness. The overriding manifestation is the marked decrease in awareness—of the environment, of what is going on around you, of your possible responses, and especially of who you are. And what is profoundly frustrating for many people is the way judgment interferes with their capacity, clarity, and sense of humor.

How Judgment Feels Emotionally

This brings us to how judgments make you feel emotionally, which is step three in judgment recognition: Learn to recognize the emotional reaction you have to judgments. You may be more aware of your feeling responses than your energetic response, or vice versa. The energetic effects limit your functioning and cause frustration, but the emotional effects of judgment often result in pain and suffering.

- Diane has just found a bad run in her panty hose and has no time to buy a new pair before an important job interview. Her judge has no mercy. She feels exposed, panicked, ashamed, ugly, and hopeless.
- Leo's father recently told him it was a disgrace that he was forty-two years old and still didn't make enough money to buy a house. Leo feels ashamed, small, afraid, and hurt.
- Melanie's ten-year-old son comes home from school complaining that his friend's mom let him stay up as late as he wanted to. Why is Melanie so mean to him? Melanie feels angry, resentful, unappreciated, guilty, and defensive.
- Paul has just come out of a private session where he realized how afraid to approach women he has been all his life, something he covered up by pretending he didn't care. His judge jumps on him: "What a phony you have been all this time, acting as if you didn't like women. You are really pathetic." Paul's newfound awareness gives way to humiliation, defeat, withdrawal, and depression.

Remember, however, that you may have completely shut off your feelings in relation to many of your self-judgments. You may only be aware that the judgment activity is a nagging, bothersome habit that you can't seem to stop and that serves no useful purpose. In these cases, it may take patient and compassionate self-awareness to allow you to reach the emotion underlying your detachment. Until this happens, it will be impossible to understand specifically how a particular judgment works on you.

Judgments may make you feel deficient, guilty, selfish, dumb, out of control, afraid, angry, ashamed, hurt, humiliated, ugly, lazy, pathetic, sad, helpless, isolated, alienated, depressed, or possibly superior, arrogant, righteous, puffed up, to name but a few of the feelings.

All of these are unpleasant states no one likes to feel. The actual sensations can be uncomfortable or unpleasant, but even more difficult are the associated beliefs and memories connected to these states. In fact, your beliefs about these negative feelings are what cause them to affect your sense of self-worth. It is the devaluation engendered by judgments that causes you to dislike yourself for having those feelings, which brings about self-rejection.

A very important insight arises as a result of this awareness: You dislike and reject yourself for having certain feelings. Whatever the reason, this fact feels like a given, beyond your control. You were never taught that feelings are just feelings, that they are not statements about the kind of person you are. You automatically assume that there is something wrong with having feelings you characterize as negative. Remember, emotions, like thoughts and sensations, are forms the soul takes on; they do not define its true nature. What would happen if you didn't reject or dislike yourself for experiencing the feelings aroused by a judgment?

As you explore through this book the ways you came to believe that painful feelings must be avoided, the possibility that you can allow the entire spectrum of your feelings without rejecting any of them will become more apparent. This will become a key to dealing effectively with the judge.

Judgments and Attacks

Let's for a moment imagine an interaction between two people in order to observe more closely the effects of judgment:

> His boss throws the papers on Bob's desk and scowls, "Bob, that's the worst piece of promotional writing I have ever seen in my life! What's the matter with you?" Bob's shoulders slump, his eyes scan the floor, and trying to catch his breath, he stammers, "Yes,

well, I-I-I f-figured that approach m-might work. P-p-please give m-me another ch-chance. I n-need this job."

In this situation, an individual received input from another person and reacted by losing vitality, awareness, and responsiveness. His functioning became distorted in a range from impulsive overreaction to complete immobilization. From the outside, it would appear that Bob had been attacked—a verbal arrow shot him down. Internally, however, Bob experienced his boss's words as simply confirming his worst fear about himself—that he is a failure. Whether he is aware of it or not, he is feeling humiliation, guilt, and desperation. Now he is caught between the attack from the outside and the feared belief about himself on the inside. The result is an inability to respond appropriately to the attacking energy.

When most animals are attacked, unless the threat is extreme or overwhelming, they respond immediately with increased awareness, energy, and presence. The resulting behavior may be fight, flight, freeze, or in certain situations, playing dead or fainting. Even when humans are physically attacked, they generally become alert and more attuned to the situation, with increased energy to take the necessary action. What we are seeing here is that judgments are a form of psychic attack in which your beliefs about yourself are actively involved. The result is not a heightened aliveness and groundedness but quite the opposite. For Bob, it is as if the threat posed were too much for his system to handle: he acted more like a child responding to an angry adult.

When you see a sluggish, diminished, or distorted response to attack in an animal like a dog or a horse, you imagine that something is wrong: the animal must be drugged, sick, or maltreated. You may suspect that something in the animal's instinct for self-preservation is damaged. But you are so familiar with experiencing judgment that when humans react by becoming disoriented, impulsive, or paralyzed, you consider this to be normal.

When you become aware of how self-judgment operates in others, you see that most people react to it by becoming sluggish and constricted or by responding in a distorted way. Something in the human psyche blocks the natural energy of self-preservation. It is as if an objective observer from the outside can recognize the attack contained energetically in the judgment, but the person receiving the judgment cannot stay focused on that aspect of it. This is what makes a judgment seem different from an attack. Focusing on judgments as attacks makes it easier for you to respond appropriately, because you recognize an outside energy aggressively threatening your own state.

However, a judgment is usually perceived as indicating something about your *inner* state—in particular, your sense of worth. You get caught up in your concern about the accuracy of the content, and this undermines your awareness of the attack. Let's look at Bob's situation again. This time, he is able to respond without getting involved in his boss's judgment:

> His boss throws the papers on Bob's desk and scowls, "Bob, that's the worst piece of promotional writing I have ever seen in my life! What's the matter with you?" Bob takes a deep breath, to keep himself calm in the face of his boss's energy, and then says, "I see you didn't like what I wrote. I would appreciate it if you would sit down with me and show me where I went wrong."

Here, Bob feels the attack but does not allow it to trigger a negative evaluation of his own worth as a person. He recognizes the real threat is not what his boss is saying but the way it tends to pull him into reacting emotionally—that is, feeling judged. To deal with this, he stays focused on the matter at hand—the fact that his boss is displeased—and disregards the harsh judgment. By speaking directly to the dissatisfaction with his writing and not the exaggerated insult, Bob is making it clear that he will not get involved in his boss's putdown. He "cuts through" the verbal attack to what is most important at the moment and thereby defends himself.

Perhaps now you can begin to see why you respond differently to feeling judged than to feeling attacked. When you feel judged, you believe you have to change yourself because something is wrong with you; when you feel attacked, you know you need to defend yourself. Let's look at how this happens.

Judgment arouses negative feelings. Each negative feeling is connected to a particular idea or belief about the kind of person you are and how people will respond if that belief is true. For instance, if your judge attacks you by saying you are ugly, you might believe that makes you unlovable, and so you are afraid that nobody will choose to be with you. Feeling helpless might lead you to believe you are weak, needy, and ineffectual, so people will be disgusted and turn their backs. You do not like to experience these old self-images, so when you are in touch with feelings connected to those self-images, you want to distance yourself from the feelings by either denying them, trying to change them, ignoring them, or withdrawing from them. So in these cases, the content of the self-judgment pushes you into feeling ugly or helpless, and you instinctively move away from those feelings. The problem is that you also move away from any awareness that your judge provoked this self-rejection and the diminishment, disorientation, and paralysis that go with it.

In the first example, Bob got caught up in not wanting to be a failure and wasn't able to stay grounded and deal effectively with the energy his boss was directing at him. When you recognize the input of the other person or your own judge as an attack, you naturally stay focused on how it is affecting you and how to stop it. In the second example, Bob used the simple practice of taking a breath as a way to stay in touch with the immediate reality of feeling attacked by his boss's anger. This helped him to respond effectively.

It is important to recognize at this point that self-judgments served a very useful purpose for you as a child for just the aforementioned reason. The sense of invasion, rejection, or hurt caused by the parent's critical energy was often overwhelming to your sensitivity. So distancing from yourself (self-rejection) dulled your awareness of the attack to help you survive what was intolerable or unstoppable. In extreme cases of abuse and trauma, the only way to survive was to completely dissociate from reality in the moment. In this case, all awareness of the feelings and sensations involved is suppressed: the child leaves her body until it is safe to return and usually does not remember what her experience was. We will see that your engagement with judgment is a mild form of dissociation, in that you lose touch with the experience of being attacked and the resulting damage. Instead, you take on the content of the judgment and the judge's perspective of what is important, and the instinctual movement to respond appropriately is blocked.

Judgments as Intentional Attacks

A judgment is an insidious form of attack because it points to a part of you that you are not comfortable with, and thus, you believe the negative assessment is justified. This belief, in turn, blocks your ability to respond to the judgment as an attack because now you are seeing *yourself*, not the judgment, as the problem. In other words, the judgment stirs up a feeling in you of wrongness, which takes you into the past and away from your experience in the moment. Thus, you cannot appropriately respond to the implicit attack.

Not only do you tend to believe the content of the judgment in some form, but what is more important, you believe that the judge (in another or in yourself) has the right to evaluate and pass sentence on you, thereby condemning you to a diminished sense of self-esteem and effectiveness in your life. This implicit agreement to allow judgment will undo any attempts at appropriate response to the attack.

Step four in judgment recognition is: See how a judgment provokes self-rejection through intentionally making you feel a certain way. Some judgments make you feel guilty ("How could you have done such a thing?"); some make you feel ashamed ("Who do you think you are, talking like that?"); some provoke weakness, disgust, superiority, inferiority, hopelessness, and so on. The fact that you react in that way is not a unique problem you have; it is built into the judgment itself. In fact, the judge says those things in order to make you feel those particular feelings. Judgments attack you specifically by generating certain emotions that will arouse self-beliefs that disarm you. Seeing this helps keep your focus on the attack and minimize its undermining effect on you.

Imagine you had an enemy and, for some reason, every time he appeared, your body became limp and unresponsive and your mind couldn't remember that he was a threat. He could then simply suggest what he wanted, and you would do it. The symptoms would

disappear soon after he left, when you recovered your awareness of
what you wanted and how he was having you do something else. If
this happened several times, you would undoubtedly think something was wrong with you. You would begin to fear that your own
recurring helplessness was more of a danger than the threat of this
enemy. But then you found out he had a diabolical weapon in the
form of a subtle perfume, which, when breathed in, caused the
symptoms you felt each time. Now you would no longer believe
there was something wrong with you; you would prepare to defend
yourself against this new weapon by purchasing a gas mask!

This is one way of seeing your difficulty with the judge: you
believe that your debilitating feelings and beliefs are what is wrong
with you rather than recognizing them as part of the arsenal the
judge uses to attack you. Understanding how a judgment causes a
certain emotional effect in you helps you see the way the judgment
works as a skillful attack.

In Session

During a counseling session with me, George was unsettled from
an incident that had happened the day before. He and his wife
worked together, and she had been present while he told his secretary he was displeased with her way of handling things. He knew
he had been intensely critical about what he felt was wrong, but
although he was not terribly pleased with his behavior, he was ready
to move on. His wife, however, was not ready to let it go and continued to go on about how insensitive and overbearing he had been
with his secretary. George found it very difficult to be patient with
her comments, however true they might have been. When he
couldn't listen anymore, he tried to tell her to stop. When she kept
harping on it, he finally did the only thing he knew other than to
explode: he completely shut her out, clammed up, and stopped relating to her. That night, he slept on his own, as he sometimes does
when he and his wife reach an impasse.

The next morning, they could barely speak to each other.
George found he was caught up in a major internal struggle. He was
aware of his anger toward his wife, but he felt considerable conflict

about it; he couldn't just let himself feel angry. As I asked him about the anger, he responded with many different explanations for why he was suppressing his angry feelings: There was nothing else he could do. Blowing up only hurt other people. His wife really was often tuned in and probably saw the truth in this situation. He just wasn't feeling very tolerant, but why did she have to go on and on and not listen to him? And so on.

Clearly, his judge was on his case about his anger. It wouldn't let him just be pissed off; it had convinced him his anger was unjustified because he had in fact done something wrong. By making him feel guilty about having anger, the judge kept him away from simply allowing the anger in himself.

I asked if he would consider letting himself express his anger toward her while there with me. He was hesitant because he didn't think it would do any good. Nevertheless, he decided to try, and though he couldn't let himself express the energy of the anger, he spoke out loud the words that sprang to mind: "You fucking bitch, how dare you speak to me that way!" He smiled, enjoying actually saying the terrible words. "And, oh, yes, there's more. I want you to just take your righteousness and shove it up your goddamn asshole!" Again the smile. George was amazed at how that cleared away his conflict, and he no longer felt in turmoil or felt any anger toward his wife.

George's judge had been making him feel guilty about the emotion of anger coming up in response to her repeated attacks on his behavior: "You fucked up; you deserve to be reprimanded. And don't you dare get angry with me." Though he spoke the words of anger to his wife, he was really defending himself against his own judge, whom he was hearing in her voice. My supporting him to ignore the guilt the attack was provoking enabled George to find the energy he needed to dispel the attack.

The groundwork we are laying in these beginning chapters on becoming aware of judgments will help you recognize that a judgment is the same as an attack as far as the health of your being is concerned. One could even consider self-judgment the original psychic auto-immune disease. Because judgment causes you to reject yourself, the basic health of your soul is at risk. The more familiar you become with how judgment works, the more it actually feels like a self-destructive disease. The goal is to reestablish a vital survival energy and a healthy immune system that will respond to both attacks and judgments with awareness, alertness, energy, capacity, and appropriateness. The movement toward that goal reflects a continuing process of unraveling why judgments have such a debilitating effect on you and learning to defend your right to your present experience with strength and vitality.

Principles of Self-Judgment

The effect created by a judgment leads to a first fundamental principle: *A judgment always touches on something you believe is true about you.* The content of most judgments is conjecture, opinion, suggestion, interpretation, accusation, or belief, but the hook for you is the way the content *indicates* or *implies* something that you think is true about your value or worth. Bob's boss was implying he was a failure without literally saying it. Bob is caught by this in the first example because he is afraid it is true. He is not afraid that his writing was the worst piece of promotional writing his boss had ever seen. That is undoubtedly not true. He is afraid of the implied judgment. Deep down, he believes he *is* a failure and is afraid of what it will mean if he is found out. The key factor is not whether a judgment is true but whether you believe that it is. The tricky part is that your belief in the truth of the judgment may be completely unconscious and may even be the opposite of what you think you believe.

> David was angry at his girlfriend, Pam, for taking so long to get ready for the prom. When she finally got into the car, he rebuked her, "I don't know why you spend an hour putting on makeup. Everyone knows it's just a cover-up for how plain you look!" Pam was devastated. Though she was strikingly attractive and acted the part—using her good looks to win attention and boyfriends— she had never believed in her own beauty. Instead, she was secretly convinced that her attractive appearance was the result of her

makeup and her pretending and that people just went along with the charade. David's cruel comment struck the deep place where this belief resided, and she felt exposed and helpless.

The clue to recognizing your hidden belief is that you are hooked by the judgmental statement. If you did not believe what is implied by the judgment in any way, then it would have no debilitating effect on you and you could defend yourself appropriately. This was the case in the second example with Bob earlier in the chapter: Bob did not believe in his boss's implied judgment and so was able to handle the attack effectively. Here is another example:

> Judy bumped into an old friend, Karen, at the natural food store.
> "How's it going, Karen? Have you got a man in your life yet?"
> Karen smiled and responded, "No, no interesting eligible male has shown his face in a dog's age. Got any suggestions?"
> Judy paused and frowned. "Lower your standards, if you ask me. You always acted like you were too good for any man who was interested in you."
> "Well, that's a pretty judgmental assessment of me." Karen paused in thought and then, looking at Judy, continued brightly, "If that were the case, it would explain everything, wouldn't it? I bet you're glad you don't have my problem!" Then she turned and walked away.

Here, Karen stays focused on Judy's attack and is not hooked by the judgment. A judgment, by definition, pushes one of your buttons—it hits a sore spot.

This leads to the second principle: *Because you believe there is some truth in a judgment, it generates self-rejection rather than self-defense.* The judgment rejects you, but you can't stop it because, on some level, you believe what it is saying. Then you are not only attacked by the statement itself but further betrayed as the judgment turns you against yourself. Unconsciously, you begin to feel more threatened by the deficient feelings and beliefs waiting to arise in you than by the attacker and thus cannot defend yourself against the actual attack. For this reason, from now on, I will refer to *judgments* as *attacks* or use the terms synonymously. This will help support your awareness of what is occurring—by identifying the true source of the threat—and mobilize your inner strength to respond appropriately. This shift in awareness from "judgment" to "attack" is one small support worth cultivating, similar to the practice of stating the attack in the "you" form.

A note here about defense: In psychological terms, a defense often refers to a way of avoiding something that is true or resisting input that would cause discomfort. This is particularly the case when behavior is judged as being defensive. The person is considered to be closed-minded. Personality defenses, especially when they are unconscious, are designed to protect a certain experience of the world, and so defensive behavior often colludes with the judge. In contrast, a healthy defense is a direct, conscious act of supporting the truth. It is based on reality now and not on an idea about yourself from the past. Defending against the judge means you have recognized that what the judge is saying is of little value when it is wrapped up in a psychic attack; what's important is that it is attacking you and you are acting to stop the attack. I use "defending" as an active step in the process of "disengaging."

The third principle is more of a warning than anything else: *If the content of a judgment is in fact true—not just believed to be true—it will be doubly hard to recognize and respond to the attack or negative valuation implicit in the judgment.* George felt his wife's statements were "true" because in fact he had been insensitive in his reaction to his secretary's behavior. However, he couldn't see that the problematic truth was not that he was insensitive but that being insensitive made him a bad person. This was the implicit truth he believed in that made it very difficult for him to allow his feelings of anger (and hurt) at her attack. He never did allow himself to feel the hurt underlying the anger.

This leads us directly to the fourth principle: *It does not matter if the content of a judgment is true; what's important is that it attacks you—it undermines your effectiveness, capacity, and sense of worth.* Once the attack is dealt with, whatever truth is involved can be understood. Real growth involves learning from mistakes and seeing the truth about what works and what doesn't. With the judge, though, the truth is only bait to hook you. The truth becomes a weapon the judge uses against you. That is another important aspect of the judge to keep in awareness: the judge has no real interest in the truth itself.

Now we have enough understanding to formulate a basic definition of an attack: *An attack is any comment or statement that triggers an internal state of diminishment—feeling smaller, less than, or devalued.* This definition complements the definition of judgment at the beginning of the chapter. No one, especially your judge, has the right to provoke in you painful or deficient feelings that cause you to reject yourself or take you away from your present experience, unless you ask for it. (In certain situations, such as therapy or spiritual practice, you may request or have an agreement to allow this kind of input in order to explore difficult feelings and their origins.)

An important note to remember: Not all statements that elicit painful feelings are attacks, and not all painful feelings are the result of an attack. In other words, just the fact that you feel unpleasant feelings does not mean you are under attack. Someone may give you the news of a friend's illness or tell you he can't accept your invitation to dinner or confront you with her desire to be more intimate with you. These types of statements may bring up uncomfortable feelings such as sadness, disappointment, and protectiveness, but there was no intention to attack in the statements made. Furthermore, if you do not take these feelings as some reflection on your self-worth, there is no attack involved internally either. You can simply receive the information being communicated and allow the feelings that arise simply to be there.

It may, however, be difficult to discern what is going on when statements hit your sore spots, setting off your own self-attack. In these cases, it may be impossible to tell if the statement was meant as an attack. Let's say you're arriving late for an appointment with a small group of friends. As you walk in the door, you overhear one of them saying in the next room, "Oh, Laura's always late." If this is indeed an accurate observation and a characteristic of your behavior that your friend has no charge or issue with, it may be that she is making a simple statement of fact, with no judgment implied.

Then again, she may have been attacking you consciously or unconsciously.

What is most important is to recognize that if you experience deficiency or diminishment associated with that issue, you are under attack from your own judge. Until you can see and feel that, it will be impossible to know if your friend was judging you. The more you are able to recognize your own internal attacks, the easier it will be to discern those coming from outside. The need for clarity and discernment in disengaging from attacks calls upon one of the inherent capacities of the soul, an open and expanded awareness.

POINTS TO REMEMBER

- A judgment or attack is a statement of evaluation that implies an assessment of one's value or worth and is felt as a rejection of one's present state. More specifically, it is any comment or statement that triggers an internal state of diminishment—feeling smaller, less than, or devalued.
- Judgments attack you by generating certain emotions that arouse disarming self-beliefs. Understanding how a judgment affects you emotionally and energetically helps you see that judgment works as an insidious attack. This helps keep your focus on the attack and minimizes its undermining effect on you.
- When you feel judged, you believe you have to change yourself because something is wrong with you; when you feel attacked, you know you need to defend yourself.
- A judgment is an insidious form of attack because it points to a part of you you are not comfortable with, and thus, you believe the negative assessment is justified. This belief, in turn, blocks your ability to respond to the judgment as an attack because now you are seeing *yourself,* not the judgment, as the problem.
- Turning your negative judgmental statements into positive ones can make you feel better, but it does not change the underlying dynamic of engaging in self-judgment in the first place.
- Focusing on judgments as attacks makes it easier for you to

respond appropriately, because you recognize an outside energy aggressively threatening your own state.

- The more you are able to recognize your own internal attacks, the easier it will be to discern those coming from outside.
- Understanding how a judgment affects you emotionally and energetically helps you see the way the judgment works as a skillful attack.
- Not all statements that elicit painful feelings are attacks, and not all painful feelings are the result of an attack.

THE STEPS OF JUDGMENT RECOGNITION

Step 1. Identify the attack or judgmental statement.

Step 2. Learn to recognize the experience of judgment through the way it changes your energetic and somatic state.

Step 3. Learn to recognize the emotional reaction you have to judgments.

Step 4. See how a judgment provokes self-rejection through intentionally making you feel a certain way.

FOUR PRINCIPLES OF JUDGMENT

- *First principle:* A judgment always touches on something you believe is true about you.
- *Second principle:* Because you believe there is some truth in a judgment, it generates self-rejection rather than self-defense.
- *Third principle:* If the content of a judgment is in fact true—not just believed to be true—it will be doubly hard to recognize and respond to the attack implicit in the judgment.

• *Fourth principle:* It does not matter if the content of a judgment is true; what's important is that it attacks you: it undermines your effectiveness, capacity, and sense of self.

EXERCISE: OBSERVING JUDGMENTS/ATTACKS

During the next week, make a list of all the attacks you are aware of—if possible, as soon as you become aware of them. Notice how each attack affects your energy, your awareness, and the physical experience of your body. Also note how the attack affects your emotional state.

Step 1. Write a phrase or brief sentence that describes the incident.

Step 2. State each judgment in the second person. This means write the judgments as "you" statements rather than "I" statements. ("You are stupid," not "I am stupid.")

Step 3. Write down what you observe about your bodily and energetic response to the attack. What sensations do you feel in your body? How has your relationship to the things and people in your environment shifted? How are your alertness and ability to respond to situations affected?

Step 4. In as simple terms as you can, note your emotional state. What kinds of feelings are provoked? How is your sense of yourself altered?

Frank felt the boards of the porch under his bare feet and the way his legs still felt stiff from sleep. The terry cloth of the robe felt soft against his genitals, belly, and buttocks as it lightly brushed the skin; in his agitated state, it was mildly arousing. Crossing his arms over his chest seemed to keep him contained and separate in some protective way. His shoulders and face still felt tense from his aborted attempt at washing the dishes. He could feel some apprehension in his chest as if there were danger lurking. Suddenly, it dawned on him that the sense of danger was caused by the recurring comments of his judge. He seemed more sensitive than usual today, and in this state, he distinctly felt that his judge was attacking him, no matter what it was saying. It was unsettling to feel the danger right inside his own head.

Frank took a breath and exhaled. He was aware that his inner tension felt at odds with what was happening around him. He could smell coffee from next door and hear kitchen sounds of Doug and Louise over breakfast. In the distance, he could hear a lawn mower and an occasional dog barking. Suddenly, a loud moving buzz caught his attention. A hummingbird was hovering over his head; it looked him straight in the eye before zipping off over the bushes beside the house.

Frank's wariness began to subside as he noticed more of the colors and sounds around him. A butterfly fluttered over the flowers in the garden below. The overgrown lawn in the backyard had a ragged, wild sense to its dark green color. A light breeze sent the soft warmth of the air past his neck, and Frank found himself starting to yawn. Stretching his arms high over his head, he filled his chest full of the morning air. He let out a loud sound as he exhaled and shook himself, feeling his body claim some space of its own. He felt at home in himself and in the day. His mind was quiet.

🌀 *Don't forget your neck. It's not fixed, and just relaxing won't fix it. Besides, that lawn needs mowing, and the wheel on the lawn mower is broken. You have things to do . . .*

Frank listened to the voice, and he listened to a mockingbird singing on the wire overhead. He took a deep breath and felt the space in his chest and the porch beneath his feet. He leaned over the railing and watched a squirrel making its way across the lawn. He enjoyed the sun warming his shoulders through the robe. The voice continued in his head, but now it was just one of the things he was aware of.

5

AWARENESS

THE MOST FUNDAMENTAL DIMENSION of our true nature is familiar to everyone in some form. This is the capacity for and experience of awareness. Awareness is what allows you to perceive reality and be in touch with your experience, whether physical, emotional, mental, or spiritual. On a physical level, it is related to your five external senses and to your internal kinesthetic senses (your ability to feel tension, temperature, pain, pressure, balance, and so forth, within your body). The physical senses register and transmit sensations to the brain, but awareness is what allows those perceptions to become a part of your consciousness.

You use your senses all the time but not necessarily with consciousness, with awareness. Without awareness, perception is mechanical and lacks the aliveness and presence of the soul. You see, but do you really notice what is around you, especially in familiar locations? You hear, but do you actually listen to the sounds and vibrations of your environment? You sense, but are you aware of your body as a sensing organ? Do you know where your arms and legs are and how they actually feel? Do you just think about your feelings, or do you actually perceive them as energetic textures and tensions in your body? Awareness brings consciousness into perception and perception into consciousness.

Awareness, however, has a more subtle aspect than conscious perception. You perceive what you pay attention to. Awareness includes not only perceptions themselves but the process of attending to them. Awareness develops as you begin noticing *what* you are aware of. In a more self-reflective sense, this means being conscious of your awareness—noticing the range and clarity of your awareness and where it is focused, or where you are focused while being aware. Here, the recognition is that your reality at any given moment is largely determined by what you are aware of. Are you at this moment wrapped up in your thinking about a judgment, memory, or plan? Are you totally focused on this book you are reading and oblivious of yourself? Or are you in touch with your own experience, aware of your body, your feelings, and your thoughts now? The more your awareness (that is, what you are aware of) includes yourself as you are, here in this moment, the more you are living in the reality of the present.

Accessing your essential capacity of awareness enables you to contact your immediate experience, which means you are more present in your life. But first, you need to develop your ability to sense yourself and to recognize where you are at any given moment. Then you expand your perception of where you are to include as much of you as possible. This may sound simple, but it is not so easy to do.

Awareness and the Judge

How does the judge limit your awareness? The judge wants awareness to be secondary to what it considers the correct perspective. In other words, it wants you to look at your experience from a point of view designed to support a particular experience of the world and of you. So it limits awareness by directing your attention along familiar paths. Perception becomes partial, and it becomes unconscious. The judge tells you what is important to pay attention to and what is not, and more important, it tries to tell you what everything you experience means.

But if you are not fully aware of your experience and how different elements of it relate to each other, how can you truly know what an experience means? True significance is not something imposed from the outside. But the judge wants to impose its own meaning on your experience, so it puts up strong, often unconscious, barriers against being fully aware. How can you know whether some part of your experience is relevant for understanding if you are not aware of it? Awareness has to come first. You must perceive, sense, and contact your experience, including your body, your environment, your beliefs, your feelings, and your self-images. At the same time, you must see why you have believed that it is important to keep your awareness limited.

You may hear your judge telling you: "What difference does it make what you are feeling in different parts of your body? You don't think with your arms or feel with your legs!" or "What your body feels like right now is not going to help you figure out what to do!" or "Stop paying attention to your own feelings. This person is feeling bad, and it is important to focus on her." If you listen, you will find that your unbiased information gathering is being constantly challenged by the judge. So the first and most fundamental ongoing practice for working with the judge is to keep some attention reserved for being aware of your body and of your process of looking and listening.

Engaging in this practice is the first and simplest step in confronting the judge. Instead of accepting its authority about what is happening and what is important, you will be discovering these things for yourself. The judge gets all its juice from directing your attention toward the past and the future, so the practice will help to locate you in the present moment in your body. Furthermore, the judge wants to restrict your awareness to the specific things that will hook you and keep you hooked. By practicing your capacity to remain aware unaffected by prejudice, bias, or preference, you are taking away one of its supports.

The Experience of Awareness

Your awareness is not only useful, it is valuable to experience as the ground of your essential nature. Awareness brings a definite quality to your experience: when it is available in an unrestricted way, your mind has a lightness, a clarity, and a cool freshness, almost like the air on a crisp fall day. Things appear bright and new as if you were seeing and hearing them for the first time. You experience the immediacy of being in direct contact with the things you are aware of: your perception actually touches them without thought, naming, or categorization. All habitual familiarity is erased, and you are just here with the simple reality of your experience.

Awareness has a sense of no boundaries, an openness from which nothing is excluded and in which things are not separate. It has no opinions, priorities, or values about what it is aware of. When you are aware, you feel awake, attentive and attuned, clear and spacious. Awareness can begin with your own breathing and the hairs on the back of your hand, and extend deep into your most hidden feelings, and wide into the hearts and minds of others.

Awareness is independent of thinking. The mind may become very quiet when you are fully absorbed in simple awareness. There can be sounds, sensations, colors, shapes, movement, silence—all without thought. You may find yourself disappearing into or getting lost in the present moment. You have lost your familiar orientation to your present experience, an orientation based on beliefs, memories, and expectations. This is common, and it is one of the qualities of awareness most disturbing for the judge. How will you act, behave, and do what needs to be done if there is no thought? How will you know who you are if you are not thinking about yourself? Should this experience actually arise, take the time simply to be with the experience and see what it is like. Do you in fact lose the capacity to move or function? How is memory related to a sense of heightened awareness? Can you be with or relate to another person in a state of unrestricted awareness?

Be forewarned that when you try to stay with your present awareness rather than getting caught up in obsessing about something that you did yesterday or worrying about an event next week, your judge will tend to attack you unmercifully. Or if you manage to pay attention to how your body feels in the moment, it will say that you did it wrong or that there is something wrong with you because of what you are feeling. "What good is sensing when we have things to think about and take care of?" Don't be surprised when this happens. Just remember that awareness is your number one tool in confronting judgment. The judge needs to control where you put your attention and what you are aware of. Beware!

PRACTICE: EXPANDING SELF-AWARENESS

Step 1. *Sensing your body:* Seat yourself in a comfortable chair. Close your eyes. Sense whatever you are aware of in your body, starting from the top of your head and proceeding down to your feet. Notice sensations, temperature, tension, emotions, energy, movement, and so on, including no feeling or sensation. Can you hold the awareness of your whole body simultaneously after you have been through all the parts? What is your overall sense of your self when you finish?

Step 2. *Looking and listening:* Open your eyes and bring your attention into the experience of looking and listening. First notice the *experience* of looking at what's around you. Pay more attention to the overall experience of looking—seeing patterns, colors, and shapes—than to anything in particular you are seeing. Do the same with listening. Be aware of yourself as someone who is looking and listening. These are two of your most common activities, but normally, you focus on what you perceive and not on the experience of looking and listening itself.

Step 3. *Awareness during the day:* During the rest of the day, when you can remember, bring your attention back into your body, becoming aware of the activities of listening and looking. Notice where you are regardless of what is occurring; don't assume that your observations about what seems to be taking place or what seems important reflect the entire picture. Notice how you feel about where you are and what is occurring.

Note: Do these moments of self-remembering as often as you can with the intention that they will happen easily and naturally. Don't be surprised if at first you have to stop what you are doing to sense yourself. Go ahead and stop for a few moments.

Step 4. *Awareness while functioning:* When you feel ready, choose an activity simple enough that you can do the task and have enough attention left to notice yourself doing it. The intention is to be able to continue functioning as you sense, look, and listen. After a while, you will find you can wash dishes, drive a car, or perhaps even talk on the phone while still sensing yourself. With practice, you will be able to maintain open self-awareness through sensing, looking, and listening as you go about your day.

You think you must use effort to make yourself aware. That's not true. Effort always restricts your awareness and you need to see how you are restricting it. It is natural and effortless to be completely aware, but you interfere. It is our nature to be aware. That is why it's possible for you to see the truth. The truth is our nature. Ultimately we are awareness.

— A. H. Almaas, *Diamond Heart Book 2,* p. 117

Hunger was gnawing at Frank's ample belly, calling him into the kitchen for his morning meal. Unfortunately, he was faced with the unfinished dishes in the sink. He considered avoiding them and just getting his breakfast, but his internal voice was back.

Don't you dare ignore those dishes. Sue will be on your case, and besides, you know you will feel much better if you clean them up now.

After putting the last clean dish in the rack, Frank opened the refrigerator and got out the orange juice, apple juice, yogurt, blackberries, bee pollen, wheat germ, bread, and jam. Next to them on the counter, he put a cereal bowl, spoon, knife, banana, peach, spirulina, and a box of granola. Then he turned on the radio to catch the morning news. Now he was ready. This was one of his favorite activities: making his morning meal.

Now let's not overdo it this morning. Guess why you have been suffering from irritable bowel syndrome and having so much gas lately. Your eyes and your mouth are way ahead of your poor intestines, and your belly shows it.

Now, wait a minute. Everything I eat is healthy, and besides, breakfast makes me feel good, so I am more likely to relax and not feel stressed. Life is just not worth living without a decent breakfast.

First the granola went into the bowl, followed by half a banana and a peach sliced up, a handful of blackberries, two spoonfuls of wheat germ, and one of bee pollen. Then in went apple juice for liquid and yogurt for texture and flavor.

What a mishmash! Are you really going to eat that mess? Yuuckk!

Frank could hear Sue's voice in his head. He let the cereal sit while he sliced a bagel and put it in the toaster and then stirred a spoonful of spirulina into a glass of orange juice.

You sure know how to ruin a glass of OJ!

This time, it was his mother's voice talking to him. He put the cereal and the orange juice on the kitchen table next to the morning paper. When the bagel was toasted, he buttered it and put it on a plate with some jam and then set it next to the cereal bowl. He checked to make sure he had everything and at last sat down to eat. Then it was the voice of the Zen master whose book he was reading:

So now, as usual, you are going to eat, read the paper, and listen to the radio all at once. Never waste a minute, do you?

6

WHAT IS JUDGED?

JUDGMENT IS UBIQUITOUS. It can arise in relation to any part of your life. You can, and will, find yourself under attack about your behavior, your relationships, your friends and colleagues, your family, your belongings, your home, your habits, your attitudes, your body, your thoughts, your feelings, your hopes and dreams, your inner work, even your judgments of yourself and others. Because of this fact, this book focuses more on the form and process of judgment than on the content. Ultimately, the many objects of self-attack are interchangeable. One moment you may feel attacked for the unsatisfying relationship you are in, and the next moment the attack has shifted to your appearance, followed by the state of your kitchen. Moments later, you are attacking yourself for your depressed and hopeless attitude about things, whereupon you find yourself righteously critical of the garden crew mowing the lawn next door. When you have a little distance, the chameleonlike quality of the judge's concerns can sometimes become quite laughable.

Nevertheless, in the interest of developing awareness of self-judgment, when it arises and why, it can be helpful to look at the significant areas of self-attack that almost everyone deals with. By occupying your mind with the specific details of your personal experience, you can easily believe that your problems are unique. They are not. We do not all find the same faults in ourselves, but the categories of faults for which we attack ourselves are remarkably few. You will discover that the judge is not very creative. Unfortunately, it doesn't need to be.

Your Body

Your body is the most visible and tangible expression of who you are and thus the easiest target for the attacks of your judge. You judge yourself about your appearance in relation to the shape and size of your body and its parts. "You're too short. . . . Your breasts are too small. . . . You have puny little biceps. . . . Your penis is pitiful. . . . You are losing all your hair. . . . Your skin is getting all wrinkled." You judge yourself for what you do to your appearance. "What a lousy makeup job. You must not have been awake this morning. . . . Your hair hasn't seen a brush in days. . . . Purple nail polish? You must be kidding. . . . It's time you worked out those blubber thighs." And of course, there is the aspect of how you dress. "You wore that shirt yesterday. You can't wear it today. . . . Those colors clash. . . . Those look like pajamas. . . . You're going to work in *that?* . . . That looks like something your mother would wear."

But appearance is only one dimension of your body that you tend to judge, though attacks on appearance are often the most constant and vicious. You also attack the way your body functions and responds. You blame it for accidents, mistakes, failures, and illness— as well as for lack of support, lack of motivation, and lack of capacity. "Just remember that your back gives out on you just when you need it. . . . You always get sick when you have a lot to get done. . . . Women love how you look, but wait until they get into bed with you. . . . You always lose your damn voice just when it's time to stand up for yourself. . . . You can't trust your body. Do what the doctor says." These attacks will become part of a vicious cycle when behaviors begin to take on an addictive quality through overeating, drugs, smoking, drinking. Those behaviors will be the object of the self-attacks as well as a way to try and escape them.

A more subtle area of attack especially relevant in the process of self-understanding is your attitude toward your body. As you pay attention to your experience, you inevitably become aware of how little you actually sense your body from moment to moment, how little you pay attention to it, and how little you trust and value it as your home. These realizations can be uncomfortable, if not painful, and often lead to self-attack. "What is wrong with you that you can't even feel your body? There must be something bad there you don't want to feel. . . . You should relax more. . . . You've got a real problem if you don't even know what you want to eat. . . . So why did you get sick right now? Are you avoiding something? . . . You care less about your body than about your car."

Self-judgment in relation to your body reflects the tendency to see things in terms of different polarities. In the area of appearance, the dichotomies are generally *beautiful and ugly* or *attractive and repulsive;* at a more fundamental level, they are *acceptable and unacceptable* or *recognized and invisible.* In the realm of body function, the dichotomies are usually *strong and weak, capable and deficient, graceful and awkward, active and passive,* or *powerful and impotent.* As far as your attitude toward your body, you attack yourself in terms of *caring and apathy, aliveness and deadness, trust and fear,* or *intelligence and stupidity.*

Your Job

How you make a living is another area of your life that is constantly available for self-attack. The kind of work you do, where you work, with and for whom you work, and how successful you are can all play a part in your judgment of yourself. As with your body, criticism in this area will often be based on comparison to others, whether they are friends, colleagues, neighbors, TV or movie characters, or your parents. For many people, work is connected to their sense of being an adult. So having a full-time job (whatever it is), keeping the job, making a living, and paying the bills are all synonymous with being responsible and grown-up. Any slippage in this area (being laid off, having part-time work that only covers the bills, or working full-time but not making enough money) subjects you to attacks about not being mature, adult, independent, and able to take care of yourself.

However you came to your job—whether you chose it, found yourself led to it, or were forced to take it—you may be attacked about that process. "How could you have chosen to work here? . . . Only a moron would have been so passive about where he ended up working. . . . I told you to do more research before accepting that offer. . . . Your lack of brains forced you to take this kind of job. . . . You lucked into this job; let's see if you can hold on to it."

Then there is the kind of work you do. For many people, what they do is a measure of their self-worth, their status, their sense of capacity and accomplishment. For others, it affects their sense of meaning in life: Do I like what I do? Does it reflect something special about me? Do I feel creative in it? Does it serve other people? Thus, it is common for you to have conscious or unconscious standards about what work you do. Even the question of whether you consider it a job, a career, a profession, or a calling reflects your investment in your work and, often, your standards for yourself.

It is important to remember that whenever you create a standard, you are comparing yourself—maybe not to others, but to an ideal—and that means self-judgment is active. The kind of work you do is the subject of self-attack when you believe it is unworthy of you, when you don't like it even if it is respectable or desirable, when you are not good at it or anticipate your own failure, or when it seems too easy or too good to be true.

Even if you are satisfied with the kind of work you do, the judge can torture you by laying down impossible standards of success. Most people are not even aware of what brings them true satisfaction, so they rely on standards set forth by the judge. To make matters worse, the judge can always change the standard and thus find some foothold for dissatisfaction and attack. To top it all off, many people's judges set much higher success standards for themselves than for others or than the situation warrants, indicating the lack of reality in their self-evaluation. So you see how self-judgment makes success a goal almost impossible to reach.

How do you measure your success? Is it a matter of getting through the day, bringing home the paycheck? Or is it more about getting beyond your anxiety and terror at failure in order to feel accomplished at what you do? Is it about the results of your work, the service you provide, or the event or object you produce? How rare it is for all three of these to coincide. When you feel you do not succeed, what does that say about you? Your judge will tell you many things: "This shows you don't have what it takes. . . . You can't really take care of yourself. . . . Now we see the result of your goofing off all those years in school. . . . No one will ever be proud of you now. . . . You should be ashamed to show your face. . . . Dad always said you would never amount to anything."

Your job also has a location, a context, and an implicit relationship with others. When the judge needs ammunition for criticizing you, it can use any of these elements: if you travel to work—weather, commuting, public transportation; if you work at home—household distractions, isolation, never getting out. The judge can find standards, comparisons, or grievances for every aspect of your work situation: the kind of office or work space, regular or irregular hours, amount of light and noise, the boss's personality, working alone or with others, contact with the public, degree of privacy, discipline, motivation, and rest. And certainly, some of the most obvious self-attacks at work come in relation to colleagues: "You are not working as hard as they are. What will they think if you finish first? . . . You can tell the boss likes her better. . . . He's never going to speak to you again because you didn't say hello. . . . You always say too much at meetings. They're going to find out you don't really know what you're doing." And of course, your judge can always turn its attacks toward others, in your mind or out loud.

Your Relationships

Self-attacks take on a life of their own in intimate relationships. Here more than in any other situation, your self-judgments are provoked, supported, and reflected. Your self-judgments and those of your partner are implicitly and unconsciously interwoven with how you experience yourself and how you experience each other. Your judgments are based on standards that define what you are looking for in the relationship, what you find valuable in it, and what bothers you about it. These standards also determine how you believe you and your partner need to be in order for the relationship to work. The standards unconsciously influence how you behave and how you respond, thereby affecting the way your partner perceives and responds to you. Attacking yourself about the relationship is basically a way to maintain or promote these standards. Though your attention in a primary relationship tends to be on what is happening in the other or between you and the other, the deciding factor in how you experience the connection tends to be your own unconscious standards.

When the relationship is in a blissful or falling-in-love stage, the judge is either silent about or actively promoting the current dynamic, because what is happening is fitting its standards. However, as time passes, real life intrudes, and the interaction no longer reflects the standards. This is when self-criticism begins. Because of the enmeshment between intimate partners, self-attack often becomes mirrored externally by the other, whether consciously intended or not. In other words, you will very often find your partner criticizing the same things in you that your judge attacks. This brings up several possibilities: Did your partner really say that, or did you just think you heard it because your judge is saying it? Does your partner really feel that way about you, or have you provoked that feeling by outwardly reacting to your own judge? Or did you choose a partner you are comfortable with because that person sounds like your judge?

These are the kinds of complicated questions that become relevant as you notice your self-attacks in an established intimate relationship. Once a certain stability or predictability in a relationship is achieved, you will experience a corresponding resistance to becoming clear about who is feeling what and why. This is the work of the judge. It believes that enmeshment is necessary for attachment, and attachment is fundamental to relationship. On the one hand, the judge is invested in attacking you for how things are in the relationship—how things haven't changed, how you are not getting what you want, how you are afraid to stand up for yourself, and how you are not a good partner. It does this by constantly shifting the blame between you, your partner, and the relationship, with no real interest in understanding the truth. On the other hand, the more you observe, the more it becomes clear that your judge is determined that the relationship not change, because that means failure. For the judge, if the relationship moves into deeper intimacy or more clarity, it means risking the discovery of unacceptable things about you or your partner. Change is perceived as threatening the existing stability, which means you will be rejected or you will find your partner unacceptable, which means the relationship will not survive.

At a certain point, you begin to realize that you are not only dealing with your own judge, you are also dealing with your partner's judge and your partner's standards that his or her judge is supporting. As you become aware of this, you are faced with just how constrained you are by these intangible forces operating in the relationship. Intimate relationship is not a two-way connection but a four-way connection in which each person is dealing with another person and two judges. Imagine what freedom and ease there might be if you were only dealing with your partner! In fact, most conflicts and difficulties in relationship would disappear if the judgments ceased. As it happens, though, most people would be terrified to let go of their standards and beliefs about how things need to be in relationship. They tend to believe that these standards determine security and satisfaction. This is the judge's approach: make sure the relationship is measured against the rules or at least those hard-won principles learned from past experience. Rather than provide fixed standards for future behavior, experience, when integrated, serves to develop your inherent capacities to be yourself and relate from that truth. How can your judge know how things should be? Is a relationship real and vital because it meets your standards or because of the unfolding mystery that connects you and your partner? True peace and satisfaction only come from knowing, being, and relating from your true nature. Following the judge's standards will not get you there.

You believe that your judge is needed to keep you safe in relationship. The more vulnerable you are, the more you think you need it to protect you. The opposite is true: the more two people are willing to be vulnerable in themselves and with each other, the less they will need their judges for protection. In fact, the health and viability of a relationship is ultimately related to the capacity for sharing vulnerability. Whenever one person in a relationship is unwilling or unable to contact his or her vulnerability in the interaction, there is a simultaneous movement into judgment: self-attack, attack of the other, or both. This is a chicken-or-the-egg situation: Do you resort to judgment for protection because you don't feel safe, or are you not feeling safe because of the presence of judgment? This is a fundamental question in dealing with the judge. We will explore it extensively as we go along.

Judgments about intimate relationship overlap with judgments about your body and your job in two of the most difficult areas for any couple to work through: sex and money. Sexual interaction generally involves intimate physical vulnerability in the context of minimal verbal communication. The less confidence in the nonverbal connection, the more you will feel isolated and exposed in lovemaking. In response, your judge will be hyperactive to fill in the gap and evaluate what takes place. Isolation tends to support your judge's high expectation of your performance (as well as of your body, your desire, your skills, and so forth) and corresponding disappointment in your actual experience. Many people deal with this situation by putting up a false front to mask their feelings, focusing on pleasing their partner, or simply having no feelings. The judge is an active agent in maintaining expectation, disappointment, denial, and avoidance.

Another area that couples tend not to communicate about is money. Money symbolizes security, power, possibility, hope, independence, freedom—many different things for people—but it always represents some fundamental support for who they would like to be. And just as with other parts of your life, the unconscious beliefs and standards you learned in your family influence how you operate around money. As long as these assumptions remain unconscious, you cannot help but assume that others share them. Not everyone does, and very often your partner has a different set of beliefs than yours. The judge is not interested in those assumptions' becoming conscious or understood; its only interest is that its beliefs and standards be maintained so your hope for yourself is not lost. This hope is maintained through attacking yourself and your partner when financial difficulties arise, as they always do.

Your Inner Work

In your external experience in the world, it is possible to minimize antagonizing your judge by staying aligned with your conditioned standards and beliefs. Many people spend their whole lives doing their best to follow the coaching, guidance, and warnings of the inner critic. Society supports this. However, if you choose to pursue inner work—the search for understanding who you are, what your life means, and what reality is—you are by necessity setting yourself directly in conflict with your judge. To explore what you believe, what you experience, why you act and feel the way you do, is to question the authority of the judge. To bring the underpinnings of your psychological reality (how you think and feel) into consciousness means potentially replacing those assumptions and beliefs with direct knowledge. This would mean experiencing that your conscious awareness can begin to take the place of accepted standards and beliefs. Then you don't need to be guided, limited, and controlled by the unconscious through your judge.

The judge cannot see this process as anything but a threat to its job and its authority. It will attack you directly and indirectly, blatantly and covertly, in an effort to maintain these deep beliefs. "You will discover horrible and unacceptable things about yourself if you continue. . . . People won't like you. . . . You will be overwhelmed by the pain. . . . It's stupid and a waste of time to be asking all these questions. . . . What's wrong with the way you've always done it?" Besides these direct attacks, the judge will try to take over the process by setting up its own standards for how inner work must be done, thereby covertly maintaining the old necessity to live up to standards. "You better learn to stop judging yourself. . . . You have to pay attention to yourself all the time. . . . You are so lazy about your meditation. . . . Your therapist wouldn't like your thinking that."

The judge engenders fear in you about your inner exploration through attacking you for revealing unacceptable motivations (fear, hatred, jealousy, desire), warning you about uncovering buried feelings (pain, deficiency, grief, disgust), and threatening you with the consequences (rejection, abandonment, alienation). This works against vulnerability in your own process. The very activities you are setting in motion in the first few chapters of this book will bring you into more awareness of and contact with your judge, which means you will be more vulnerable to the feeling of being attacked. This is not enjoyable or comfortable. Your judge will say it is bad and must be avoided. But without the willingness to bring the judgment experience into consciousness, face the attacks directly, and defend your right to vulnerability, you cannot undertake inner work in a meaningful way. The most you can do is gather information in your mind. You cannot open to the fullness of your experience and the deeper knowing that brings self-understanding.

Self-Distrust

In order to challenge the judge and disengage from its attacks, you will confront different levels of concern that underlie your self-judgment. The first relates to your perception of your functioning as expressed in the areas of body, job, and relationship, as described earlier in the chapter.

On this level, you constantly question yourself in relation to your capacities, functioning, relationships, acceptance, rejection, ability, success, independence, and so on: Do I have what it takes to work, have friends, a partner, be attractive, and so on? Do people really like me? Can I win the approval of my boss, my partner, my parents? Are people talking about me behind my back? Do I have the willpower to succeed in life? All these questions can be reduced to one basic issue: How am I doing? The underlying beliefs that drive the constant questions and attacks are: I am lacking something important, I can't do it right, I'm a failure, and I don't have what it takes.

The unconscious reality underlying these beliefs are the lack of contact with the soul's true nature. This lack of contact is experienced as something fundamental missing, which manifests as a loss of self-esteem. The bodily experience is of a deficient emptiness. What is needed is to stop the self-attacks and simply be with the emptiness, allowing it to become the spaciousness of the soul's true nature and the openness in which all needed essential qualities can arise.

The next level is more central and more disturbing. The questioning focuses on what you feel like underneath all your activity:

Am I grown up? Am I big enough to handle my life? Am I always this tired? Why do I feel so small? Who says I need anyone's help? How come I am so alone? Am I always this afraid? These questions are more about the polarity of grandiosity and deficiency. The basic issue is: What's wrong with me? The underlying belief is: I am small, weak, helpless, defenseless, vulnerable, and alone.

Here what is needed is the ability to tolerate this fundamental experience of the conditioned self as you explore what the true nature of the soul is. At this deeper level of inner work, as you uncover your beliefs and experiences about who you are, you recognize the judge has a profound distrust in the fact of your existence in the moment. It must justify, relate, define, explain, and analyze who you are, comparing you to the past and measuring you against the future. The judge believes you must rely on past beliefs, standards, and guidelines in order to continue to exist. It does not believe that if you let yourself feel these scary feelings of deficiency you will survive. Its ongoing belief is that nothing good can or will happen in the present by itself. This distrust fuels its attacks on your efforts to understand who and what you are.

Maturing does mean learning from past experience, but the judge does not help you grow from past mistakes or successes. It insists that you relive the past by maintaining a fixed sense of who you are. What you learn from your past experience then becomes limited by your conditioned sense of self. The judge says you cannot question what you assume or believe; in fact, you cannot even bring this conditioning into awareness. According to the judge, doing that will cause too much pain, be too shameful, cause others to reject you, make you wrong, or be overwhelming. This is not learning what works from your experience; this is suppressing your experience to preserve a limited perspective on life.

Why does the judge feel this is necessary? And why do you continue to participate in its perspective? Because you have no trust that what you will discover about reality or true nature has value or goodness to it. You have forgotten your soul nature, and now the unspoken belief is that what arises in your inner experience will bring you harm or make your life unlivable, unless mediated (censored, shaped, rejected, or approved) by the judge.

Stopping Expansion

This distrust manifests blatantly in the judge's reaction to your experiences of expansion. *Expansion* here refers to situations when you try something new, succeed at something you've never done before, stop a self-destructive habit, speak up in your own defense, recognize a truth about yourself, take on a new responsibility, and so on. The expansion is a shift in your sense of who you are or who you have taken yourself to be: who you are becomes a little bigger, includes a little more than it did before.

What does the judge do with these moments? Most everyone has experienced some sort of contraction after they expand: some letdown, some fear creeping in, some shame about being bigger, some withdrawal from the expansion. In one sense, this is part of a natural cycle of expansion and contraction. However, the contraction is seldom seen as part of the normal flow of the unfolding soul.

More often, your judge reacts to the expansion; its attack causes an exaggerated ebb and undermines or undoes the new sense of self. The contraction is now evidence that something is wrong. Instead of being a breather before a return to the expanded sense, it becomes proof the expansion was a mistake. "You look really stupid having asked for that raise just before a twenty-point drop in company sales. . . . You felt good about getting all that applause, but just imagine what people are saying behind your back. . . . You know you are going to start smoking again just like every time before. . . . Just because you did a good job, don't let it go to your head." This is how the judge provokes distrust in your ability to expand, grow, and change. Once you recognize how the pattern works, it is more possible to see it for what it is—an attempt to undermine your self-confidence and trust in your capacity to grow. The judge is effectively denying your soul and its living, dynamic potential. You don't have to accept what it tells you.

POINTS TO REMEMBER

- The judge has a profound distrust in the fact of your existence in this moment. It believes you must rely on past beliefs, standards, and guidelines in order to have a right to exist.
- Whenever you create a standard, you are comparing yourself—maybe not to others, but to an ideal—and that means self-judgment is active.
- Your body is the most visible and tangible expression of who you are and thus the easiest target for the attacks of your judge.
- Addictive behaviors are often the object of self-attacks as well as a way to try to escape them.
- The kind of work you do is the subject of self-attack when you believe that it is unworthy of you, when you don't like it even if it is respectable or desirable, when you are not good at it or anticipate your own failure, or when it seems too easy or too good to be true.
- Intimate relationship is not a two-way connection but a four-way connection in which each person is dealing with another person and two judges.
- Your self-judgments and those of your partner are implicitly and unconsciously interwoven with how you experience yourself and how you experience each other.
- Though your attention in a primary relationship tends to be on what is happening in the other or between you and the other, the deciding factor in how you experience the connection tends to be your own unconscious standards.
- Whenever one person in a relationship is unwilling or unable to contact his or her vulnerability in the interaction, there is a simultaneous movement into judgment: self-attack, attack of the other, or both.
- The more two people are willing to be vulnerable in themselves and with each other, the less they will need their judges for protection.
- You need the willingness to bring judgment into consciousness, face attacks directly, and defend your right to vulnerability, so you can undertake inner work in a meaningful way.

Exercise: Identifying the Focus of Self-Attacks

Look at your growing list of self-attacks and begin to organize them according to the various areas of your life where attacks are common: body, job, relationship, and so on. Make a separate list for attacks aimed at your self-awareness and self-exploration. Notice which are areas of heavy attack and how attacks in different categories relate to each other. What are the similarities and differences?

Exercise: Observing Self-Attacks on Expansion

The next time you are aware of an expansion in your sense of self, notice what happens afterward. Be aware of what your judge is saying to you and of any shifts in the felt sense of your body, your energy, and your behavior. If it is helpful, write down the event or opening that caused the expansion, then list the judge's attacks and whatever you notice has changed in you as a result.

[T]he less free a person is from his superego, the more his relationships are determined by it—not only in the choice of partners but also in what transpires in the relationship. If the superegos [of the two people] complement each other, we have a stable relationship. But it is stable only as long as there is no growth or change. . . . In the majority of cases, stable relationships are ones in which the two superegos can live together without too much friction. In other words, they are superego relationships and not real ones. In fact, often the individuals involved dislike each other but they still stay together because of the dominance of their superegos. This is the situation when relationships are based on dependency and insecurity. In other cases, the couple cannot stay together although they love each other, because the superegos don't get along. This explains those cases in which a couple experiences difficulty when their two sets of parents don't get along; because their superegos, as a result, cannot get along. So a couple can spend their whole lives together but never really come into close contact because it is the superegos that are in relationship.

— A. H. Almaas, *The Work on the Superego*, p. 9

Frank looked at the food ready to fill his belly, the newspaper with its bold headlines attracting his eyes, and the radio with intelligent voices pouring information into his ears. Suddenly, he was struck by the fact that he was stuffing himself from all directions. At the same time, he recognized a need for the security he felt from having all systems being fed—as if some important support would disappear if any of the three were missing. Was he trying to drown out his judge by overloading himself with input? Or was he simply doing what he wanted by making himself feel secure? He didn't know, but his hunger felt more important than figuring it out, so he took a big bite of cereal and washed it down with juice.

Immediately, he coughed and sputtered, and there was Sue's voice in his head.

> *When will you ever learn not to drink right after you take a bite! You are in such a rush to get everything in. Can't stand a little peace and quiet, can you?*
>
> *Hey, quit telling me what to do. Who cares if I cough? If I want to eat, drink, read, dance, and sing all at once, I will. I don't have any problem with doing it all, so why should you?*

These arguments in his head were so familiar. It felt as though nothing new would ever come of it, and he felt trapped in his defensiveness. Frank took another bite and then just sat and chewed slowly without tasting, listened to the radio without hearing the words, and stared at the paper without recognizing anything. He became aware of a hunger inside that he didn't often feel, deeper than hunger for food. He realized he felt this hunger now that he was no longer preoccupied with his multiple inputs. Had it always been there?

> *Frank, this is dangerous territory. You don't know what will come up or what it means, but it will be bad, believe me. Now snap out of it and eat your breakfast.*

Frank ignored the voice as the gnawing sensation grew more prominent and demanded his attention. The awareness made him nervous, but at the same time, it felt so deep in him that something relaxed by simply acknowledging it. Did this mean that if he didn't do three things at once, this hunger would appear? Or was it some reaction to his judge? He didn't know. At the moment, the hunger felt more real and more interesting than his usual thinking. It was distinctly uncomfortable, and though he didn't like it, he felt no need to push it away. For now, that was OK.

7

ACCEPTANCE

As you begin to be more aware of your inner process, you realize that you are constantly evaluating, assessing, reacting to, and commenting on your experience. This is a central way you make your feelings, thoughts, and behaviors your own. Your judge puts its familiar stamp of approval or disapproval on them, providing orientation and perspective while reinforcing the belief that what you are experiencing in the moment must be constantly evaluated.

Questioning the attitude of self-rejection that underlies all judgmental activity opens up the possibility of—and longing for—a different way of being with your experience. What if your judge did not react to everything you do and every way you feel? What if you did not take a position on whether your experience was good or bad? What if you could just let your experience be what it is without needing to change it? For the judge, this is inconceivable, but there is an aspect of your true nature that supports such a possibility. This is the quality of acceptance.

Acceptance and Rejection

Acceptance is generally considered to be the opposite of rejection. If a university accepts your application rather than rejecting it, then the university has approved of your qualifications and welcomes you as someone it wants to teach. So to reject means to push away, deny, or negate; to accept, in usual terms, means to move toward, approve of, or affirm. If you are acceptable, then you have made the grade, you are OK.

The problem with this definition of acceptance is that it still operates within the world of judgment, assessment, and evaluation. Acceptance means something positive, rejection something negative. You need acceptance to offset rejection, and if you are acceptable, it is always possible you will later be found unacceptable. Acceptance on these terms is conditional on some criterion. So the familiar usage of *acceptance* is, in fact, closer to approval, the opposite of rejection, than to true acceptance.

True acceptance means stepping out of the world of assessment altogether. It is exactly the experience of neither rejecting nor approving. Where rejecting and approving are actions of moving away from or toward one's experience, accepting is not an action at all. It is nonaction: a state of Being without attitude, simply allowing experience to be as it is.

Acceptance does not mean you approve of your experience, think it's OK, like it, or are happy with it as it is. Acceptance is not an expression of any kind of evaluation or interpretation. It simply means you can allow your experience to be exactly as it is. There need be no justification or effort to defend, deny, protect, or promote what is there. Acceptance means you get out of the way and stop taking a position. You don't approve, you don't reject; you don't push away your experience, you don't try to hold on to it. If you like it, that's accepted; if you dislike it, that's accepted. Whatever it is, your soul is simply there with the experience.

The State of Acceptance

Your soul spontaneously relaxes as it senses the arising of acceptance. There is release and letting go throughout the body as the experience of inner rejection drops away. Each cell seems to open and breathe with the space to simply be itself. Your soul feels bathed in a delicate, refreshing liquid that nourishes and welcomes you into a sense of profound relaxation. You feel relieved of an ancient burden of struggle and feel it replaced with an unquestioned sense of belonging. You belong here and now exactly where you are, as a part of everything that is. At the same time, you feel fully accepting of what is here; you welcome it without preference or condition.

At first, acceptance is experienced in relation to efforts to control experience. It allows what was being resisted or rejected. This is felt as the letting go of holding and reactivity. As the state of acceptance deepens, it goes beyond relaxation to include all aspects of experience, including tension and contraction. Acceptance is the fundamental nonattachment to any physical, emotional, or energetic state. The various permutations of inner experience—such as rejection, doubt, curiosity, sadness, fear, joy, satisfaction, anxiety, and worry—are all experienced as natural arisings in the soul. Each has its place and can be understood and appreciated. None is better or worse than another.

When this true acceptance is felt for whatever is arising, a natural flow of transformation in the soul becomes apparent. You notice that all manifestations of inner life come and go. If there is no reaction to what arises, it will unfold in its own natural cycle and pass away as something new takes its place. This flow of Being has an innate intelligence that responds exactly as needed in relation to the whole life of the soul. The spontaneous, nondefensive functioning of inner life is the gift that acceptance offers to your soul. Some call it the state of grace.

Control and the Functioning of Being

The fundamental belief that blocks your access to the state of acceptance is that you need to control your experience. This belief is reinforced by the recognition that much of what happens to you is beyond your control. So many things could go wrong or take you by surprise, not to mention your need for things to be a certain way for life to feel safe, comfortable, and manageable. You take every opportunity to maintain some control over your world. In particular, you have learned one thing over the years—that at least you can always control your inner experience.

If you don't like something that happens and you can't change it, you can pretend it doesn't matter, withdraw and stop caring, or decide you really do like it after all. If you want something and can't have it, you can shift to wanting something else, resent the world for denying you, or decide never to want anything again. The irony is that the biggest barrier to a smoothly functioning life is this constant effort to manipulate your inner experience. How did this come about?

When you were an infant without conscious awareness or control of yourself, there was a spontaneous and natural flow to how you interacted with life. This flow was intertwined with the responsive presence of your mother. Together they expressed the simple beingness of true nature and the natural way the individual soul is part of reality. If hunger arose in you, she sensed it and fed you. If she wasn't around, your body responded by becoming agitated in an effort to get a response, and if that was not enough, you cried out and mother came. When she arrived, you relaxed, were fed, and later slept. The right attunement between you and your mother resulted in a natural ebb and flow of energy: tension and relaxation, expansion and contraction, activity and rest, excitement and calm.

As a physical, energetic organism, you had a certain capacity at that time to tolerate frustration. This charge could build to a certain point before it needed a discharge through some form of gratification: holding, feeding, burping, crying, throwing up, or eliminating. If all went well, the environment and your body functioned together to bring an appropriate discharge. As you grew older, your capacity to tolerate discomfort increased and gratification could be delayed, which reflected a growing organismic strength and cohesiveness (referred to psychologically as ego strength).

Crisis Intervention

However, if, as often occurred, mother and the environment were not attuned to your needs, the frustration would build and not be released, and the charge would become overwhelming to your undeveloped system. If overwhelm due to hunger, cold, colic, isolation, and so on persisted past the point of tolerance, your very survival was in danger. In this context, your soul responded by shutting down your sensitivity to the frustration or charge. Whatever the intolerable feeling, you would numb yourself to it in order to carry on. This amounted to crisis intervention in an untenable situation.

This shutdown occurred to varying degrees in everyone; it circumvented the natural cycle of charge and discharge by aborting the process. Instead of a real discharge, a freezing of the charge in the physical, energetic, and psychic system occurred. From then on, the cycling of tension and relaxation happened in a more limited field, trapped within the bounds of the frozen energy. Thus, you came to define yourself based on this early contraction against your own experience. You learned that you could not trust the natural flow of tension and relaxation because of the overwhelm that resulted from the unsupportive environment and unresolved frustration. Deep down, you believed that rejecting your immediate experience was fundamental to survival.

Now, as an adult, you continue to reject your experience through judgment and manipulation, believing that you must still control yourself. As if you were some poorly built machine, you believe that your nature is flawed, defective, and out of touch with the natural world; you must be coaxed and coerced in order to work right. You are convinced that there is no natural process in you— no flow of true nature—that will contain and successfully orchestrate the changes in your inner reality. To further justify the need for inner reactivity, your judge constantly reminds you that the environment is uncontrolled and threatening. Should you relax that activity, you tend to expose yourself to the infantile sense of overwhelm. This will also activate the judge, causing it to issue its prime directive, "Something must be done!" You feel compelled to take action, figure out what to do, or at least feel bad about yourself. If all else fails, you can always eat something and numb out again.

Acceptance means a return to the natural, spontaneous flow of your own being. The judge considers this a direct threat to its control. "If you can't have an opinion about your experience, you might as well not even have it. How can you know what it means to you if you don't evaluate it? How can you relate to your experience if you can't decide whether to reject it or not? You can't improve unless you know what is good and what is bad, what to go after and what to avoid."

You are used to relating to your experience based on historical assumptions of what is important, what is meaningful, what is good, and what will help you. This approach seems so necessary, it is hard to imagine life without it. Acceptance of your experience without judgment or evaluation would disrupt this familiar orientation. The judge is afraid that you would be left at the mercy of external forces: a passive recipient or observer with no choice and no preference, no discrimination and no control. It will strongly discourage such openness: "You can't just let yourself trust reality, especially when you know things are painful, scary, or get you into trouble. That's not only naive, that's stupid!"

Acceptance and the Flow of Reality

Acceptance can only arise when you recognize the extent of your own distrust and self-rejection. You must see the judge's constant fostering of self-doubt. Eventually, you must uncover the way your present experience is completely colored by what happened to you in those first months of life. This makes it possible to recognize that you are not that infant and you no longer need your mother or the physical environment to provide self-regulation. What you are is a soul whose true nature supports being in your life without manipulation and judgment.

With this understanding, acceptance becomes a viable alternative to approving or rejecting your experience. As you let go of the need to change things or make them different, this state of Being emerges and opens the soul. To accept how you are feeling means to let your experience be what it is without commenting on it, reacting to it, or jumping to conclusions about it. Intense feelings may arise, as well as the experience of being a child who feels overwhelmed by them, but you do not stop, judge, or believe what arises. They are seen as simply an expression of your soul's unfolding at this moment. You open and surrender to the movement of your life.

The feelings themselves were initially rejected by you as a young child because they were overwhelming. This pushing away of the feelings has kept you in a child's relationship to them, for fear they will drown you. However, a lifetime of rejection has made the fear of being overwhelmed the *most* overwhelming feeling. Remember, your nervous system is no longer that of an infant, so the feelings themselves are much more tolerable than they were for you as a child. When you allow yourself to feel them directly, you discover that the fear of the feelings is much worse than the feelings themselves.

Acceptance is the heart opening and welcoming what you are. To the freshness and immediacy of awareness, it adds the qualities of intimacy and flow—a sense of release and the feeling of being washed clean of holding patterns, tensions, and resistances to what you are at this moment. It permeates you with a cool, gentle freshness, soothing the familiar internal agitation of your inner activity.

Life Lessons

Georgia arrives home after a hectic day at the office, and before she knows it, she is feeling irritated at her partner. She feels upset that he's on the phone when she comes in; she sees that the flowers in the dining room have started to wilt and he hasn't even noticed; she finds his clothes strewn about the bedroom, and the bed is not made up. She finds herself torn between complaining to him and giving him the cold shoulder to teach him a lesson. She notices she has judgments about each: complaining seems weak and manipulative in playing the victim, and shutting him out seems unfair and unsatisfying because he won't even know what he did wrong.

As Georgia considers all this, she notices how tense and frustrated she is. What she really wants is to collapse in his arms and be held. Immediately, she feels the reaction of her judge: "Don't even consider it! How humiliating, showing your neediness and helplessness. He'll find you disgusting."

Usually, such a profusion of voices and feelings would put her in a state of confusion, upset, and overwhelm. She would feel frozen and shut down, unable to act at all. This time, however, Georgia goes into the bedroom and, after pulling up the sheets and blanket on the bed, takes some time to lie down, close her eyes, and simply allow each element of her inner process; she accepts each feeling, judgment, and thought without getting engaged or trying to stop it. As her inner state unravels, she senses her breathing as a way of staying present and not reacting.

Gradually, her body calms down, and her mind slows from its

mad rush. It is now possible to connect with the truth of what she's feeling with less reactivity and judgment. She feels a sadness and longing arise and with it associations of childhood and the desire for the comforting presence of her mother. The feeling of neediness intensifies and threatens to overwhelm her. Georgia pays attention to her physical sensations and simply allows the feelings and images to come and fill her, without reacting. Flashes of isolation in a crib and being small and alone in an empty room come and go. Tears well up and flow down her cheeks. After a while, the intensity begins to subside. The childhood identification dissolves as she continues to rest.

Georgia's body feels open and light, as if all inner contraction has been purged. Her breath is deep and nourishing, and she feels more relaxed than she can remember feeling in weeks. She is aware of a gentle ease and an intuitive appreciation for herself and for where she is in her life. As her partner finishes his phone call, she gets up feeling grounded, refreshed, and ready to join him.

This is an example of how your true nature can support you through the quality of acceptance. You don't have to like your experience; you simply don't resist it. Resisting your experience is the same as not trusting the movement of true nature—believing you must control things to ensure movement because you do not experience the larger flow of reality. By not resisting, you don't get stuck or fixed on a particular feeling or concern, so your experience is able to flow and transform more easily and naturally.

Remember, acceptance is not something you do. It is not an action you take. If you try to stop rejecting, stop feeling, or stop judging, you feel it as a contraction inside. You end up trying to be different, which continues the rejection of where you are now. In the same way, judging the judge does not get rid of it. It only perpetuates the system.

All you can do is recognize the rejection, control, or judgment and feel how it operates to cut you off from your experience; then acceptance comes as an expression of opening to the truth of what is there. "What is there" in one sense means recognizing that you are part of a larger flow of Being; you are not isolated. So acceptance means opening to this larger reality and experiencing that its movement includes you. The flow of true nature controls you whether you know it or not.

Acceptance means relaxing into your own experience so that a natural process of unfolding can occur. However, it does not preclude action. It simply allows reality to be more apparent because it is not clouded by judgment or preference. Then reality can support true action through you. In this way, acceptance supports the action of Being by exposing behavior that both engages judgment and keeps you isolated from the larger flow of reality.

Your soul must undergo a deep shift in consciousness for your experience to be fully accepted. Becoming familiar with the many elements of true nature supports this transformation. As you are aware of and stand up for the truth of your experience, the inner frozenness of self-rejection is melted bit by bit. And through these moments of letting go, the flow of acceptance arises as a natural balm to soothe the aching harshness in your soul.

PRACTICE: OBSERVING YOUR REACTIVITY

Choose a simple activity that you do on a daily basis, such as brushing your teeth, getting dressed, making up your bed, eating lunch, or taking a walk. Make sure it is physical and relatively brief. Do that activity each day for a week with simplicity, care, and attention. This means taking your time, being aware of yourself, completing the task without rushing, and being open to your ways of resisting the activity. Notice the tendency to skip the activity, do it halfheartedly, rush through it, or be preoccupied as you do it.

Can you learn to trust yourself and the flow of the universe enough to relax and be open as you do this daily task? What gets in the way of trusting that there will be time enough for what needs to be done? What aspects of the activity are most difficult to do without engaging in commentary, reaction, or judgment? Is it possible simply to observe your inner reactivity when it is there? If you have some success, you can expand this practice to other activities.

Sue lay awake for quite a while before opening her eyes. It was nice just to lie in bed. She wished she could stay there all day. Her life felt too demanding to think about at the moment. She could hear Frank in the kitchen with the radio on.

🕸 *Every time he is in the kitchen, he has the news on. He's addicted to it. So what if he knows a lot more about what's going on in the world than I do? I don't care about every move the Bosnians make and how the Republicans are going to get rid of another government handout. Why can't he play some music?*

Speaking of music, what a lousy CD I bought yesterday!

That'll teach you to listen to a client's recommendation. You should take it right back today after you return the video and go exercise. You are going to exercise, aren't you?

Sue didn't know what she wanted to do. She felt tired already. She opened her eyes and looked at the ceiling. The first things she saw were cobwebs and then a familiar crack in the paint.

🕸 *What a mess this house is. I knew we should have had the landlady paint this room before we moved in.*

Watch out. You are getting yourself depressed.

I already am depressed. What will Frank think if I say I want to stay in bed? I think he hates me.

Of course, he does. But he would never say so. He's too nice a guy.

"Frank, would you please come here?" she called out as she sat up in bed. After a moment, the door opened, and he stood there regarding her quietly with a curious, intent look on his face. The look caught her off guard, but not knowing what it meant, she ignored it.

🕸 *Can't you ever eat without stuffing yourself with information from the radio at the same time? You know it's why you get indigestion and have so much gas, don't you? I've got a headache, and I feel lousy this morning. Be a sweetheart and make me my coffee. I'm going to read in bed for a while.*

Frank walked over to the bed and sat down on Sue's lap, putting his arm around her with a big smile. "You called me sweetheart. That's the nicest thing I've heard all day," and he gave her a big kiss. "All I've been listening to since I woke up is my judge giving me a hard time!"

8

ENGAGING THE JUDGE

YOU HAVE SEEN THAT your ability to identify judgments as attacks and respond to them appropriately and effectively is usually blocked. This is because, although some part of you recognizes the attack as dangerous and responds to ward off or minimize the emotional and physical effects of the incoming energy, simultaneously another part of you believes in the judge's authority. If you look closely, you will see that though it may not like the judgment, this second part believes it needs the support of the authority and is afraid to let go of the connection with the judge. This part is more interested in getting the judge to change the judgment or, better yet, take it back.

This means that your normal reactions to judgment are not true defenses against attack: they are engagements. I call these reactions engagements because they tolerate the judge, accept its terms (that it is the authority and can pass judgment), and endeavor to minimize, deflect, or argue with the judgment. What they don't do is put an end to the relationship altogether.

All engagements avoid the fundamental effect of attacks on you. This effect is to bind you into a debilitating relationship with the judge. Engagements accept this relationship and, in fact, preserve it, thereby buying into the judge's world. Because judgment intentionally provokes self-rejection through evoking a negative self-image, engaging the judgment means becoming involved in this self-rejecting process and accepting this negative self-image. Engagements are active modes of self-rejection provoked by a judgment. When engaging, your focus is not on rejecting yourself; your focus is on dealing with the judgment. But the self-rejection is implicit through the very fact of engaging the judge in relationship. To truly defend against an attack—that is, to disengage—would be to see the judgment as an unacceptable invasion or intrusion and take whatever action is needed to end it. Clear and simple. This would mean not being involved with the judge at all.

Modes of Engagement

However, we start from where you are now. You continually, and most often unconsciously, engage judgments or attacks. There are three basic modes of engaging an attack—counterattack, rationalize, and absorb or collapse. All buy into the judgment but express it differently. As you become aware of this process, you will see that you tend to favor one, depending largely on your own learned survival style.

Counterattack. In this mode, you attempt to *fight back* and *defeat* the judge. Your attempt is to throw the energy back where it came from and at the same time direct more firepower at the attacker. The desire is to respond so intensely that the attack will stop, which you believe requires wounding the attacker. This behavior usually involves *blaming* others and completely rejecting any deficient feelings in yourself. The energy is explosive, intense and quick—"shot from the hip" and often "below the belt." Your body generally feels energized, taut, and highly reactive. There is usually no thinking involved, just action. However, counterattacking doesn't achieve disengagement because the result is an escalation of the interaction—and continued avoidance of your real experience.

An example of attack-counterattack:

> "Who did your hair? I'll make sure never to go there!"
> "You don't have to worry because you couldn't pay him enough to go near what's on your head!"

Frank counterattacks his judge in the chapter 4 episode, and he and Sue counterattack each other in the chapter 10 episode.

Rationalize. In this mode, you try to *justify* or *explain* yourself, to *argue* your way out of the judgment. The response feels flat, lifeless, and mental, as if denying the reality of being attacked. You are solidifying your outer walls, shoring up weak spots to prevent the attacking energy from penetrating and exposing the alleged deficiency. The body may feel stiff and dry, even wooden, if you are aware of it at all. You will notice that what you say never completely answers the judgment—there is always a more perfect answer just ahead—and in this way, the engagement never stops. Men are particularly prone to this form of engaging, which is experienced as withdrawal from emotional contact with themselves or others.

An example of attack-rationalize:

"How come you never remember to get me flowers?"

"Well, I never know how to choose the right kind, and besides, my sense of color is really bad, and it never seems like a good present because they only last a few days."

Frank rationalizes his judge's attacks in the chapter 2 and 6 episodes.

Absorb or collapse. Here, you give up internally, replacing opposition with compliance in an effort to appease the attacker and make the situation OK again. This response is most evident in the activities of *placating* and *complaining*. There is usually a dramatic loss of energy, a feeling of hopelessness, and often depression. The body may reflect a sense of collapse with rounded shoulders, caved-in chest, and curved-under pelvis (your tail tucked between your legs). You tend to continue the engagement by linking the judgment to all kinds of other issues, thus exaggerating your deficiency and failure. You turn molehills into mountains. This seems to be a more socially supported way for women to engage than for men. It is often experienced as feeling needy for approval and unbroken emotional contact with others.

An example of attack-absorb:

"How come you were a hundred fifty dollars off in balancing your checkbook again?"

"I'm a failure. I've probably bounced five checks, and I'll never make enough money to be able to take a vacation!"

Sue demonstrates the absorbing engagement in the episode with this chapter and in the chapter 14 and 16 episodes.

Survival of the Child

Energetically, these three modes exemplify the three responses available to a young child in the face of parental judgment, criticism, or threatening demands: fight back, shut out, or give up. All are responses to an experience of threat to the child's psychic survival. These modes are analogous to the basic survival responses to physical attack: fight, freeze, faint (flight is number four).

In order to understand a profound turning point in a child's development, let's consider one thread of the complex tapestry of early childhood. She often feels attacked or condemned by parents on whom she is dependent for physical and emotional nourishment and protection. Many times her parents' attitudes, words, and actions do not reflect or support her inner reality. She feels hurt, rejected, criticized, ignored, abandoned, manipulated, or attacked. In those moments, she is caught between her emotional response of instinctually moving away—to break off the connection with the attacker/parent, the source of hurt—and her physical dependency and helplessness urging her to stay, to maintain the relationship with the attacker/parent at all costs.

Over time, every child gives up a certain part of her soul to satisfy the relationship demands of physical survival. The breadth and depth of her field of consciousness become less and less because she must identify with the dependency of her physical needs. This blocks her natural instincts of self-preservation as relationship preservation becomes the priority. In other words, the need for connection with the other becomes more important than the need to maintain contact with her true nature and thereby with her soul.

The child cannot use the fourth option of flight, breaking contact, or running away, because she is dependent on her parents for survival. She is neither big nor strong enough to stop the attack without endangering the relationship; nor can she understand the larger context so as not to experience it as an attack or threat. Understanding the child's dilemma will help you to see that your engagement with the judge reflects a childhood pattern: a survival mechanism learned to ward off the energetic intensity of parental judgment or attack without threatening the ongoing relationship with the attacker. To establish your independence, you internalized your relationship with your parents as a psychic support, and the survival mechanism of engagement was internalized as part of that process. Now you engage with your judge in your mind the same way you did with your parents long ago.

Engagement perpetuates your relationship with the past because it results from the belief that you are still in the life-threatening situation of the child. You are now an adult without the physical dependency needs of a child, but you are still psychically dependent because you came to believe you had to be in order to survive. An important step in disengaging is to recognize that what makes you sensitive to an attack now and limits your response to it is an experience from the past. That earlier experience tells you nothing about what is true now.

All three modes of engagement leave you emotionally and/or energetically engaged with the attacker—the way the child was with her parents. (This is not to say that the parent-child relationship is primarily characterized by a sense of compromising self-denial, but the particular dimension that resulted in internalized self-judgment certainly was.) Engaging the judge is, at its deepest level, an act of self-rejection or self-avoidance, consciously or unconsciously. You are often left silently resentful—filled with impotent anger or rage at the injustice of it all. All too commonly, the resulting state is depression.

Engagements Need Your Support

By studying your own experience of engagement, you can learn a great deal about how you support the judgment process. You will begin to notice that the attack cannot have a sustained effect if you do not engage. Let me repeat that. Judgments will not work in their intended ways unless you engage them. The usual notion is that you are just a victim or recipient and have no power in the situation. In fact, you actively maintain the judgment process through engaging it. You support it by believing it is necessary. We will explore more why this is. For now, you want to use your awareness to discover your own involvement, hopefully without judging it or reacting to it. You want to see truthfully what takes place.

In Session

Doug reported an incident with his woman friend Gloria. While walking in a department store, they arrived at the bottom of the up escalator at the same time as another couple. Gloria slipped in front of the couple, but Doug decided not to rush, so he let them go ahead. When they got upstairs, Gloria started goading him about being passive and letting other people get ahead of him: "Why do you always let others take advantage of you by playing the good boy?"

In describing the incident, Doug couldn't understand why she couldn't see his point of view. He knew that she was speedier than he, always in a hurry, wanting to get ahead. He didn't see the need to rush, and he would rather be polite and be considerate of others. Maybe he was slower than Gloria, but that didn't mean he was passive. Furthermore, the couple was black, and he didn't want to create any feeling in them that he felt superior because he was white . . .

Doug was rationalizing. No matter how many responses he came up with to Gloria's question, he never seemed satisfied that he had answered her criticism. It continued to bother him. This is the distinctive energy of the rationalizer. What he doesn't say or even recognize is that he is feeling attacked.

I asked what bothered him about the interaction with Gloria. He said he just couldn't understand how she was unable to see his side of things. What was it like to feel not understood? He didn't like it, especially because she kept criticizing him for being too nice, as if he were too accommodating to others to take care of himself. He indicated that she often criticized him for being too caring.

Doug realized he felt hurt that she often interpreted his concern for others as weakness. Now he could see that he had felt attacked by her question—that it hurt him to be misunderstood in his intentions. Until this point, he couldn't stop engaging the attack because he was rationalizing his responses to avoid feeling hurt. Thus, he kept it going, without realizing the part he was playing.

Once he recognized that he was feeling hurt, Doug was able simply to attend to that feeling, notice that he had felt the hurt at other times without realizing it, and that it made him sad. It was not clear whether he would recognize such an attack from Gloria in the future or be able to disengage from it, but at the moment, he was no longer engaged in this recent incident.

Being able to recognize when you engage an attack immediately offers you an avenue of disengaging—simply to stop the engagement activity. This is a real option, but it is more difficult than it might at first seem. What is perhaps more helpful now is to continue to develop your awareness of yourself and the ways you engage. In addition, knowing which mode is your most familiar style can help expand your awareness.

Centers of Engagement

Each mode of engagement roughly corresponds to one of the three "centers" in the body: the belly, the head, and the heart.

Counterattacking is a belly reaction—instinctive, fast, without thought or feeling. The underlying assumption fueling this engagement is that survival depends on strength and power. The childhood belief of those who engage in this way was that the only way to stop the attack was to fight back, to resist, not to be taken prisoner. For whatever reason, not fighting back felt too devastating to endure. The central polarity here is *strength and weakness.*

By counterattacking, you unconsciously hoped to have your own strength recognized, preventing further attacks by intimidating others. But this requires showing that the attack has no power over you and that you are not at all vulnerable to it. This means that if you are one who counterattacks, your response must be immediate, and you will tend to have little feeling or awareness of yourself at the time.

To stop the cycle of attack-counterattack, you will need to step back from that instinctual show of force long enough for something else to happen. What will help you is to slow down. When you don't react immediately, there is time for you at least to notice the attack and begin to feel how it affects you. In other words, you bring in more awareness of your heart and head centers.

Counterattackers find vulnerability especially difficult because to them it implies weakness. Though many people do not regularly counterattack when others criticize them, almost everyone does when they are involved in the power struggles of a sustained intimate relationship. When someone knows how to push your buttons, it is very hard not to automatically reciprocate: you counterattack by pushing the buttons in the other that you know so well.

Rationalizing originates in the head center and tends to be quite mental and out of touch with feeling or direct action. If you habitually react in this way, you probably learned as a child that what was most respected was the power of the mind. Your greatest hope for avoiding judgment was to justify yourself and hopefully convince your parents through reason that you were right. Then maybe they would accept and approve of you. The worst thing you could do was to become irrational or emotional, plead, or throw yourself on their mercy, for that would only prove that you had no logical support for your position, that you were wrong. Feelings had to be hidden, and no action could be taken without careful forethought.

The central polarity here is *right and wrong*. So to break the rationalizing engagement will mean letting go of the primacy of the mind. If you are a rationalizer, you must practice being aware of your heart after being judged, or noticing what your body wants to do. For you, thinking replaces all other activity and basically blocks any awareness of yourself in the moment. It is particularly difficult for a rationalizer to feel the pain of the attack because pain implies there is something wrong with you. Rationalizing is probably the most common form of engagement in public situations or hierarchical relations (for example, boss/employee).

Absorbing or collapsing is a reaction of the heart center, stimulating such strong emotional patterns that thinking clearly or taking action becomes all but impossible. The assumption fueling the absorbing engagement is the childhood belief that what is most important for survival is love and attention.

The polarity most active here is *good and bad*. The good parent is the source of love, and you must be the good child to deserve it. When you were a child, feeling the loss of love through a parent's judgment seemed life-threatening. Therefore, the most important goal was to continue to see your parents as good and accept their view of you in order to regain the love. You found that the best way to recover their love and the sense that you were good was to feel how miserably bad you were. Then they would comfort you and say it wasn't so bad, that you were really a good child. So feeling bad was a way to get love, forgiveness, and sympathy and avoid painful judgments.

Shifting out of absorbing as engagement will involve giving up your belief in your unlovableness. If you collapse under attacks, one challenge is to become aware of the external reality of the situation (develop a more detached mental awareness) rather than be overwhelmed with a feeling state. Does your sense of badness, failure, or hopelessness accurately reflect the reality of the situation? The most difficult challenge, however, is to be able to mobilize energy to support yourself. As an absorber, taking action on your own behalf implies the presence of self-love. Absorbing is probably the most common engagement of your internal judge.

Inner Engagement

You are probably most familiar with absorbing as a reaction to your own judge because, when you engage in this way, you feel most directly the effects of being attacked. You feel bad about yourself, often ashamed and guilty. You obsess about your failures, your bad qualities, your gloomy future, your lack of friends, and so on. You feel caught in a downward spiral and find yourself retreating and perhaps shrinking. Moving away from collapsing or absorbing the attack feels as if it would just open you up to more attacks. Your only choice is to hide in your deficiency.

In this form of engagement, you believe the only way to stop the attack is to attack yourself first. So you accept and even confess your inadequacy, in the hope that others will proclaim your goodness, or at least forgive you, for you can't. In many cases, the hope for escape from attack is long gone, and all that remains is a certain familiarity with being bad, deficient, needy, helpless, or a failure. Engaging your judge through collapse is a way of giving up the effort to be adult and returning to your childhood world with your good parent and your wish to be loved.

But your inner process can also take on the other forms of engagement. Rationalizing is a fairly familiar mental activity for many people, but they don't necessarily connect it with being attacked because generally there is little feeling component in their rationalizing. However, whenever you find yourself explaining your actions, justifying your feelings, or trying to figure out the right response, chances are good you are engaging an attack. In absorbing, you get lost in your emotional state, while in rationalizing, it is easy to get lost in fantasies. You can stay away from unpleasant feelings by playing out endless scenarios of what might have happened or how it might be in the future.

At these times, it is less important to actually work something out than it is to avoid the attack and the feelings it brings up. But since the attack continues to exist in the background, you can't stop the fantasies. Sometimes, rationalizing is experienced as a mental obsession with an experience you had or might have as you desperately seek the perfect resolution for the situation. That sense of not being able to let go of something indicates the presence of an underlying attack that has not been addressed. Rationalizing keeps you engaged.

Least obvious of the internal engagements is the counterattack. How do you counterattack your own judge? Basically with the energy behind statements such as, "Who cares what you think. . . . I'll show you who's boss here. . . . Don't tell me how I'm supposed to be or what I'm supposed to do. I'll do exactly what I want to do." Notice that the belief may be that this type of defiance is separating you from the judge: "I am pushing it away and claiming my own independence." However, the strength of the action derives primarily from opposition to or rebellion against the power of the judge. The illusion of independence is achieved only by fighting off the attack. For this reason, maintaining the sense of strength and sepa-rateness is *dependent* on pushing away, which means keeping the fight going, which means engagement.

One manifestation of this internal counterattacking engage-ment is self-destructive behavior. Your judge believes you should not drink (your parents drank too much) or smoke (it causes lung can-cer) or eat sweets (you will get fat, and no one will like you), so your counterattacking engagement of these attacks is to do exactly what you are not supposed to: you drink, smoke, or eat sweets. You are saying "fuck you" to the judge. "I'll do it if I want to, and you can't stop me!" It's a power struggle, and inevitably addictive behavior of this sort results in even stronger attacks by the judge as you suffer from the effects of the self-destructive behavior. Even though you recognize that the behavior hurts you, you resort to it in an effort to get back at your judge. You are acting out of your resentment and hatred of feeling dictated to and treated like a child. But you are only escalating the engagement with self-attack.

Each of these modes has its own history, assumptions, and char-acteristics, and they may seem mutually exclusive. But remember, these definitions only provide a conceptual framework for helping you explore and understand judgment in yourself. Do not feel con-fined to one of these categories. Everyone will have some experi-ence with each mode, though the particular details may vary from person to person. What is important is that you begin to see the rather predictable nature of the patterns that support inner attacks.

How Engagement Feels

The more you become aware of engaging attacks, the more you will be able to recognize the energetic sense of being engaged. Being engaged can have a sticky feel to it, like flypaper: once you are in it, movement only makes it worse. You try to go on to other things with your mind and your energy, but you keep getting pulled back to rationalizing or obsessing about something that happened. You are not satisfied with anything, can't complete things. You find you can't let go of something when you are done; you keep fussing over it to make it perfect—when actually what you can't let go of is the engagement in your mind.

Another aspect of this engagement state is a sense of confinement. You may find yourself feeling downright claustrophobic as the attack and your engagement of it leave you nowhere to turn or move: you feel trapped, closed in. Or your breathing may be constricted, which you might not notice until you slow down and find that it takes a conscious effort to breathe deeply. A third quality of engagement is a feeling of murkiness, of being in cloudy or muddy water. You can't get clear about what's going on or what needs to be done. You feel confused, easily distracted, and ungrounded, as if things around you won't come into focus.

Another flavor of engagement is a subtle but constant sense of frustration (associated most often with counterattacking). This is similar to the stickiness but includes a dose of irritation and agitation. It is as if everything rubs you the wrong way no matter how much you try to relax and calm yourself. You can't quite get mad because nothing is really significant, but the frustration won't go away.

Other qualities of engagement include depression (absorb/collapse) and rigidity (rationalize). Depression carries that heavy, lethargic, apathetic quality. You have a hard time summoning up energy to do anything, and nothing seems to matter all that much. Why not just watch TV? Rigidity feels tight and stiff both emotionally and physically, as though you have no flexibility in your joints or in your responses. This is a variation on the sense of confinement, but rather than feeling trapped or closed in by something outside yourself, the feeling seems more internal—a sense of inner crowding, of being brittle and hard.

You are probably familiar with all these energetic qualities, but now you can see that they may be manifestations of being engaged with an attack—indicators of self-judgment. It happens like this: You experience an inner attack from your judge. It affects you and continues to affect you as you unconsciously engage it by counterattacking, rationalizing, or absorbing. Meanwhile, you go about your life and feel compulsive, constricted, not very focused, and slightly depressed. Is this state related to the attack and the inner engagement? Absolutely.

Recognizing engagement is a refinement and deepening of your awareness of the energetic and emotional effects of judgment that we looked at in chapter 4. You see that the particular effects are related to the way you engage the attacks. With some practice at noticing your own process, you will come to recognize the qualities of your own state of engagement. You may already be noticing that you are operating in this state a large percentage of the time. Some people live most of their lives in this state and take it to be normal.

Engagement in Daily Life

Engagement is evident in the extreme on most TV sitcoms. Often, 90 percent of sitcom and soap opera interaction is judgment and engagement: attack followed by counterattack, rationalize, and absorb. In some comedies, the main form of humor is counterattack. (On the other hand, one of the most satisfying types of humor comes from a real defense against attack because it supports the soul's truth.) In "real life," engagement is an accepted form of social interaction, very apparent in casual conversation and gossip. Consider how much of superficial conversation consists of complaining or berating yourself (absorbing), explaining or justifying your behavior (rationalizing), or criticizing or putting down others (counterattacking). I refer to these all as engagements rather than attacks because, if explored in yourself, these behaviors usually arise in reaction to your own self-judgment. However, they could certainly be both.

Recognizing attacks and engagement behavior, and the self-rejection implicit in both, is a gradual process. At first, you do not feel the self-rejection or attack in what you are doing because it is so familiar and it supports the ways you are used to thinking and behaving. Over time, as self-awareness develops, you naturally begin to experience how painful it is. This means you are becoming aware that the attack and engagement behavior does not support you. You recognize that, though familiar, it perpetuates a self-destructive process. You start to value yourself in a new way, different from what is supported by the attacks. You don't want to continue that form of self-rejection. This is the natural movement of working with judgment. Judgments that you didn't notice last year because they felt familiar and acceptable are now painful and upsetting, though others may continue to find them normal.

Thus, in exploring your engagement of the judge, little by little you become aware of the amount of time you are affected by attacks, often without knowing it. For instance, you probably use many common activities to act out your engagement of attacks and, in that process, reject yourself. Have you ever eaten to fill a collapsed state, watched TV to avoid depression, told your story to a friend to rationalize away an attack, played a mean game of racquetball or yelled at other drivers in traffic to counterattack your own judge? As you begin to recognize your own engaging behavior, you may begin to notice you have been under attack without being aware of it and without knowing what the attack was. You then have the opportunity to reflect back on your experience to see if you can discover what happened and how you felt attacked.

This is a difficult stage in the journey: staying with the discomfort and feeling of entrapment to understand the truth about judgment. It is tempting to look for quick solutions, convenient interpretations, or more comfortable experiences. Supporting yourself to stay with what is true is not easy. Awareness requires the perseverance of your own personal will to move toward freeing your soul of engagement and self-attack.

POINTS TO REMEMBER

- Your normal reactions to judgment are not true defenses against attack: they are engagements. Engagements endeavor to minimize, deflect, or argue with the judgment, but they don't put an end to the relationship itself.
- To truly defend against an attack—that is, to disengage—is to see the judgment as an unacceptable invasion or intrusion and take whatever action is needed to end it. This means not being involved with the judge at all.

- There are three basic modes of engaging an attack, all of which buy into the judgment but express it differently. They are:

Counterattack: An attempt to *fight back* and *defeat* the judge, to throw the energy back where it came from so that the attack will stop. This behavior usually involves *blaming* others and completely rejecting any deficient feelings in yourself. It doesn't achieve disengagement because the result is an escalation of the interaction—and continued avoidance of your real experience. The body center is the *belly;* the focus of concern is the polarity of *strength and weakness.*

Rationalize: An attempt to *justify* or *explain* yourself, to *argue* your way out of the judgment, in order to prevent the attacking energy from penetrating and exposing the alleged deficiency. It doesn't achieve disengagement because what you say never completely answers the judgment. There is always a more perfect answer just ahead. The body center is the *head;* the focus of concern is the polarity of *right and wrong.*

Absorb or collapse: Opposition is replaced with compliance in an effort to appease the attacker and make the situation OK again. This response is most evident in the activities of *placating* and *complaining.* It is often experienced as feeling needy for approval and unbroken emotional contact with others. It doesn't achieve disengagement because you tend to keep linking the judgment to all kinds of other issues, thus exaggerating your deficiency and failure. The body center is the *heart;* the focus of concern is the polarity of *good and bad.*

- The engagement modes exemplify the three responses available to a young child in the face of parental judgment, criticism, or threatening demands: fight back, shut out, or give up. All are responses to an experience of threat to the child's psychic survival.
- Engagement perpetuates your relationship with the past because it results from the belief that you are still in the life-threatening situation of the child.
- Being able to recognize when you engage an attack immediately

offers you an avenue of disengaging—simply to stop the engagement activity.

- An important first step in working with engagement is to develop your awareness of yourself and the ways you engage. Knowing which mode is your most familiar style can help expand your awareness.

Exercise: Identifying Modes of Engagement

In both your internal and external life, recall some of your recent experiences of feeling attacked and explore which mode of engagement you used in each case. Consider social, work, and intimate situations. Do you respond similarly in all types of interactions? Which situations evoke which modes? Notice if you use one particular mode most of the time.

Exercise: Observing Engagements in Social Situations

The next time you are at a dinner party or other social activity, pay particular attention to the presence of attacks and engagements in the conversation. How does it feel to pay attention to that level of the conversation? Do you find yourself participating? What can you do to avoid supporting that kind of interaction?

The ego automatically and unconsciously responds to the superego with repression of parts of the personality, to defend itself against its painful attacks. An effective way to deal with the superego is to learn to defend against its attacks in a different way, without having to use repression and the other unconscious defense mechanisms of the ego. The method has to be conscious and intentional, in contrast to the habitual automatic ways that can only foster unconsciousness. . . . For instance, if the man responds with: "Father, it's not true I am feminine and weak. Tenderness is good and does not mean weakness or femininity," then he is being reasonable with a superego that is not really rational. Also, he probably has tried this response many times but without success because in this response the man is on the defensive; he is trying to justify his feeling and to account to somebody else for its being okay. Any justification already implies some guilt, and so it won't work.

— A. H. Almaas, *Essence*, pp. 137–138

Sue stiffened with surprise at Frank's unexpected behavior. She did not respond to his kiss and felt uneasy after the comment about her calling him sweetheart. After all, she had not meant it in a loving way. It was simply a habitual way to manipulate him into doing what she wanted. She felt guilty about that and wondered if he was making fun of her.

Watch out, Sue. You can't trust this openness. You know you don't deserve to be treated lovingly. After all, you were just complaining to him, and besides, you are feeling crummy as usual. He's doing something strange, so don't let him get to you.

Sue was aware of this familiar voice, and she was aware of Frank sitting on her lap, staring at her with a very open, loving look. She didn't know what to do or what to make of this situation. All she could manage was to take a breath and exhale. Sue felt less tense but more rooted to the spot, unable or unwilling to do anything.

Look, just push him away. You know he's too heavy to sit on you. Tell him you can't deal with this now. If you don't, you'll be sorry later. He just wants something from you, and he's worked out a new strategy to catch you off guard.

Sue realized how often she listened to that voice, doing and believing whatever it said. It was familiar, and she was tempted to go with the familiar. However, at the moment, she was more interested in what was here now: Frank's look and that last comment he made about his own judge. *Boy, I know exactly what he means.* Without thinking about it, Sue leaned forward and kissed him. Her hands reached inside his robe, feeling his warm skin as they slid around his back and squeezed his flesh. Her body suddenly felt alive and hungry, and his felt full, strong, and responsive.

After an extended kiss, Frank pulled away, smiling, and said, "Take it easy, my neck is out, and I don't want to make it worse . . ."

Here goes, now he's going to blame it on you and then withdraw. I told you this was a mistake.

". . . Are you sure you have a headache? You don't feel like you have a headache. You feel good enough to eat!" And with that, he slipped off his robe, gently pushed her down onto her back, and climbed on top of her.

9

PERSONAL WILL

THE JUDGE BELIEVES THAT it knows what is best for you, how you need to be, what you need to pay attention to, and what is wrong with you. The more you study it, the more you see it has a mind and a will of its own. To free yourself from this constant controlling quality of the judge, you need to understand and use your own will. But having your own will does not mean getting into a battle of wills with your critic. Having your own will means experiencing the essential soul quality of personal will.

The following story shows some of the stages that occur in activating personal will. The italicized statements mark significant points in Dorothy's process in relation to this quality.

Life Lessons

Dorothy was an ambitious young woman who had started her own business producing annual reports for growing nonprofit corporations. She was smart, intuitive, and hardworking as well as skilled in writing, business communication, and financial statements. She drove herself hard and developed a successful business. Dorothy liked being a success because her father had always praised her accomplishments and paid special attention to her when she did well. She became aware that her judge did the same thing. It motivated her to push herself and praised her when she succeeded. "Each time you land a new account or hand in that finished report, you really prove you are worth something," it would say to her.

For the first few years, she enjoyed the hard work, the long hours, and the feeling of urgency to get things done. Her judge was her constant companion and support, pushing her on if she ever grew weary, lonely, or anxious. *At some point, as Dorothy began to feel a desire for a personal life with social time, she became aware of how little she knew what she wanted or what it might look like.* She also noticed that when an acquaintance would ask her how she was doing, she always answered in terms of her work. *She realized she did not know how she felt;* she could only evaluate her state in relation to how far along she was in her work or how difficult it was.

Time passed, and one day *she found herself wanting to take a break in the middle of the day.* "You can't do that; there's too much to do, and besides it's a waste of time," said her judge. She agreed and continued working. A week later, the desire came up again, and though she didn't leave work, she felt unsettled enough to get up from her desk and go stand at the window and watch the world outside. *It felt as though a spell were being broken,* and she stood for fifteen minutes absorbed in cars going by and people passing before her judge managed to break into her consciousness: "What is going on? You are getting lazy! Get back to work before you get in any worse trouble!"

As she returned to her desk, she was much more aware of how her body ached and how much at this moment she did not want to write a euphemistic report about some faceless organization and its money. For the first time, she realized *she was in touch with how she felt in the moment,* unrelated to how the work was going. *It was a little scary because her feelings didn't match what she was supposed to be doing.* Her judge chimed in, "Now you see why personal feelings only create problems. You've got to keep busy and stay focused on your goals and what you have to do. Who knows what will happen if you start letting yourself feel things? You might never want to work again. Then where would you be? Listen to me, this personal feelings stuff is a disaster waiting to happen." Clearly, if she wanted the judge's support, she'd better keep pushing.

The problem was she had been doing that for two and a half years, and though she had some money and a nice place to live, she couldn't enjoy it. She was always working and wasn't eating well or getting exercise. At this moment, *she felt sure that things would have to change, though she didn't know how.* She wondered where she would find support since she knew her judge wouldn't like it if she began putting time and energy into personal concerns. The rest of the afternoon, she found herself periodically stopping to sit and wonder what it would be like to make space for herself. During these pauses, *she found herself noticing many things in her office that she had been completely ignoring:* the wrapper from a sandwich she had bought last week, an early draft of a report strewn in a corner where she had dumped it, a poster curling up where one thumbtack was gone, an empty coffee cup on the windowsill and another one on the file cabinet. The third time she paused, she suddenly noticed right in front of her on the desk the rose her landlord had left her two weeks ago on Valentine's Day, now long dead as it sat in an empty glass.

This was the last straw. *She got up and spent the rest of the afternoon cleaning her office.* "Well, it's about time you paid a little attention around here. This has hardly been a professional office, I must say." Dorothy could hear her judge trying to take credit for what she was doing on her own. *She didn't care; she knew why she was cleaning. And when she was done, she felt open and clear and happy, not because things were more professional but because she had done what needed to be done and she liked her surroundings now. For ten minutes, she just sat in her reading chair, enjoying her office and being aware of how she really felt there in the room in a solid, simple way. It had nothing to do with making something happen.* Rather than return to working, she decided to take herself out to dinner as a beginning to her new life.

Waking Up to Reality

Dorothy first must see how little she is in touch with herself and how her judge has been the guide, support, motivator, and director of her life. She feels she is doing what she wants to do, but her desire is motivated by wanting the support of the judge (her internalized father). Gradually, she awakens to the fact that she has no personal life and no inner life separate from her work and her judge. This process of recognizing her lack of self-direction and self-awareness reflects an awakening of essential will. It is the personal will that is being activated as you begin to question what you have taken to be reality, as you realize that your experience is limited and does not necessarily reflect what is true for you.

Even as she is waking up, she is too dependent on the support of the judge to change anything. When she can't help herself and breaks the pattern of habitual activity, she steps outside of how she knows herself. But the judge is quick to reassert its position and bring her back. Dorothy complies but now can no longer accept at face value what it tells her. She is faced with the possibility that what is underneath this facade is a very dissatisfied woman. What if she actually doesn't like this work she has created for herself? She becomes aware of major hindrances to seeking her own grounding in life—fear of not knowing what is supposed to happen or what will happen and fear of losing the judge's support.

Again, her personal will surfaces, this time in giving her a certainty that she must move in a new direction in spite of the obstacles. This is another characteristic of this soul quality. Personal will supports you in discovering what is true for you and then provides a sense of confidence when you are aligned with that truth—even when it includes not knowing. Having connected with this sense of personal necessity, she begins to notice more immediate aspects of her reality, such as the things in her office she has ignored while being totally absorbed in accomplishing her work. This, too, is an expression of her personal will grounding her in what is real in the moment, inside and out.

The more she is aware of this external reality, the more she is moved to respond to it. At this point, her will manifests in taking immediate action to clean her office. When you are grounded in your personal will and recognize that something needs to be done, you feel moved to do it—not so much because you want to do it or should do it, but because it needs to be done. This doing is a natural, spontaneous act. There's no need for a judge to push you. You simply feel good to be part of reality taking care of itself.

The last piece in Dorothy's journey in relation to personal will is sensing the actual feeling of will in her own body. Having acted from her own will rather than her judge's, she finds a natural rest that has a sense of satisfaction and spaciousness in it. In particular, she is aware of feeling present in a simple, solid way. When you are in touch with your personal will, you feel here, physically grounded in the moment. Your body feels solid and definite, with clear edges and internal density. You know you are here in this place at this moment and nowhere else. The mind may be quiet or busy, but you are not in the past or the future; you are just here now.

So we have seen three specific manifestations of personal will: a definite, concrete sense of your own physical presence; a certainty and confidence in your actions; and a knowledge of what is true and what is needed. When you experience your own will, it is obvious without thought that these manifestations are all expressions of one inner reality—a solid, unshakable clarity of Being. As your experience of this develops, you recognize that personal will also gives you a certain steadfastness in what you do. Knowing that a particular thing needs to happen in your life is no different from intending it to happen, and that is the same as your commitment to making it happen. You feel a clarity of purpose that can resist the pulls and pushes of the judge. Just as Dorothy felt her judge trying to take over her action of cleaning, you hear your judge's attempts to manipulate you and are not moved by them. This is not being stubborn or bullheaded about action; there is no effort to ignore reality. On the contrary, personal will is always open to and depends on contact with reality. In interacting with the judge, your personal will exposes how the judge must manipulate reality in order to maintain its power.

Will and the Judge

Will builds on awareness and acceptance. You perceive as fully as possible your current reality and align yourself with that. This means being in touch with physical reality: the concrete definiteness of your own body, the air you breathe, the food you eat, the house you live in, the car you drive. If something is broken, you fix it; you don't walk by it for months, hoping it will go away. Will also means being in touch with your feelings, your needs, your thoughts, your beliefs, and your judge. You realize these things don't have ultimate reality, that they are merely a part of your reality you must be in touch with and deal with in a realistic way. When you see that a friend at work is always attacking you as a way to make conversation, you ask yourself whether you want this; if not, perhaps you ask him to stop. If this doesn't work, you consider whether you want a friend who is always attacking you; if the answer is no, maybe you stop relating to him, even if it is socially awkward.

How does the judge attack your will? Primarily by telling you that nothing will work unless you apply effort, struggle, and use discipline. "You can't just sit there; you have to deal with this. Everybody is watching you; what are you going to do? Look what happened to you last time. Why do you think it will be different now?" The judge is constantly distorting reality to get you to pay attention and feel a certain way. When you attempt to slow down and not act rashly, the judge will call you a wimp, a sissy, chicken shit, or weak. It says you are being lazy or irresponsible because you are not doing enough, you are losing control, you are going to be left behind, you won't be ready, you will miss your only opportunity, and so on. The judge affects will more than any other quality of your true nature. It actively attempts to separate you from your grounding in reality. By constantly telling you that you are deficient, weak, passive, timid, needy, helpless, the judge makes you believe that you need it for support. If you turn your back on it, the judge says you are rigid, controlling, too independent, overconfident, cocky, self-centered, and arrogant; therefore, you need to be cut down to size and learn your place.

Staying in touch with your personal will threatens the judge's power. If you begin to trust yourself and the experience of being with your own truth, then you will not need the support of the judge. As you cultivate your sense of steadfastness in reality, you develop the patience to allow things to unfold and reveal their truth to you rather than allowing the judge to impose its beliefs, priorities, and values on your experience.

The personal will works in concert with awareness by providing the determination to sense, look, and listen. As your personal will develops, you will have more capacity not to engage your judge when it delivers a familiar attack. How would it be simply to listen to the judge without response—to commit to doing nothing but following your own breathing? If the judge cannot make you act or react, it is lost; it has no power.

PRACTICE: THE SITTING PRACTICE

This is a progressive practice to cultivate personal will, the capacity simply to stay with what is happening in the moment.

Step 1. Find a place in a crowded, busy location where you can sit undisturbed, such as a bench in a shopping mall, train station, or a busy downtown street. Sit comfortably and quietly, without moving or speaking for at least fifteen minutes, just watching and listening and being aware of your own body. Notice all the life and energy that flows around you and that you can just sit in the midst of it and do nothing. You may get interested in things you see or snatches of conversation you overhear, but your task is to keep bringing your awareness back to your own body, your own experience of just sitting.

Step 2. Now try this practice in a setting of nature that has little human intrusion or activity, perhaps by the ocean, in the woods, or in a nearby park. Notice how different the pace and intensity of energy and movement are. Be aware of what pulls your attention in this setting. Continue with the intention of always coming back to self-awareness.

Step 3. Try this sitting practice in your own home, perhaps your bedroom or living room. Do it for at least fifteen minutes and notice how your mind is pulled by all the familiar associations with what you see, the things you are reminded of that you need to do, the memories stirred by seeing things you may not have noticed in a while. Try to keep your body relaxed and quiet. There is nothing to do during this time. Do you find it harder to bring your attention back to the simple activity of sitting, breathing, and sensing yourself when you are in familiar surroundings?

Step 4. Sit *with your eyes closed* for fifteen minutes in a quiet place in your home where you won't be disturbed. You might want to turn off the phone. Now there is no visual input or distraction. What is left is you and your own mind. You become faced with the countless ways your mind wants to distract you from simply sitting and being quiet. A good aid to keep you focused is to follow your breath, and if you like, you can also put your awareness on sensing your arms and legs. Whenever you find yourself in the past or future, in far-off places, thinking of complicated tasks, or dealing with your judge, just bring your attention back to your breathing or your awareness of body sensation. Remember that the only thing you are doing right now is sitting.

Consciously choosing to be still and not do anything outwardly (or inwardly) is the practice at the heart of this experiential sitting. Sustaining the practice will activate your will to support simply being and not doing. Remember, this practice is not designed to encourage any particular outcome or experience—easy or difficult, pleasant or unpleasant. You may find it quite delicious and relaxing to stop doing, or you may find it very uncomfortable not to move around, adjust your body, or get engaged with what's in your mind or outside you. You may be bored, anxious, sleepy, or excited. You may have any number of different experiences. Personal will is the source of your ability to stay connected to and aware of whatever is happening in your experience.

It is valuable to do sitting practice many times, even daily, for it will strengthen your ability to be quiet inside and not be swayed by the various kinds of energy you encounter inside and outside yourself.

*The moment we say "no" to our experience, we are using false
will. True will is simply letting go of the false will that wants
to take our experience somewhere else.*

*So when we are willing to be completely in the moment,
we have a better chance of seeing what is actually there, what
is actually happening. If we are saying, "No, I don't want this,
I want it to be different," that blocks the experience and gives
us less chance of seeing the truth clearly. So when true will is
operating, it enhances our awareness of what is there. It allows
us to have a more complete and full perception. Only when we
have this complete perception can we truly understand what is
there.*

— A. H. Almaas, *Diamond Heart Book 2,* p. 120

Frank and Sue lay on the bed after making love. The process felt incomplete, as was so often the case for them. This time, he lost his erection once he got inside her. She felt ripped off as usual, unable to have her own pleasure because of his problem. They were both silent. The atmosphere was thick and uncomfortable.

☾ "So what's the problem this time, Frank? Why can't you stay hard?"

"Why can't you show some pleasure in having me inside you? You always look kind of pained, like you wish I was someone else!"

"Oh, so now it's my problem? Who's the one who hasn't wanted to be sexual for three years and comes so quickly I can hardly take a deep breath?"

"Go fuck yourself. You make me so mad!" Frank rolled over away from Sue and wrapped his arms around himself tightly.

"Now, don't clam up on me, Frank," Sue demanded, starting to feel helpless in the face of his withdrawal. She was very familiar with how he could isolate himself and how frightened and needy it made her feel. "Why don't you go ahead and say whatever you have to say. I'm tired of you sitting on your anger." She paused, then added, "Look, I promise to just listen and not respond."

Frank said nothing for several minutes, and then he sat up, took a deep breath, and began.

"Yeah, well, it's true I hate your guts right now. ☾ You're always waiting like some vulture to blame your lack of pleasure on me. You love it when I blow it because then you can gloat and make it all my fault. Your real problem is you can't give yourself pleasure; you are totally dependent on the man coaxing you along the whole way. Well, fuck you! I've got enough deficiency of my own without having yours blamed on me, too. Don't you think it's hard enough living with a wimpy little dick like mine? I can't control it. I can't depend on it or trust it to follow through or stay hard. I don't know what's going on with it or what it needs. How would you feel making love when your main tool might up and die on you right when you need it most? I feel fucking helpless. Like I'm castrated, no balls, might as well go live in a monastery. Suze, it's just so goddamned humiliating."

Sue reached over and put her hand on his chest, and he burst out crying. What a morning! First he was so spontaneously loving, and now this. It was intense to witness all the pent-up rage trapped in his judgments about her and himself, rage that covered all the hurt and pain he fought so hard to conceal.

10
BEING THE JUDGE

SO FAR, WE HAVE been examining judgment from the point of view of the one being attacked. This is important because it is from this position that you begin to notice judgment and the suffering it causes. But both sides of the judgment process exist inside you. A full exploration of judgment also requires seeing things from the viewpoint of the one who is attacking. This means knowing yourself as the judge.

You may already be aware of the times when you take on this role: criticizing others and putting yourself down. You may even find that feeling superior to others is a more familiar experience than feeling deficient or unworthy. Whether familiar or not, with growing self-awareness you will recognize times when you are invested in being judgmental, even when you wish you were not. So an important step in working with the judge is to learn why you feel obliged to play the judge.

The Judgment Loop

As we saw in chapter 8, the judgment process is actively supported by both the judge and the one judged. Their mutual dependency creates a closed loop of self-judgment. The judge needs the one who is judged and vice versa. If you tend to consider yourself superior to others, you will likely end up in relationships with people who lack self-confidence. Should you commonly identify with being put down, you will feel more comfortable relating to someone who likes to criticize. In either case, you will unconsciously gravitate toward your opposite because this reinforces your sense of who you are. In other words, you find someone to play your helpless child or your judge in these externalized versions of the judgment loop.

Once you are identified with either the judge or the one judged, you are caught inside the loop. You must stay there; otherwise, you lose the support of the other end of the loop. In a relationship, stepping out of a complementary role can upset the status quo. If you are Mr. Superior and one day you start feeling unworthy, your partner, Ms. Inferior, may get upset and try to boost you back up to your familiar lofty self. This is life inside the loop.

Since the judgment process goes round and round inside the loop, either acting as the judge or acting as the one being judged can start the process going. Often, your judge starts things by attacking you. But the more you see how the process actually works, you realize it can start from the other end as well. You can feel "attacked" by someone who is under attack when that person's behavior tends to pull you into the judgment loop.

If you are around someone who is acting out absorbing engagement—feeling persecuted, helpless, extremely dependent—it can be very difficult not to become his judge. He might say something like, "You think I am disgusting, don't you?" Thus, he makes you his judge and then relates through absorbing engagement. Sue's behavior in the episode preceding chapter 16 is a good example of such an interaction. This pattern is common in intimate relationships as the two people unconsciously fulfill expected roles. The judgment loop easily becomes part of the familiar dynamic of the relationship, where it is invoked by either person playing either role: judge or judged. Internally, this process happens in a similar but less obvious way.

The loop is what you are in when you are engaged. The closed nature of the loop makes engagement feel confined and stuck: you can't see beyond your engagement and can't find your grounding. In fact, when you are trapped in the loop, the only way to get some relief without disengaging is to switch roles. You change from judged to judge or vice versa.

What does this mean? It means you become the one who feels powerful instead of the one who feels powerless. If you have just gone through an experience of feeling attacked, perhaps without knowing it, and the sense of helplessness and shame that arises is difficult to tolerate, it is not uncommon to find yourself becoming critical of others or aggressively ordering them around, be they employees, spouse, children, pets, or objects. In this way, you temporarily escape your own powerlessness at the judged end of the loop and take on the powerful state of the judge. It doesn't matter if the external situation is different from the one that made you feel judged (this generally makes it easier to switch roles, in fact), because the judgment loop is inside you wherever you go.

In Session

In a private session, Jim related a recent experience of seeing himself attacking other people harshly. He was in a café one morning, feeling good and enjoying the sunshine and coffee smells. As he approached the counter, he caught the eye of someone sitting at one of the tables. Immediately, he noticed himself stiffen, contract, withdraw inside, and start looking around with a wary eye. He was also aware that his mind was busy making derogatory remarks about different people in the café—comments that put each person down. He was very familiar with that kind of inner commentary but had never before noticed how negative it was.

Jim was a little disturbed recognizing this, but he was also curious about what was going on. By sensing himself as he waited for his cappuccino, he realized how vulnerable he felt being seen by that person. He felt weak and exposed and certain he was being judged. The vulnerability became intolerable as he saw his own judge in the eyes of everyone in the café and imagined them mocking him. At that moment, Jim realized he was seeing his own weakness in them. He knew that his automatic way to shut down his feeling of exposure was to become the judge and attack others. In the session, he was able to see that, as the judge, he had felt strong and in control rather than exposed and weak, so by becoming the judge, he avoided feeling attacked for his vulnerability.

As the judge, you feel right, strong, in control, and willing to be aggressive to make yourself heard. You know what is happening and what is supposed to happen. This is a dramatic contrast to how you feel when you are the one being judged: weak, helpless, small, deficient, and unworthy. It is no wonder that a favorite escape route from such feelings is to become the judge. Why be a prisoner if you can be the prison guard? Of course, this is the ego perspective based on the conditioning that life is made up of complementary roles—that you must be one or the other and that they are mutually exclusive.

True nature is not based on division, separation, and exclusion. Being your true nature embraces all qualities and all experiences. You had to learn as a child to divide your experience into roles and relationships, possibilities and limitations, ideas of self and other. Children internalize these perspectives through playing games based on observing how people relate to each other: "Tommy, you're going to play the bad boy who didn't do his homework, and I'll be the teacher who gets to yell at him and make him stand in the corner." They learn the roles of the personality prison. In this book, we are exploring the possibility of leaving the prison altogether.

Usually, when you are playing out the judge role with its strength, control, knowledge, clarity, and rightness, you don't see yourself as judgmental. You feel full of conviction and feel it's necessary to take this position, so you feel justified in behaving and thinking the way you do. However, this sense of conviction and necessity does not arise from the grounding in reality of the personal will but from the need to avoid the discomfort of being attacked. You know this is so when you get charged up about your position, tell someone what ought to happen, feel righteous about what you know is true, or communicate by attacking people. When you feel attached to how things unfold and defensive about why, you know you are not feeling the ease and clarity of resting in the larger truth of reality. In most cases, being judgmental of yourself or of others covers up a sense of deficiency, often arising from the experience of being attacked. (From this point of view, counterattacking constitutes a shift from being judged to being the judge.)

It is difficult to see yourself being the judge and not react by calling yourself bad, wrong, cruel, or heartless. However, this reaction means you are the judge judging your judge—and you are still caught in the loop. The first step in breaking out is to be aware of the truth without reacting. Remember, this judgment loop is all in your mind, and some part of your identity is connected to each end.

Your deepest or oldest connection is with the one being attacked, the child, but in order to survive, you learned to be like your parents through internalizing the judge that you originally experienced in them. You alternate back and forth and identify with one end of the loop or the other. To continue to deepen your understanding of the judging process, just as you looked at engaging the judge, you must consider your experience being the judge. These are some important questions we will look at: How does it feel to be the judge? When do you become the judge? Do you show it or hide it? Do you get something out of judgment? What motivates the judge?

Recognizing the Judge in You

One dimension of exploring the judge in yourself is to identify how you feel when you are being the judge, just as you did with experiencing judgment in chapter 4. On a somatic level, you can recognize when your judge is becoming dominant by noticing any of the following physical symptoms:

- A change in your voice to a higher pitch, faster rate, or louder volume
- An increase in the rate and depth of your breathing
- An awareness that your heart is racing and beating harder
- A sensation of tightness in the muscles of your arms, legs, neck, face, or gut
- A feeling of being charged up, ready for intense action
- Tension between the shoulder blades
- A strong physical sense of needing to discharge energy
- A narrowing of your awareness to focus on what you believe deserves criticism

Certain attitudes and stances characterize the judge on a cognitive level as well. Any of the following thoughts or feelings tend to indicate a critical frame of mind:

- Conviction that things are not being done the right way around you
- Certainty that others lack the capacity or motivation to do what needs to be done
- Distrust of others' motives; disappointment in their failings
- An intense need to hold your ground and defend your territory
- A stubborn focus on making a point or correcting details
- Belief that you will have to do it by yourself, without others' help

Neither of the above lists is exhaustive. Nor will you necessarily experience being identified with the judge in these forms. What ways are most familiar to you? What makes it difficult for you to recognize your identification with the judge?

Roles of the Judge

To recognize yourself as the judge, it is helpful to know different forms that judging can take. These are the roles in which the judge hides out, such as conscience, motivator, guard, and mirror. The functions these roles serve are important for your life. Unfortunately, you learned these roles by modeling yourself after your parents or guardians, and inevitably, this modeling included an element of self-rejection. So each role is colored by the judgment implicit in the relationship you had as a child with your parents.

For example, when you are making a moral evaluation of an action taken by yourself or another, you find it hard not to judge the person as well as the action. "There must be something wrong with me to have done something bad like that." Not only that, but you tend to encourage guilt as a form of punishment for "wrong" behavior: "How will I learn if I don't feel guilty?" You don't trust that you can learn without being threatened. Your experience of conscience is based on moral standards instead of a direct knowing of your actions and their effects. And you use guilt and punishment to support these standards rather than your own love for supporting the truth.

Similarly, to get yourself to do things that take effort or that you don't like to do, you have learned to motivate yourself. Perhaps you do it by offering yourself a reward. Or you scare yourself by focusing on the negative consequences of not acting. You may coax, persuade, cajole. The underlying assumption in all of these styles is that you must incite a desire for something better or a fear of something worse. Either way, motivation is based on rejecting your present state.

This same pattern of judgment and self-rejection is the basis of other roles such as counselor, guide, authority figure, guard, evaluator, and mirror. If you are focused on providing self-approval, determining appropriate behavior, or giving yourself direction, you are likely to miss the attitude of the judge underlying these functions. So one step in discovering your own activity as the judge is to notice your attitudes and assumptions as you act out these roles in your life. As you allow more awareness of being the judge, it is possible to explore how you experience yourself when judging and why you experience yourself in those particular ways.

Judgment and Speaking Your Mind

You are inevitably forced to confront your own judgmental nature when you give feedback to someone or say how you feel about another's behavior or actions. One of the major barriers to straightforward communication is the fear of judgment and rejection in either giving or receiving feedback. Can you express strong feelings about a situation or person without being judgmental or being afraid that others will see you as judgmental?

Four particular concerns are relevant in this situation. First, can you separate your feelings about the other person from your judgments about that person? To do this would mean that if you were hurt by what someone said, you would stay focused on how you felt and not get caught up in judging the person as bad, manipulative, or untrustworthy. If you didn't like a choice someone made, you would just say that and not try to justify yourself by explaining why that choice was wrong or bad. If you believe there is a better way to do something, you say that without calling the other person a jerk for not agreeing with you. You will discover that all judgments are based on and fueled by personal feelings. Focus on communicating the feelings and you will bypass the need for judgment.

This leads to the second concern. Should you wait until you are sure of not being judgmental before you say something? If you wait until then, you might never say anything—at least, anything juicy and alive. It is a good practice to become more aware of your own judgmental habits, and you can develop skills for minimizing critical commentary and harsh feedback. Nevertheless, real communication must be spontaneous and alive; too much planning and carefulness will kill it. At some point, you have to plunge in and learn by doing. The best learning comes through being open to feedback from others, not trying to prevent any need for feedback. You will make mistakes, step on toes, and undoubtedly embarrass yourself at times, but these are useful experiences and not reasons to keep your mouth shut. What is most important is that you are truly interested in communication and learning to be real, not in winning or being right.

Sometimes, it is not possible to separate your feelings from your judgments, so expressing yourself will include your judgments. So the third concern is: Can you own your judgment as you express it? This means being willing to acknowledge your reactivity and engagement—the feeling that something is hooking you. Remember, there is nothing wrong with judgment; it is a common human capacity and activity. You do not have to feel defensive about having judgments (even though you will, and others will want you to be). Everyone has them, lots of them. The difficulty in communication and interaction occurs when people don't own their judgment and instead act as if they were speaking an objective truth and often believe they are doing so. Obviously, if you do not recognize your own judgment, you cannot own it.

When you realize you are feeling judgmental about someone—you are convinced he has screwed up or believe she is wrong—the most effective first step is to say nothing. Judgment seldom serves a constructive role in any interaction, unless expressing it exposes hidden feelings. How does it affect you to keep it to yourself? Do you fester with it? Do you end up turning it back on yourself? Is it possible to explore in yourself what is driving the judgment without reinforcing it or adding further judgment? By sitting with your experience, you may be able to separate your feelings from your judgment.

However, there are times when revealing your judgments and reactions to the other person seems important or perhaps unavoidable. When you must speak and let the other know what is going on with you, it can be helpful to ask the other person to listen and not respond. At these times of intense feeling and judgment, expression is more about revealing you and your state of reactivity and less about giving the other useful information: "I am having a major judgment that you are out to lunch on this one," or "When you say that, I get very judgmental and can't help but feel you're a weak, disgusting crybaby!" Framing your comments this way can bring a degree of self-recognition into your communication that allows more space for real contact. The other can feel you in your judgment rather than just the judgment.

The fourth concern is a tricky one: How can you keep from hurting the other person with your comments? In one sense, you do not have the power to control whether or not someone else feels hurt. That is controlled by the other person's history and development. On the other hand, the more sensitivity you have to the person and the situation, the more you can be heard and make contact with the other through your speaking. Provoking hurt in the other is not an effective way to communicate or bring about change. Attacks are certainly more likely to cause pain than a direct expression of feelings, but there is no guarantee that your feelings (even without judgment) will not wound the other. Sometimes, evoking pain is part of telling the truth, even when done in the most tactful and attuned way. Ultimately, avoiding hurt cannot be the primary concern in honest communication. At the same time, communication without compassion simply won't work in the long run.

The Power in the Judge

We have noted particular ways you feel when you are being the judge, such as aggressive and focused, right, strong, in control, big and powerful, certain about what you know, and capable of influencing others. You might not be conscious of feeling these ways while judging, but chances are your behavior reflects it. However, having these feelings does not necessarily mean you are being judgmental. Just as you learned that certain roles imply an attitude of judgment, similarly, you have learned that these assertive feelings arise when you are being judgmental. In fact, most people find it difficult to experience aggressive, powerful, self-assured strength without identifying with the judge.

In our society (movies, TV, advertising), powerful strength is often associated with harshness, violence, control, and intimidation. Even when it is the good guys who are strong, their intent is to defeat the other, impose their will, demand retribution, and so on. When you were a child, the times you experienced aggressive strength in your parents were most often when they were angry, and often enough, they were angry at you. Few role models exist in this culture, and probably fewer in your personal life, of positive, powerful strength being used in an open, supportive way that does not put anyone else down. What is the last instance you can remember?

Because of this conditioning, expansive, self-assured strength can easily be associated in your mind with intimidation, control, threat, punishment, revenge, and even cruelty and hatred. Internally, this means being the judge, the mean one. The association will cause you to consider yourself bad, mean, and cruel when you notice you are feeling strong and aggressive around others. This kind of strength will only be acceptable to you if you are fully justified, which usually means responding to evil, correcting an injustice, or protecting someone else.

The painful association of strength with meanness becomes especially clear when feelings of excitement, passion, and expansiveness spontaneously arise in you. At these times, you can be alive and strong as long as you aren't aware of yourself. If you or anyone else notices, self-consciousness takes over, and you react to the strength as bad, shrinking away from the expansive feelings. You prefer to be small, weak, and powerless because you believe that also means being good, sensitive, caring, and lovable. On the other hand, if you don't want to shrink away from your strength, you have to distance yourself from others you think would judge you or be threatened by you. And what better way to distance yourself than by judging others for not understanding you! In this pattern, self-awareness actually seems to undermine your own living, expansive strength because of your beliefs associated with it.

Now is your chance to challenge those associations and beliefs. Allow yourself to be aware of the judge in you without reacting. Just see it and hopefully see it in action. It is good to make an effort to stop attacking yourself and others, but what is more important here is to be curious about that part of you. What happens when you become the judge? Why do you act that way? What deeper feelings are motivating that activity in you? The judge, as we have seen, is the watchdog over unacceptable feelings. Why is it so important to keep those feelings down? Only by taking the part of the prison guard can you truly understand why you keep some part of you behind bars.

To experiment with this, find a private place to explore saying out loud the judgmental things you often hold back. "*I know what is wrong with you, and I know exactly how to fix it!*" The judge part of you generally has to be somewhat covert about expressing itself because you believe "it is not nice" to be openly critical. This commonly leads to suppressed anger and frustration fueling the judgmental statements. Thus, when your judgment of the judge is suspended and you allow yourself to be the judge overtly and fully, you will often feel both relief and unfamiliar energy. A great rush of pleasure can arise from this power of judgmental authority, as well as pain at recognizing how much you want to attack.

How is it that the power of judging can feel good? Is this just because the feelings have been suppressed and revenge is sweet? Is it because wielding power over others is naturally pleasurable? Or is there something inherently enlivening disguised in judgment? If you recognize a sense of rightness in the experience of the judge, it may be you are sensing your natural vital strength, a real part of you that has been trapped in judgmental behavior. Perhaps one reason you continue to be judgmental is to access that part. Be curious as you explore.

What Motivates the Judge

Making space for your judgmental feelings and attitudes will naturally open you more to seeing the judge's point of view. If you accept
this view at face value, it will simply lead to more involvement in
the loop through attacks, self-rejection, and engagement. However,
being curious about what makes the judge tick can lead to considering what is useful about criticism and attacks. What exactly is your
judge trying to say to you? It is possible to ask your judge this question. When you are not rejecting your judge, you can allow it to
speak through you about why it acts the way it does and why it treats
the child part of you so harshly. In fact, if your judge has such an
opportunity to speak without being in attack mode, it can offer
valuable perceptions and questions to explore and increase your
awareness.

This kind of exploration depends on the openness of self-
acceptance and the support of your personal will. The biggest fear
in opening up to the judge is that you will discover that you are in
fact bad, selfish, and cruel. You will find out you really are hateful
and uncaring. Certainly, allowing the judge to speak its mind may
reveal such feelings, but it is also possible that it can tell you why it
feels that way. You always act out of a belief that what you are doing
is the best thing to do, and this includes your being the judge. The
problem is that you have lost touch with the judge's original motivation: how it—and you—came to believe that being harshly critical is the most effective course of action. Reconnecting with the
deeper concern of the judge lays the groundwork for accepting this
critical part of you and thus for understanding why it continues to
operate as it does.

Developing a sense of compassion for the judge is a powerful
element in transforming the judgment loop. You need to know what
it is attempting to do and why it feels it is so important. What you
will find is that the judge does not trust that you have the capacity
or resources to handle things without its help. It feels great pain
about the weakness, helplessness, and neediness of the young part of
you. In particular, it is convinced that danger lurks in the child's con-
suming need for love. This impassioned hunger has always caused

problems. As a result, the judge feels an urgency to protect, warn, restrain, and subdue the child.

It is striking how the judgment loop takes on a radically different quality when the judge is able to express its own vulnerability—its fear and helplessness about trying to care for this hopeless child who never seems to learn. From the judge's point of view, the child part of you has absolutely refused to grow up, refused to stop needing and complaining, refused to learn to take care of itself. It feels that its job will never end. It is tired and feels unappreciated for what it has been doing. Until the whole situation is accepted and understood, the judge has no choice but to carry on doing what it can. Are you aware of a part of you that feels this way?

Being aware of yourself as the judge takes time. It cannot be faked. And it cannot be allowed until you feel that it is safe to do so. This means feeling enough grounding in yourself or support from a teacher or therapist to hold your judge. As we have seen, it has access to most of your aggressive, expansive strength, so before giving it rein to speak fully, make sure you have a good solid anchor. You can always begin by noticing the judge in others and experiment with being curious about what you see and feel.

The process of opening yourself to accept and hold the judge within you is a vital step toward reclaiming the essential qualities that are imprisoned within it. The most central of these is the inherent strength and authority to stand on your own without the constant presence of the internalized parent as judge.

Points to Remember

- Once you are identified with either the judge or the one judged, you are caught inside the loop. Since the judgment process goes round and round inside the loop, either acting as the judge or acting as the one being judged can start the process going.
- When you are trapped in the loop, the only way to get some relief without disengaging is to switch roles. You change from judged to judge and back again.
- In most cases, being judgmental of yourself or of others covers up

a sense of deficiency, often arising from the experience of being attacked.

- Judgment hides out in various roles you learned from your parents, such as motivator, conscience, guide, and authority, as a result of the judgment implicit in the relationship you had with them as a child.
- All judgments are based on and fueled by personal feelings. Focus on communicating the feelings and you will bypass the need for judgment.
- There is nothing wrong with judgment; it is a common human capacity and activity. You do not have to feel defensive about having judgments. But if you bring a degree of self-recognition into your communication that allows more space for real contact, the other can feel you in your judgment rather than just the judgment.
- Most people find it difficult to experience aggressive, powerful, self-assured strength without identifying with the judge.
- If you recognize a sense of rightness in the experience of the judge, it may be you are sensing your natural vital strength, a real part of you that has been trapped in judgmental behavior.
- If your judge has an opportunity to speak without being in attack mode, it can offer valuable perceptions and questions to explore and increase your awareness.

EXERCISE: UNCOVERING THE JUDGE'S COVER-UP

Choose a time when you find yourself looking at someone, or others in general, in a critical way. Stop and feel yourself. Are you bothered about something? Could your criticism of others be related to a way you are feeling criticized by yourself or others at the moment? If you can identify your own feeling, what about that feeling makes you shift into attacking others? In the future, you can use your critical attitude as an indication that your own feelings need attending to. This can lead to experiencing yourself more honestly and intimately.

EXERCISE: UNCOVERING THE JUDGE'S GIFT

Consider an incident when you have felt attacked by someone else. After the fact, take some time to sit with what was said to you. First, clarify what the implicit attacking statement was. Then see if you can set that aside for the moment; that is part of your history. Now consider what else was being communicated in the attack. Can you get in touch with any awareness about how the other person was feeling, what you did to provoke that person's judge, or something that you are not attending to in yourself that concerns this person? Any of these or other things can support greater awareness and appreciation of yourself, the other person, and the relationship between you.

EXERCISE: LETTING THE JUDGE SPEAK

Choose a time when you are aware of a self-attack and take a moment to clarify the attacking statement, using the "you" form and being particularly aware of the tone of voice appropriate to that attack. If you can and are willing, try saying the statement out loud with that tone of voice. Repeat it several times and let yourself elaborate on the attack if the judge has more to say. Notice what you feel. The focus here is on getting in touch with how it feels to be the judge more than on the particular content. If you feel some energy there as you say it, explore why you are saying it. How does it make you feel to be speaking this way, saying these things?

Frank felt washed clean by the tears. It was definitely a big release to put out all his judgments of Sue and himself. He couldn't help but feel that suppressing that anger was connected with his impotence. As he sat up and looked at Sue, he could sense how much pressure he usually felt under when making love: to be turned on, to be hard, to get her turned on, to stay hard, to help her have an orgasm, to enjoy his own. It made him feel like a little boy being pressured to do it all right so everybody would be happy.

As he explained this feeling to Sue, he could feel himself getting quite indignant about treating himself this way. He felt a desire to stand up for himself and tell those voices to get lost!

"I don't need your help, thank you. In fact, if you show your face, I'll shoot you!" The thought of doing that made him smile. He pulled out an imaginary pistol and began firing in different directions. He could feel strength and capacity in his belly and arms—a warm aliveness that made him feel he could take care of himself. He didn't need anyone, any voices, any judges telling him what to do. Putting away the gun, he turned to Sue and let her have it verbally: "And I don't need you to tell me how I'm supposed to be either. I'm tired of all of my judges, inside and out. I'm going to stand up for myself!"

With that, Frank stood up on the bed and let out a whoop. He pulled Sue up and began dancing with her. She looked surprised, but she joined right in and they bounced around until they tripped on the blankets and collapsed laughing in a pile. While he was still breathing hard, the voice in his head started up again.

Don't you think you're acting a little silly? You haven't changed anything but your mood. Wait until you make love again and then see how much she likes you. Remember, you've still got that wimpy little pecker that won't follow instructions.

Frank clapped his hands loudly together and cried out, "Begone, you worn-out record!"

Sue was getting used to these spontaneous outbursts. "Who are you talking to?"

"Guess. My friendly, ever-present judge. He doesn't like that I got my life back. Yeah! And I got back my passion for you." With that, Frank grabbed her and they rolled around amid the sheets and comforter, screaming and giggling.

11

STRENGTH

THE MORE YOU EXPLORE your inner experience, the more you feel the judge's dominating strength and energy. When the judge is in full force, it is aggressive, sharp, penetrating, intense, big, and intimidating. Even when it doesn't feel large and concentrated, the judge appears seductive, pervasive, insidious, manipulating, and able to thwart any defensive strategy you might attempt. These powerful qualities affect you completely apart from the content of an attack. You feel controlled, powerless, and defeated in the face of them.

When you realize that the original source of this experience was your parents, perhaps in an angry or controlling mood when you were very small, the dynamic becomes more understandable. What they were saying didn't matter; they were far bigger and stronger than you. Though the content has become more adult and sophisticated as you have grown up, the original energetic experience remains: "The judge is bigger, quicker, and more powerful than I am."

This conditioned experience is one of the major barriers to confronting the judge. As long as you feel that your judge has all your physical and energetic force at its command—even if you know you are in the right and stop engaging—you still believe that it can overpower you with size and energy alone. As you have seen, this is one of the primary reasons you continue to become the judge: to access that feeling of power and strength.

Essential Strength

This brings us to the next quality of your true nature, strength. How do you usually define strength? For most people, it is force, power, hardness, muscle, intimidation, intensity, massive energy. On a physical level, strength is pictured in our society as a contracted arm muscle: tense, hard, and solid. When you want to feel or appear strong, you usually tighten your body to create that sense of solidity and hardness. The problem is, this results in rigidity, inflexibility, and defensiveness. In contrast, if you have no feeling of density, tension, or forcefulness, you tend to consider yourself weak. For most people, it is difficult to feel strong and fluid, strong and open, or strong and vulnerable at the same time. These qualities can seem not just difficult to experience together but mutually exclusive: "If I am vulnerable, the last thing I am feeling is strong!" As it happens though, you have learned about strength from the judge, and *it* operates with nothing but false strength.

True strength is not about being massive and muscular and intimidating. Strength arises out of your very aliveness, the dynamic flow of your soul. It is an expression of the vital, juicy, dynamic quality of being a living, growing organism. It is the sap and the blood of your true nature. It flows through you, feeds you, moves you, awakens your vitality, and expands your horizons. Real strength gives you a sense of capacity more than power, a sense of initiative more than brute force. You feel you can do anything, but you feel no pressure to *have* to do anything. In contrast, false strength demands action. Often, people feel strong when they work out or get excited; they are charged up and full of energy. This energetic strength, however, needs an outlet: you have to do something to discharge the energy; otherwise, you begin to feel restless, confined, and irritable.

With true strength, you feel you have the courage to open yourself up to life and all its possibilities. You are willing to take risks, be seen, go for what you want. You experience your mind as bright and intense and your vision as sharp and clear. There is no hesitation, no hanging back, no ambivalence.

When this strength flows through you, it is expansive and full of life, but it is also very precise and appropriate to what is needed. It can be as strong as a bulldozer, as hot and flowing as lava, or as delicate and precise as a needle. No energy is wasted, and you enjoy total flexibility and responsiveness. You feel a directness in dealing with your life: simplicity combined with a no-nonsense quality. Above all, you experience an immediacy of meeting the moment as it is, unencumbered by expectations, hopes, or prejudices: "I am here, passionately alive in my life."

Strength Destroys False Beliefs

Strength in your soul serves life—your life. It protects life, not by erecting barriers and preserving the past the way the judge does but by eliminating what is not true to reality. This essential quality protects life by supporting its flow, allowing the natural process of destruction and creation, dying and being born. Essential strength can be like fire—intensely alive yet always burning through what it touches, cutting through defensiveness aimed at protecting old beliefs and ideas.

This particular characteristic of true strength makes it much more powerful than the false strength of the judge because it has no positions or attitudes to hold on to and defend. This uncompromising truthfulness also makes strength more disturbing to consider as part of your own experience. Much of your usual sense of security, capacity, and confidence is based on familiar and dependable beliefs and experiences. You know how things work and what to expect. Opening up to this spontaneous, vital aliveness of the soul can be terrifying. Essential strength will not allow you to rest inside the comfortable structures of your familiar self. "But how do I know," you ask, "that something new and better will arise if I let go of my cherished beliefs? How do I know I will survive without those structures? How do I know the judge is not right?"

Only when the old beliefs about what supports, directs, and protects your life are given up can you see what is really true. This is the very experience that strength brings as it cuts through the old and familiar: you see that you are the source of life; you are full of the living capacity to be and move and function; you are born each moment with the juice of the universe flowing through you. And you don't need anyone, especially a voice in your head, to tell you what is real and what is important.

What Remains of Strength

What has happened to this inherent quality, with its energetic potency, life protection, and vital truthfulness? Largely, your true strength has gone underground, been suppressed, or become disguised in much more limited forms. Let's look at what has substituted for essential strength in your familiar experience.

The quality of vital energy surfaces at times during sexual contact and in physical activity, whether sports or manual labor. In these realms, the vitality exists mostly as a physical energy related to bodily activity or emotional charge. You feel robust and alive and excited when infused with this energy, but it is dependent on the condition of your body and the particular activity. Here, the aliveness of essential strength is reduced to an energetic vibrancy lacking a deeper intelligence or truthful clarity.

What of the life protection aspect of strength? It has been taken over by the judge. Remember, the judge appeared at a time when you needed an inner voice to help you survive by maintaining a connection with your parents. So the soul's instinctual survival energy was directed through this internalized parental voice toward physical and emotional protection. In that role, the judge became the part of you that feels capable, strong, clear, decisive, and energetic—the one that knows what is best for your own well-being. However, this protection was based on learned beliefs about what was good for you, how you needed to be, and what you shouldn't do. So the strength you feel being the judge is in the service of old beliefs and ideas. Its quality is tense, harsh, and punitive. Though aggressive and motivating, it is really a false strength. Over time, it has lost any connection to what is real and true for the survival of your soul. In fact, now the judge protects an image of you by attacking what is real in you.

Anger Versus Strength

What of the capacity for revealing the truth by burning through what is false? This is a rare experience and, for many people, only a dream. And yet it is the very nature of strength: being the blood of the soul, it flows from the truth of what is real. Without this relation to truth, strength will always be rigid, hollow, and short-lived.

If you are like most people, you have lost touch with your potent truthfulness and only taste its fullness when you allow yourself to directly embody your anger (an uncommon experience in itself). Unrestrained anger is the closest you get to the unapologetic directness of essential strength, for only in anger are you willing to challenge the beliefs and structures that limit your life. When your frustration has built to an intolerable level, some part of you says, "No more!"—and you let loose, you seethe, you explode. In that fullness of refusing to be limited by the frustrating circumstances, your essential strength is called upon to break the constriction and speak your truth. At this moment, you become aligned with your own truth and access the strength to voice it. But anger speaks out of frustration and focuses on the frustrating obstacle. When angry, you are seldom aware of yourself; you are intent on influencing the situation. Your mind is obsessed with the story of how you were wronged, so the strength that is activated seems less important than the need to be heard and felt.

For this reason, anger is the cork in the bottle of true strength. Anger calls upon your vital aliveness and gives you access to its power. At the same time, anger defines itself through resentment and frustration and refuses to let go of its object. So even when you feel strong and powerful after a burst of anger, the tendency is to dwell on your own success and righteousness and not simply experience your juicy, bright fullness.

But anger can be a doorway to strength. The challenge is to focus on the bodily sensations generated by the anger: feel the energy of the anger itself and don't focus on what you are angry about. If you can let go of needing the story as a support, then you can begin to taste your own vital, expanded capacity with its clarity and certainty—with no apologies. You will experience a sense of irresistible vibrancy and heat, a potency that can't be denied. Thus, anger can be an opening into your essential strength, if it is contained and embodied without being unconsciously discharged on others or yourself.

But this is where the judge comes in and reasons with you to stop you from feeling your anger. It will say things like, "You have no justification for being angry; it won't make any difference, and it's probably your fault anyway. . . . You scare people when you are angry and will probably hurt someone or destroy things. . . . You get out of control and make things worse than before. . . . It is cruel and ugly and heartless to let your anger out on innocent people; how could you even think of doing such a thing?"

Even if you do allow your anger, you may first experience it as a feeling of frustration, a sense that your energy is blocked or stuck. This is the anger and the resistance against the anger meeting head on and knotting up your energy. This holding back of angry feelings is particularly strong in the shoulders, neck, and jaw. If this is your experience, start by getting a sense of the two forces opposing each other. You will generally feel one—the anger—that wants to move from inside your body out and the other that is working against it to hold it in. When you can feel the struggle, breathe deeply and focus on allowing the energy of the anger to move through you. Don't force it and don't move your body; simply imagine relaxing the surface tension that stops the expansion from happening. You may begin to feel rising heat and an increase in energy and size. Anger makes you feel bigger if you don't get trapped in your angry thoughts. And when you get bigger and fuller, the source of frustration tends to dissolve, and the anger gives way to assertive strength.

Standing Up for Yourself

When you taste the sense of capacity, focus, and initiative in true strength, you recognize that it removes the internal barriers to acting and being effective in your life, to expanding and growing, and to being independent. The judge will quickly attack such autonomy as selfish. "If you don't need anyone, who will care about you? . . . You'll get too big for your britches. . . . Nobody likes someone who is so full of himself. . . . You sound pretty arrogant to me. . . . Get realistic and realize no one likes a show-off. . . . Wait until the first storm hits and then see how independent you feel."

You have a long history of suppressing your true strength, and the judge will remind you of every one of the reasons why you had to cut off that energy. Activating this part of you, however, is absolutely essential to making any real headway in disengaging. It is your lifeblood, and it has been totally sucked out of you by the judge. To regain it, you must actively take it back. You need to learn to get righteously indignant about the robbery and tell the judge to back off and shut up. Disengaging from judgment can become a reality only when you can come from your strength in defending against the judge's attacks. It doesn't matter whether it manifests as a blast that wipes the judge out of your mind, a curious child exposing the judge's nakedness, or a clear, solid presence staying focused on what is real and ignoring the rest (as Bob did in the second example in chapter 4). Remember, strength engenders responses that are appropriate to what is needed.

By using true strength, you will bring the judge down to size. The judge's strength is fake, rigid, inflexible, mechanical, and is no match for the strength of your inherent aliveness. That strength is far beyond the intimidation of the judge. It is like an exploding demon in the service of truth. When you first experience it, this intensity and spontaneous power is often frightening. It may feel destructive and out of control, and the judge will do everything to convince you that it should be avoided. But with practice at allowing your excitement, your aliveness, your passion, your indignation, and your heartfelt courage to stand up for yourself, you will come to trust that true strength supports who you truly are and that what it threatens most is the falseness of the judge.

PRACTICE: CHECKING FOR ALIVENESS

Whenever you think of it, stop what you are doing and remind yourself that you are a living organism full of pulsating blood and vital energy. Notice whether or not that feels true. Take three deep breaths and with each, imagine you are exhaling with intensity *out your eyes*. Move your shoulders around and spread your fingers wide and then make fists. Do this three times. Don't worry if you don't feel strength or aliveness. Often, we must start by feeling the lack of a quality before we can feel the quality itself. Simply allow whatever is there without reaction or judgment. Practice awareness and staying with your experience.

Every time the individual succeeds in defending against the superego, a certain amount of aggressive energy is liberated and can manifest as anger. This is why anger is frequently experienced simultaneously with the process of defending oneself. In other words, the anger that was directed by the superego toward the ego is now in the possession of the ego, to use for whatever purpose it chooses. We have observed that when a person is engaged in the process of disengaging from the superego, she is strengthened and endowed with more energy. In fact, one is strengthened not only by reowning one's anger, but also, and more fundamentally, by integrating the essential aspect of Strength, which is the energetic basis of the emotion of anger.

— A. H. Almaas, *The Work on the Superego*, p. 6

Frank and Sue were sitting on the back porch, enjoying the late summer morning. She was drinking her coffee, and he had herb tea. She cupped her hands around her mug as she began to speak.

"You know, I was thinking about how judgmental I felt about you after we tried to make love earlier. When you were so mad, you made that comment about how I don't know how to pleasure myself. I am really scared about that. I don't feel very good at giving over to pleasure. I constantly complain about the things that keep me from enjoying myself in food, sex, and relationships, but I think that complaining just covers my fear about letting go. About the only time I really let go is playing tennis; I become a different animal—no fear, no holding back, total involvement.

"I was thinking about my family, and I can just hear my mother saying while I was growing up, 'Too much fun will just cause trouble,' 'You can't trust your body because you will do things you regret. Trust me,' and 'Life is hard work; it's not supposed to feel good.' I say those same things to myself all the time.

"I remember once I started making a game out of my math homework, and I showed Dad how much fun it was to find the right answer. Mom ordered me to go back to my desk and be serious. 'Homework is not to be played with.' "

Sue paused and sipped her coffee. Frank sat in the sun with his eyes closed, listening.

"Dancing on the bed naked with you this morning brought back a memory I had totally forgotten. One time when I was about six, my aunt and uncle were over for the evening. After dinner, I was dancing around the living room to some Elvis record, having the greatest time. My uncle was enjoying me so much he got up and danced with me. Then it was time for me to have my bath before bed. He volunteered to help because my parents were talking to my aunt.

"He helped me undress and wash myself in the tub. I still remember standing up in the bath while he rubbed soap all over my body. I was giggling and laughing, especially when he put the bar of soap between my legs. Then I happened to look up, and there was my mother standing in the doorway, watching. She asked what all the fun was about, but I could tell she was not happy. After that, she was always saying to me how I had to act ladylike and I shouldn't get too excited or happy because someone might misunderstand."

12
WHY JUDGE?

❧

AS YOU TUNE IN to the inner judging process, you may experience
the judge as an omnipresent voice, hovering in the background,
speaking familiar phrases. As you notice what it is telling you, you
recognize that it is drawing from a huge reservoir of standards, ideals,
reprimands, and prohibitions that first appeared in childhood. It is
easy in most cases to see that these judgments are what you heard
from those around you as you were growing up. These are statements your parents used often or on significant occasions, things said
to you by older siblings or schoolmates, warnings and reprimands
spoken by relatives, guardians, or teachers—every one of them
tailor-made to fit your specific situation or experience. It is this arsenal that your internal judge has gained access to and is using as blackmail and threats to prevent you from living a full, joyous, and
peaceful life.

The most significant fact about all these judgments and standards presented to you by the judge, besides their effectiveness in
diminishing you, is that they are not derived from or directly related
to the present moment. These admonishments stem from pro-
nouncements that were relevant to your functioning and survival
from age one to six. They were warnings about things you had not
yet learned for yourself, reprimands to keep you out of places you
should not be, standards to help you act like the person your parents would be proud of, threats to stop you from doing things that
would scare or upset adults, insults to motivate you to do things you
didn't want to do, and all manner of statements to keep your

natural aliveness from disturbing the status quo. This was all part of what is called civilizing and socializing a child—developing in the child a conscience and an orientation to living in our society. In the process of learning to control your emotions, behavior, and energy, the judge became your conscience, reinforcing the ways you learned to govern yourself to live in the world.

These original standards developed when you were a helpless and inexperienced child learning to live in a world run by adults. Now you are an adult living your own life, interacting with other adults, yet you continue to live by those same standards. The obvious question is, Why is the judging process so tenaciously effective if it is operating with ammunition that is long out of date?

The external relevance of the original standards is gone, but the internal relevance remains and keeps you unconsciously believing you need those standards and evaluations in the context of your present concerns. The judge uses current words and issues to appear relevant, but its underlying message is the same one you heard when you were very young. During that time, you internalized the judge and its standards to keep your parents with you and to give you a sense of protection, safety, and imagined power over yourself and reality. This is the key to understanding the power of the judge.

In Session

Joanne brought into a session a struggle she had been having with her judge since the previous night at work. She started her shift as a midwife while a labor was in progress. She began her story by saying the birth was quite difficult and she didn't do well; she could have done better. I asked to hear more, wanting to know how much of this assessment was accurate and how much was an attack. She said the baby was showing signs of stress when she took over, and it was important to get him out as soon as possible, but the dilation of the cervix was proceeding slowly. She was familiar enough with this kind of situation to know it was serious but not dangerous. However, the nurses helping her were not so knowledgeable and were quite anxious. They felt as if things were in crisis and that Joanne wasn't doing enough. She, meanwhile, was staying calm and in control, though obviously not feeling supported by the staff.

Finally, one of the nurses convinced her that a doctor must be called. Joanne sent her off and continued supporting the labor. The baby began to descend and Joanne was beginning an episiotomy to help the baby out more quickly just as the doctor arrived. This woman was very aggressive and immediately took the birthing out of Joanne's hands, continuing to cut the mother while saying Joanne wasn't working fast enough. Within two minutes, the baby was out. Joanne had withdrawn into the background and felt somewhat ashamed of herself.

It became apparent that Joanne was attacking herself for not being aggressive enough. Clearly, her engagement with the attack was to absorb and accept it as true. My questioning revealed that she, in fact, felt she had been taking appropriate action; the baby was coming out, and she felt confident that it was not an emergency requiring such aggressiveness on the part of the doctor. In talking about the experience, it became clear that she felt she had done fine but felt unsupported by the slightly hysterical nurses and pushed aside by the doctor. Joanne felt she was not trusted and her knowledge was not appreciated by the staff, but because the doctor took over and produced the baby, she attacked herself. This was more familiar and less threatening to her than to feel hurt and angry with the way she was treated by the staff. The more she saw that, the clearer it was that this had been her birth, she knew what she was doing, and she would have done fine had it not been taken out of her hands.

At this point, I asked Joanne how she was feeling. She said that now her judge was attacking her for not having realized something so obvious sooner. Seeing that, she was able to tell her judge to leave her alone. I agreed that there was no reason to attack herself for not seeing the truth of the situation sooner, but I was curious as to why she hadn't. What got in the way? I asked her to remember exactly what she felt when the doctor came in. Joanne recalled that she felt fine when the doctor first arrived and asked a few questions, but she felt pushed aside, ignored, and invisible once the doctor took over. She felt small and helpless, as well.

I asked if this was a familiar feeling. Joanne said, "Yes, I felt that a lot as a child with my father. The only thing my father cared about was work, and the only thing I ever did with him was work around the house. But he was controlling, wanted things done right, and was very impatient with everyone. Each time he would tell me to do something, he almost never showed me how. I would begin, and he would take over and finish the task. I never got to finish anything and never got to feel as if I could learn anything myself or trust my own capacities to accomplish things."

At that time, it was true that she didn't know how to do certain things, but she was never given the chance to learn. I asked if the incident with the doctor felt similar, and she said, "Yes, it felt exactly like that: a 'big' person who knows what to do stepped in, took over, and finished something for me, and I was left feeling totally unseen, small, helpless, and incapable."

Here, we were getting a very clear picture of how the circumstances of the previous evening had so powerfully replicated painful experiences from Joanne's childhood. It was now obvious why she had attacked herself rather than see the truth of what was happening. The attack about not being aggressive enough was designed to (1) suppress the feeling of no support from the nurses and (2) avoid challenging the belief she learned from her father—that she was incompetent. The attack accomplished this by provoking the familiar feeling of being small and helpless she had felt as a child.

After exploring how this incident played directly into that old pattern with her father, I asked Joanne to look at the ways the incident was not the same even though it had evoked that ignored, rejected child self-image in her. She thought a few moments and then said, "First, I knew what I was doing last night. I was not ignorant like I was as a child. Second, I saw that the doctor was not acting like my father; she was just doing what she felt was necessary, and it had nothing to do with me as the midwife." In other words, the doctor was not making some statement to her about her competence or lack of it. Last, she realized that the doctor was not in control as her father had been, nor was she voiceless as she had been with her father. She could actually have told the doctor she was doing fine if she had wanted to. The latter would have been a more unfamiliar action, however, than giving up and feeling helpless.

These insights helped Joanne to let go of the sense of experiencing herself as a child in this incident and allowed her to see more of the truth of what had occurred. The two attacks—for not being aggressive enough and for not recognizing the obvious—turned out to be doorways to understanding much more about her experience and would undoubtedly affect her awareness and functioning in the future.

An attack usually directs your attention outward toward the events, obstacles, or behaviors you are facing or are involved in. Listening to the content of the attack, you believe that the judgment is relevant to what you are doing and that you must listen for your own good if you are to be the person you want to be or live the life you want to live. As long as you remain focused outward (on others, on the environment, on your behavior, on your problems), you will unconsciously cling to that parental power and the sense of safety it provided, which keeps you engaged with the attacks and at the mercy of the judge. The route of disengagement is to look more carefully at your own inner experience rather than attempting to alter your external experience. This was demonstrated in the example of Joanne. Only in this way will you come to understand why you feel you need the judge around—why it has such a powerful presence in your life.

Living Out Your Parents' Desires

As you have recognized, your judge arose in the environment of your family, particularly your mother and your father, or whoever else may have been around if neither of them was present. You could not help but take their actions and words as representative of how life is, so you internalized their statements and attitudes as part of your inner environment, most notably as the judge. Because of this process of internalization, you still live out of your parental environment, and it is difficult to separate your sense of yourself from your parents and their desires and expectations of you and of themselves.

The more objective you can become about what the situation was when you were growing up, the more clearly and intelligently you can deal with your judge. Often, when a mother is relating to a child, she is expressing her own needs, fears, and expectations about life through that relationship. Furthermore, her action toward the child may lie anywhere on a continuum from simply dealing with her own needs to responding to those of the child. Thus, what the child receives in the interaction may be irrelevant for him, partly appropriate to his situation, or exactly what he needs. Unfortunately, the child is unlikely to be able to tell the difference, and though he feels the pain of irrelevance or inappropriateness in the parent's behavior, he will inevitably attribute it to his own failing. In other words, the lack of awareness and presence in the parent becomes part of the child's judge.

As a child, you could seldom recognize the lack of attunement in your parents, but as an adult, you can. The more you are aware of your own difficulties in living, working, and relating, the more you can become aware of what was missing for you as a child in terms of recognition, support, guidance, or appreciation. Learn as much as you can about how your parents thought, felt, and behaved in your family. As you come to recognize what your parents wanted and expected from you, you can compare this to what you yourself needed as a child and assess how they did not match up. This will help you understand what you did and didn't get in the way of help and support, and why you responded the way you did. As you do this, you can question your internalized conscience to determine how it affects you and whether it supports you. Can you recognize that your judge treats you with the same lack of attunement as your parents did long ago?

One method of continuing this exploration is to look at the larger concerns behind the judge's attacks. Attacks fall into two broad categories: those designed to maintain control over "bad" or unacceptable parts of the self and those designed to move you toward your ideal of what a good person should be. One could say, then, that the judge is always moving you either away from something or toward something; it is never content with your being where you are.

Keeping a Lid on the Negative

You learned early in life that certain subjects were best not talked about (such as defecation) or had to be carefully disguised (sex, for example). These "unacceptable" parts of your experience were aspects of your natural, instinctual vitality, and they threatened your parents and environment because they were spontaneous, energetic, and untamed. Which specific expressions of your aliveness you came to experience as not acceptable or "bad" depended on your family and on your personal history. These were parts of you that you couldn't just get rid of and perhaps didn't want to, but they caused problems, brought strong negative reactions, or were considered morally unacceptable.

One of the major jobs of your judge became the task of keeping a lid on these parts. Unless you consciously bring these taboo parts out into the light of day, they will tend to be a major unconscious weapon your judge will use against you. Sooner or later, you are bound to recognize that your aliveness itself has been imprisoned and deadened out of fear of revealing the badness in you. *Good* and *bad* are themselves highly suspect terms that must be questioned with vigor. *Bad* sometimes is used to refer to things that feel good— particularly pleasurable sensations and things that feel good without a reason or justification. Look closely at what your judge is saying when it begins castigating you for some part of your present experience it considers bad. What exactly is the badness?

Most people consider "negative" emotions to be bad—feelings such as anger, hatred, jealousy, envy, greed, hurt, sadness, and fear. In general, their badness is determined by how they affect others. If your parents deplored hatred or greed, or if they had difficulty tolerating your explosive energy when you were angry or your tears when you were sad, you learned that these feelings were bad. This inevitably led to avoiding, hiding, or denying these feelings when they arose in you or learning to condemn yourself for having them. Sometimes, this external judgment was combined with your own discomfort about feeling emotions like hurt or fear; if your parents had been compassionate or accepting, it would have helped you to bear the feelings. You would have learned that such feelings may be painful or difficult but not bad.

Not only were certain emotions, behaviors, and actions recognized by you as unacceptable; at times, you felt *yourself* to be unacceptable. This rejection by your parents often related to something you didn't understand. In an effort to explain the rejection to yourself, you adopted labels used by others such as *wrong, bad, weak, unlovable, needy,* or *helpless.* (Some of these terms relate more to internalizing how others saw you than to what you experienced yourself. After all, what does wrong or unlovable feel like other than rejected?)

In each of these feelings, the negative or unpleasant quality is dominant because it represents a distinct and painful experience associated with being rejected, unwanted, or ignored. You came to believe you were rejected because you were weak or needy. Thereafter, if an experience brought up weakness or neediness, you were certain rejection would follow. Now, to keep you from feeling rejected, your judge actively attacks these negative feelings about yourself to stop you from feeling them. At other times, if you think, feel, or act in ways it finds unacceptable, the judge may use these feelings (and the implied rejection by others) as blackmail to threaten you and make you stop: "If you come out and say what you want, people will think you are needy."

There are, however, two "negative" emotions that are seldom condemned by the judge. In fact, these two feelings, shame and guilt, almost never arise except in response to judgment, so they are powerful tools used by the judge to control your inner life. In fact, the judge uses these feelings to condemn the unacceptable parts of you.

Shame and guilt are secondary feelings that get attached to more immediate aspects of your experience. Then they negatively affect your relationship to those aspects. In this way, the judge uses shame and guilt to undermine self-confidence, self-love, and self-respect. For instance, if you were told it is shameful to hate someone or feel envious of another person for what he has, shame will become attached to hatred and envy. Then when you find yourself hating someone, or someone else notices your envy, the shame will be a blow to your self-esteem. Similarly, if early on you were made to feel that speaking up for yourself was interfering or taking something away from someone else, you may find that every time you speak up in public, you feel guilty. Two of the most familiar generic statements of the judge are "You should be ashamed of yourself" and "It's your own fault."

The Positive as Unacceptable

Badness is not limited, however, to negative emotions or even strong energetic states such as aggression, enthusiasm, sexual arousal, or anxiety. What seems unacceptable may be surprising. A common example is the childlike innocence that is revealed in truthfulness, curiosity, openness, and the desire to know. Children are more in touch with the mystery of life and not as constricted by the orderly boxes into which adults try to fit it. The child of three or four learning to name what she sees may constantly ask what things are or why they are the way they are; for instance, "Why is the sky blue?" If the parent is impatient or is uncomfortable not knowing the answer or gives a too-adult answer, the child may feel she shouldn't have asked. The curious child of five or six may ask about subjects such as divorce, death, God, love, hate, and sex organs. If these subjects provoke anxiety in the parents, the child may come to believe there was something wrong with asking questions as well as with the subject itself. Furthermore, parents often find the direct questioning by a child very threatening because it may expose secrets or taboo subjects that have been carefully avoided or protected by the family. Because of this, the qualities of curiosity and truthfulness can easily become part of the perceived badness that must be avoided.

In other cases, what is not acceptable may be the embodiment of some "good" quality—such as love or joy or vitality—in too energetic or expressive a way for others to accept. Any quality that people lack or about which they have ambivalence will be hard to tolerate in a pure form in another person. Children are very sensitive to this intolerance in their parents and easily conclude that something is wrong with the quality itself. In this way, the judgment process may suppress basic human experiences so a sense of accept-ability can be maintained. As an adult, you may find it hard to under-stand or accept that you judge your own positive feelings, such as love and joy. After all, these are such good things. But this is a com-mon form of self-attack, one that your mind can make more accept-able by making it sound reasonable, such as: "The problem is not that joy is unacceptable; the problem is that it is selfish to be happy for no good reason and when lots of things still have to be taken care of!"

Feeling Versus Expressing

An important consideration here is the difference between experi-encing an emotion or thought and expressing it. One of the charac-teristics of early childhood is that experiences are immediately expressed: sadness brings tears, anger brings kicking and screaming, joy brings smiles and dancing. This is both delightful and problem-atic. The child has yet to learn any control over his emotional impulses. Part of growing up is learning to control self-expression—not say-ing everything that comes into your mind and not always expressing your feelings such as dislike, revulsion, fear, or desire because it is not appropriate in many situations. For a child, this is difficult to grasp. Often, learning to suppress the *expression* of a feeling or thought leads to suppressing the feeling or thought itself. "If I shouldn't express my anger, that must mean my anger is bad," or "If I can't express it, what's the point in feeling it?" This latter suppression is what affects you most deeply. Your contact with your soul nature is diminished much more by blocking the experience of your thoughts and feelings than it is by blocking their expression, because you learn to distrust the spontaneous movement of your own responses to life.

Another aspect of growing up is learning to experience the value of your own experience whether or not anyone else sees it, responds to it, or approves of it. A child's growth is dependent on interaction with and mirroring from parents and the world in gen-eral. Expression is important because the child needs to communi-cate, be heard, and be understood. Furthermore, developing her own sense of self depends on having her feelings reflected back to her so she can learn to recognize them. Feelings not acknowledged by others will not be perceived or integrated.

So if appropriate interaction and mirroring happen, the child will gain the confidence to know and appreciate his own feelings. This confidence becomes the foundation for developing a sense of autonomy in which feelings support self-understanding as well as interpersonal communication. If, however, expression is thwarted, the child will grow up believing that in order to have meaning or validity, emotions must be expressed so they can be seen and reflected.

The Judge as Behavior Police

Society actively supports the judge's job of making you conform to appropriate and civilized standards. Challenging the judge in this area must not be taken to mean giving yourself license to act impulsively or any way you want. Such behavior will almost certainly reactivate the judge in a big way, possibly disrupt marriages and jobs, or even land you in jail! The task here is to develop an adult's capacity for feeling something without expressing it, thinking something without saying it, and knowing clearly the difference. Your judge may tell you they are the same thing—"If you think it, that is as bad as doing it"—but that is left over from the experience of the child or a moralistic stance still rooted in the perspectives of childhood.

Your suppression of feelings includes both the judgments you internalized about the feelings and the frustration you felt as a child about not being able to express yourself. Therefore, allowing your suppressed feelings to surface will require making space in yourself to hear that frustrated child and perhaps even seek out safe places in therapy or with a good friend to let yourself express what has long been held back. Conscious expression can be important for getting in touch with suppressed feelings. However, the ultimate goal is to develop the capacity simply to feel and not express—a difficult skill. The child in you gets no satisfaction from such a practice. But you as a living soul can recover your fullness and aliveness through having the inner space and strength to allow all parts of your experience, at the same time recognizing what is appropriate for expression in the world. Then you can fire the judge from one of its major jobs: that of policing you and instructing you in what is OK and what is not.

The Ideal Self

You not only had to struggle to avoid proscribed feelings and behaviors as a child, you also had to learn what was required from you in order to be liked and accepted. Usually, this related to certain aspects of you that were seen and appreciated by your parents (your intelligence, attractiveness, sweetness, cleverness, obedience, determination, and so on). These qualities were then molded and others added in accordance with your parents' desires for how you should be and your experience of who they were. The result was an ideal but distorted sense of yourself on which you unconsciously became fixed. You have been trying to match this ideal ever since, convinced that it is the key to your happiness. Unfortunately, by constantly comparing yourself to an ideal standard, you conclude that self-improvement is necessary for self-acceptance. You have come to believe you are not learning skills and behaviors just to live more effectively but to be a better human being so you can feel acceptable. You subtly and unconsciously reject yourself almost every moment, certain you are by your very nature imperfect and in need of improvement.

This imagined ideal self became an internal image of how you should be so everything would turn out all right and you could relax and be loved, accepted, appreciated, and taken care of. It includes personal standards for action, thought, feeling, behavior, appearance, and accomplishment. Thus, the ideal self is a goal that orients all your activity—the direction your life takes, what needs to happen, and how you relate to yourself. The biggest difficulty with pursuing your ideal self-image is that *it doesn't work*. Although striving for the ideal as a child may have brought you parental approval, it did little to give you inner peace; the strain of constantly comparing yourself to the ideal was exhausting, lonely, and anxiety-provoking. Now, as an adult, when you no longer live and interact primarily with your parents, there is even less likelihood that you would feel happy, secure, or satisfied if you achieved your ideal sense of self.

You can never reach an ideal; it is always just beyond the horizon. Even if you do achieve some element of it, the satisfaction won't last, so you tend to believe you didn't do it well enough or get it quite right. Motivating you toward this unreachable ideal is the other major job of the judge. It keeps egging you on to reach that perfect image, never letting you rest or feel satisfied. Even though the ideal may be worthy and good, at some point, you must question how good it is when you use it as a way of continually rejecting yourself now. Compared to an ideal, you will always find yourself lacking, deficient, or not good enough in the moment.

The ideal self is the foundation for most of the standards and rules by which you live. The judge is the part of you assigned to maintain those standards. What you so easily lose sight of is that standards are appropriate for effective functioning in action and interaction but are not relevant for self-evaluation. For that, you need compassion, awareness, and understanding. Unfortunately, you grew up believing that standards applied to everything, especially yourself.

By becoming aware of the standards you hold yourself to in all kinds of situations, you can learn much about how the judge works on you every day. Some of these standards relate to habitual patterns for doing physical tasks. Though originally learned for efficient functioning, these patterns have become rote actions supporting a feeling of safety through familiarity and predictability. You can hear this in the way the judge talks to you about how to brush your teeth, wash dishes, make up the bed, get dressed, and so on. Other standards appear in the constant watchfulness you have over yourself in social situations to make sure you don't look foolish, don't do anything inappropriate, don't attract attention, or don't say anything stupid. All these judgments are based on standards you have internalized in relation to your ideal self. Standards affect your social life, emotional expression, intimate relations, work behavior, recreation, personal health, and even your private thoughts.

The infamous *should* is a critical term here for pushing you on toward impossible standards. Though *should* can be used to denote "what is appropriate or needed," it is most often a term that expresses critical judgment, such as, "There is something wrong with you if you don't." It is useful to see through each "should" statement to the underlying negative statement within it. For example, "You should be more caring" hides within it the statement "You are selfish," which is the actual attack. Here also you see how promoting an ideal self can perfectly mesh with the attempt to avoid bad parts of you, by setting standards that reject and deplore those parts.

Recognizing What Blinds and Binds You

The judge served the survival needs of the child through these two primary functions: preventing her from acting in ways that would cause rejection and encouraging her to act in ways that would bring acceptance, love, and care. Because these choices were particularly related to your parents and family situation, they are obviously either going to support you to choose situations similar to your family later in life or create great tension in you when the environment doesn't match what you learned to live with as a child. As long as you are unconscious of what you have internalized, you will be in the familiar situation of blaming yourself or blaming the environment for not producing the results your judge wants. As you recognize the historical roots of your perspective on yourself and your life, you begin to notice that this outlook is not allowing you to see or respond to the world and yourself in the present.

To begin to unravel the webbing that binds you to self-judgment, you need curiosity about how this fascinating logic of self-perception developed. You need a willingness to wonder about what unusual turn of events caused you to need to watch yourself so closely. And especially, you need a certain lightness and sense of humor to keep from being drawn into the deadly seriousness of self-improvement.

POINTS TO REMEMBER

- The key to understanding the power of the judge is knowing that you internalized the judge and its standards to keep your parents with you and to give you a sense of protection, safety, and imagined power over yourself and reality.

- As long as you remain focused outward (on others, on the environment, on your behavior, on your problems), you will unconsciously cling to that parental power and the sense of safety it provided, which keeps you engaged with the attacks and at the mercy of the judge.
- The route of disengagement is to look more carefully at your own inner experience rather than attempting to alter your external experience.
- Your judge treats you with the same lack of attunement that your parents did long ago.
- Shame and guilt almost never arise except in response to judgment, so they are powerful tools used by the judge to control your inner life.
- Your contact with your soul nature is diminished much more by blocking the experience of your thoughts and feelings than it is by blocking their expression, because you learn to distrust the spontaneous movement of your own responses to life.
- By constantly comparing yourself to an ideal standard, you conclude that self-improvement is necessary for self-acceptance.
- Motivating you toward unreachable ideals is the other major job of the judge. It keeps egging you on to reach that perfect image, never letting you rest or feel satisfied.
- What you so easily lose sight of is that standards are appropriate for effective functioning in action and interaction but are not relevant for self-evaluation.
- As long as you are unconscious of what you have internalized, you will be in the familiar situation of blaming yourself or blaming the environment for not producing the results your judge wants.

EXERCISE: SEEING HOW YOU ARE YOUR PARENTS' CHILD

Take some time to write about what your parents wanted *for* you and *from* you. Who did they want you to be and why? How did they communicate that, and how did it affect you? Are you living out their dreams, trying to accomplish what they failed at, rebelling against what was so important for them? How are you your parents' child?

Exercise: Noticing What Your Parents Taught Your Judge

Explore the ways in which your judge acts like your mother and your father. How does the way you relate to yourself reflect how they related to you?

Exercise: Making Room for What's Excluded

Make a list of parts of you that you feel must be kept hidden, not spoken about, or not given any attention. This may include emotions like hatred, selfishness, or jealousy; behaviors like farting or masturbation; fantasies like killing your partner or voting Libertarian; parts of your body like the penis or clitoris; or other parts of you such as your soul, your aliveness, or your curiosity. Be aware of any parts that you may not want to know about yourself. How is it to write these things down and consider them as part of you?

Exercise: Questioning Self-Improvement

Make a list of all the ways you are involved in self-improvement, including diets, exercise programs, reading, studying, classes, workshops, even meditation or other spiritual practices. How much are these activities based on an effort to make yourself better? What standards do you use to determine if you are getting better?

The ego functions through emotional dependency, and you call it love. Even when you are by yourself, not married or in a relationship, or in a group, you are still relating to your mother—the mother inside you. You relate to your superego, and your superego is always beating you up. Why is your superego beating you up? Because it makes you feel that your mother is around. When you were a child your mother was always judging you. So every time you feel like a little kid, your internal mother comes and beats you up. Then you feel secure. You might complain, but you feel secure.

— A. H. Almaas, *Diamond Heart Book 1*, p. 185

Sue looked at Frank, and he looked different. He had surprised her so many times this morning, and now this memory had come back to her that connected to so many things in her life. "You know, Frank, I always wanted to be a dancer. I realize now that, after that incident, I felt too inhibited by my mother's fear."

Sue dropped into silence as she turned her thoughts to how this same incident had affected her sexuality. There she was, enjoying the pleasurable sensation in her genitals without any thought of "sex." She was much too young. Her child's mind couldn't understand what was wrong about it, but her mother's look had made it very clear that it was wrong. It had been impossible for her to separate pleasure in her genitals from the feeling of wrongness. She had never been able to figure out what was wrong: Was it someone giving her pleasure, giving it the wrong way? Was it enjoying herself? Was it being happy with her genitals? Dancing too much? A man liking her too much? What was it? Finally, something inside her started to relax as she understood where the feeling of wrongness might have originated.

Sue felt open and light in her heart for the first time all morning. Then, as she sipped her coffee, she noticed she was feeling very curious. "You know, Frank, I am amazed at that memory and what I've understood from it, but I'm more amazed at this whole morning. What has been happening? I don't understand what is going on."

⚙ *What are you doing talking like this? There's nothing going on, and asking about it will only cause trouble. Looking for hidden meaning is opening a can of worms!*

"There goes my judge. At this moment, it sounds like a windup toy with my mother's voice. Now you—you seem the same but also like someone I have never seen before. I feel a little of that toward myself. I love what is happening, and though it doesn't make sense to me, it doesn't matter in the usual way. I don't care if it makes sense, and yet I feel very curious about what is really happening. ⚙ Then again, a little voice says I must be crazy."

Frank sipped his tea and smiled a mischievous grin. Then he spoke in a deep, authoritarian voice: "Yes, Susan, you are definitely crazy. Sexuality is a very big deal, and you just recovered a memory of serious incestuous abuse. We need to find you a survivors group immediately. You obviously have important work to do on this issue. This lightness you are feeling is a sign of a serious problem, clearly some kind of neurotic defense against hidden sadomasochistic tendencies." They both burst out laughing.

13

JOY AND CURIOSITY

ONE FUNDAMENTAL QUALITY IN human nature that cannot exist around the judge is joy. You can recognize this by noticing how naturally joy arises in children—and how unusual it is in adults. It is the quintessential quality of a happy childhood. Joy is at the heart of play, freedom, lightness, spontaneity, and fun. These qualities are associated with a time when you had no responsibility, and you believe you had to give them up in order to become grown up. Meanwhile, your heart longs to feel as light and free as it naturally felt at an early age. One of the greatest sadnesses your heart holds is the loss of that joyful experience of life. As you travel the path of confronting and investigating your judge, an important challenge is to recover your heart's delight in the wonder of life and of yourself.

Lighthearted, radiant happiness can only manifest itself in an internal environment free of restraint. To be joyful means to let your heart go, let it blossom and radiate. It means you are not just satisfied, content, OK, acceptable: you are transformed, overcome, by the magic of your heart's delight. You are so full of pleasure at what you feel and what you are experiencing that you are overflowing and glowing, dancing and singing. Joy is such a profoundly heartfelt quality that it can never be understood by the rational mind. The practical part of you finds it silly, light-headed, and defenseless. If joy is allowed, it completely undoes the mind; it bursts forth with such radiant sweetness and energy that no reason can explain it and no rules can contain it.

Joy is closely linked to desire. You desire what you take joy in, and the heart is filled with joy when it receives what it desires. For this reason, you have grown up believing that joy is a result of getting what you want. There is some truth in this belief. When you first receive something you truly desire—be it a new car, an elegant dress, a gourmet meal, a night with your lover, or a deep insight— your heart is naturally overjoyed. For a moment, you have come closer to what delights your heart.

The joy, however, does not last. Its very nature seems to be impermanence. Within days, hours, or even minutes, your heart is no longer content. And so desire leads you on in search of the food that you hope will feed your hungry heart. Only after much searching and many disappointments do you begin to realize that the heart's own freedom is what gives it joy. Each object of desire was simply something that at the time seemed necessary for the heart to move freely—but you mistook it for the source of joy itself. This is why you always know that events and situations, people and places do not cause joy. At best, they remove a barrier to joy's arising. The true source of joy is the heart's knowing and being itself without restraint.

Totally antithetical to the state of happiness and joy are the serious and cautionary, restrictive and threatening qualities of the judge, which permeate your life with worry and fear. The judge exists in a world of boundaries and standards. Things must measure up. Spontaneity is not allowed. "If you cannot maintain control over the environment and other people, you must at least always control yourself. Otherwise, bad things will happen, the least of which is being inappropriate and looking silly, the worst of which is doing something disrespectful, dangerous, and selfish." The judge is intent on separating right from wrong, good from bad, and useful from frivolous— and joy is the epitome of what is frivolous and useless. To the judge, joy may be good, but only if there's a good reason, and it is right only if you deserve it. Most of the time, joy just causes problems because of its irrationality, irreverence, and uncontrollability. As far as the judge is concerned, being joyful is seldom warranted and generally overdone even then. "You get along fine in life without it, so better to avoid the feeling altogether."

Joy is a movement of the heart, easy and playful, full of love and delight. The heart moves toward things not because it needs them but because it loves them. It is happy and enchanted and radiates that feeling to others. "Look what amazing things there are to see and appreciate!" For the lighthearted, the world is full of wonder and fascination, with endless discoveries waiting around every corner.

Joy Brings Curiosity

A joyful loving of the world naturally brings a heartfelt desire to know the world. From joy arises curiosity. Curiosity is the open-hearted fascination with life, love expressed as a desire to know life intimately: to examine it, listen to it, watch it, taste it, take it apart, and swallow it. You see this quality of curiosity in a child as she takes great delight in each encounter with her world. She has no goal in mind but to know what she comes in contact with. This is a wondrous movement of the heart with the mind going along as support.

In contrast, most learning in school and as an adult is a goal-oriented mind game that completely excludes the heart. You learn in order to function and improve, make money and be efficient, avoid pain and suffering, or find out how to get what you want. There is little desire to know just for the sake of knowing, to discover the truth for its own sake. Learning often feels like a burden or a chore, something that is good for you. Curious learning as an expression of loving life has been lost.

As with joy, the judge has been instrumental in suppressing your natural playful curiosity. "Curiosity gets you into trouble by sticking your nose into places you don't belong. . . . You'll never learn what you need to if you just follow your heart. Look at all the heartache you've suffered in the past. . . . Think about it. You can't trust your heart to know what it's doing. . . . You've got to get serious; after all, it's your *life,* not some game. . . . If you only did things because you loved them, learned things because you were curious, you'd still be playing around in the sandbox. . . . Grow up and stop acting like a kid!"

The presence of the judge continually undermines your capacity for open and lighthearted exploration. It restricts the easy flow of the heart, and the heart is the source of the natural movement of the soul. Without joy and curiosity, life is a serious chore, a task fraught with heaviness and even morbidity. You may study all the right things, do what is good for you, be thoughtful, generous, helpful, and caring, but life has no sparkle. It remains rather dull and uninteresting. Without the presence of joy, you will not be moving from your heart in a creative and spontaneous way, so you will never be in touch with what your heart truly wants, what it is you truly love in your life.

Joy Brings Freedom

What your heart takes delight in can at times seem irrelevant to the pressing needs in your life—a luxury or an indulgence for which you don't have time or energy. Yet in the larger picture, life is not worth living without joy. What is the value in a human life if the heart has not been touched? When you are moved by that effortless and carefree happiness, all concerns and worries seem meaningless and irrelevant. You know at that moment that life is an amazing revelation that can only be celebrated. No suffering or misery can take away the mystery and wonder of what is.

In the state of joy, suffering and misery are not denied but are seen as passing manifestations of the surface layers of reality. Ironically, many people believe that pain and unhappiness characterize the deepest realms of the human soul, yet joy brings such buoyant gladness into the heart precisely because it springs from the depths of true nature—touching that place where Being is unbounded, undivided, and inseparable from love.

The more you cultivate curiosity—your desire to know your own experience simply for the sake of discovering the truth regardless of the consequences—the more you can challenge the judge's efforts to limit and direct your exploration. Again and again, the judge will present you with "received wisdom" about what things mean and why they are the way they are. If you are truly curious, you will not accept its statements but will want to find out for yourself, to question your assumptions and past beliefs about reality. You will want to know now, in the moment, what is actually true. As you discover the freshness of your present unfolding experience, you experience joy at knowing your own heart and mind. The more you uncover and let go of your investment in childhood experiences of yourself, the more you remove the restraints from who you are now and who you might become.

As each limitation in your mind is relaxed, a bubble of joy is released. As your internal boundary cracks open, a light, sweet delight escapes. Each taste awakens the heart further to its own love of being whole and true and real. As more constrictions are loosened, the heart's joy deepens, boundaries dissolve, and the bubbling of newly discovered freedom gives way to the rich, soft quiet of an awakened soul. Beaming in the blissful rapture of a ripening joy, the heart rests in the truth.

Nothing is more powerful in combating the judge in a loving way than the heart's longing for and knowing of the truth. As the joy in being who you truly are is recognized, the heaviness and seriousness of self-judgment becomes more and more vivid and intolerable. Where once the judge could suppress the joy with rules and standards, fear and pain, now the judge discovers that its weapons are useless against a heart that is totally carefree, more radiant than the sun, and untouched by fear.

PRACTICE: OPENING TO A PLAYFUL HEART

Find a playground where you can sit and watch neighborhood kids play. Give yourself at least a half hour to observe the children come and go. See how they interact, make up games, and find ways of playing and having fun. If possible, allow your heart and body as well as your mind to watch them. Can you touch into the children's perspective—their pacing, their focus of attention, their sense of scale and priority? How is your heart affected by attending to the world of children? Are you aware of your experience's being dampened by the presence of the judge?

PRACTICE: ENCOURAGING CURIOSITY

Choose a time when you can listen to a few friends talk about themselves. Notice their implicit assumptions and beliefs about who they are and what their experiences mean. See if you can be curious about why those attitudes are there and where they came from. Imagine what it would be like to have a child's curiosity about why they talk, act, and think the way they do. What stops you from really wanting to know more about who they are and why they feel the way they do? Whom would it threaten if you were to ask the questions people rarely think of or dare to ask? Can you begin to notice your own unquestioned relationship to your experience?

Joy is curious. Joy is curiosity. As you love the truth, or as truth loves the activity you are engaged in, truth shines. That shining of the truth is the joy. You are being the truth, investigating the truth, loving the truth, and your joy is joy in the truth. . . .

When we are curious we are completely whole, happy. We are doing what we are made to do. We are not engaging in the things that bring us more and more suffering and frustration. We are engaged in something that frees the heart and the mind without even seeking that freedom. The process itself is the freedom. . . . You are free every moment that you are completely curious. You're completely in love, and who are you in love with? Who knows? You're just in love. Whatever happens to be there, you're in love with it. You're completely in love with yourself, with your existence. You're completely in love with whatever is presented to you; you love it so much, you want to know everything about it.

— A. H. Almaas, *Diamond Heart Book 1*, pp. 240–241

Sue was driving as they headed for the park that afternoon to go on one of their favorite walks. She was happy, singing one of her made-up songs that Frank would try to hum along with. Suddenly, she had to slam on the brakes to avoid hitting a car that was taking forever to make a left turn. The brakes squealed as Sue swerved. She was able to stop just in time, barely missing the rear end of the car turning.

Frank let out a cry as the sudden stop jarred his neck. "Christ! ☙ Woman, I can't believe you still haven't learned to drive! You trying to kill us or something? Ohhh, now my neck is really shot. Damn."

All the lightness in the air had vanished. Sue was in shock, clutching the steering wheel for dear life. She drove the car at a crawl as they both caught their breath and tried to stop shaking.

☙ *He's right, you know. What is wrong with you? You never did learn to drive. Feeling so good and you nearly get everyone killed! You ought to be ashamed of yourself.*

   God, I feel like Mom was right. Feeling good just gets me in trouble.

Tears began to roll down Sue's face as she held herself together to drive. Under her breath, she was saying to herself, "I shouldn't be driving. . . . It's too much for me. . . . I'm too little." As soon as Frank calmed down and noticed the state she was in, he suggested she pull over. She refused because they were almost there, so they rode in silence until they reached the parking lot.

"All I can hear is this voice saying, ☙ 'You should be ashamed of yourself, feeling so good and pretending you know what you're doing!' What can I say? I just feel miserable." She was blubbering now as Frank held her in his arms.

"It was bad enough almost hitting that car, but what you said went so deep in me. I feel like I'm five years old and I did something very wrong. I didn't mean to. I was feeling so good, and then *blam!*" She sobbed, holding him tight. "I feel devastated—blamed for something bad. The sensations of being little are so vivid, like I'm reliving it. I'm so upset I can hardly breathe. ☙ 'You should be ashamed of yourself.' It sounds like my father's voice. He's standing over me, telling me how shameful I am." She gradually caught her breath and calmed down enough to look at Frank and reassure herself that he was not her father and that she was safe being with these vulnerable feelings.

14

LOOKING DEEPER

YOU NOW HAVE A sense of how to recognize at least some of your self-attacks. You are beginning to see how you engage those attacks and what it feels like to do the attacking. Finally, you have become aware that many of your judgments are carried over from your early childhood. All of these are necessary steps in the process of disengaging; they lay the groundwork for the more challenging work of defending yourself against the attacks. However, you may have found yourself wondering in all this exploration: What is really going on here? Who am I when I am attacking, and who am I when engaged with the attack? How did this dynamic originate? Before focusing on defending, we will take one more deeper look at the actual judgment interaction.

In Session

Paula wanted to understand why she was still having such a hard time being around her mother. She always felt uptight and critical of her when they interacted in relation to her mother's business. Even when her mother seemed to be trying to be open and sharing, Paula found herself feeling tense and not wanting to be there. She felt disappointed in herself for not having learned to act like an adult and for being so bothered by her mother. Paula could feel that her judge was attacking her about having this problem, but she couldn't find any way not to agree with her judge. (After all, what was the problem?) I asked her how she actually felt toward her mother, and she said, "Angry. I just feel angry all the time." She judged herself for that because she couldn't understand why.

Paula is clearly experiencing herself as a child with her mother, angry at her and not wanting to be with her. She does not like to feel herself this way and so focuses on how she would like to feel— her idea of being grown up. She is not able to understand her anger because she is not willing to feel herself as the child who is angry.

I asked her how she had felt with her mother as a child growing up. She thought a while and said, "Unsupported." Her mother always criticized her, was never satisfied with what Paula did, and always focused on the fact that there was more to do. Paula never felt seen by her mother, never got any compassion or warmth from her. "It wasn't even that my mother was vicious or anything, she was just always wrapped up in what she felt needed to be done and how to do it. There was no room for me and what I wanted or needed." I asked her how it was for her to be aware of the situation she grew up with. She said it made her sad. I observed that it must have also been pretty frustrating to have always been focusing on her mother and her needs and demands. She simply nodded in agreement.

Paula was now becoming aware that she was still operating with her mother as if she were that young child. This child is small, unseen, unloved, controlled, and frustrated by a mother who is self-centered, driven, and preoccupied.

I asked her if she felt this might have anything to do with the anger she was feeling toward her mother now. She replied, "Yes, of course. I can't stand having to do anything for my mother these days. But I'm still committed to helping her out with her business. I can't stop now. That would let her down." As she said this, she became aware of how frustrating a bind she was in.

The situation was no more resolved by the end of our session, but Paula was no longer judging herself. She felt some compassion for what she had had to put up with from her mother all her life. She could understand her readiness for that to change. And now she could see that this change would require her willingness to face the feeling of abandoning her mother. This explained why her anger felt uncomfortable and unacceptable, because to feel it fully would bring up her desire to turn her back on her mother. Her judge attacked her for having that desire and made her feel guilty for even considering such a selfish act.

If you want to understand the power behind your judge's activity, you must learn to observe yourself closely as you experience an attack. This kind of awareness is not easy. It requires your will to stay present and not get lost in your usual engagement, your awareness to sense your body and your reactions, your courage and strength to face difficult feelings, and your curiosity to be open to what you find. It helps if you have a time and place to be quiet and stay with your internal process or perhaps find someone to support you in exploring.

In-Depth Self-Exploration

To experience yourself *under attack* rather than lost in *engaging the attack* requires shifting your focus away from the outside and toward the inside: from the judge and its story to yourself and how the judgment affects you. The task here is to choose a self-attack you have noticed recently and explore how it works in you. The following is an example from my own life of how this might work:

> I notice that when I imagine future projects for myself, my judge tells me, "You are too ambitious, you're selfish, and you think you are better than others." This always leads to engagement as I try to decide if the judge is right and try to justify myself. Instead, this time I consider what happens to me when I feel the judge talking to me like this.

Observing your experience this way will begin to expose more of the emotional layer of your experience. As soon as you notice what feelings are provoked by the attack, you can speak them, write them down, or list them silently to yourself.

> I notice I feel resentful, trapped, ashamed, and restless. I can feel that I worry about how others are seeing me. I withdraw and want to put my attention on something else. I recognize that in

order to follow through on projects, I have had to stop feeling myself.

Staying with those feelings, you will undoubtedly sense that being made to feel this way is a familiar experience: it has happened before, perhaps many times.

> This pattern goes back all through early adulthood, around most activities in which I got involved. The dynamic would arise when I was learning something new, was excited about it, and wanted to teach it or show others what I had learned. I wasn't usually aware of the attacks then, but now I can feel that they happened many times. Usually, I imagined that other people were judging me, and I would avoid them or act detached in order to shut down my own feelings in response to what they might say or do. I am aware of a painful irony of wanting to share what I am excited about but needing to wall off my heart because I'm afraid I'll be attacked for being ambitious and selfish. I feel a hurt in my heart.

Allowing yourself to stay with whatever feelings come up will tend to open you to associated feelings and beliefs about this situation. You may discover a different or deeper understanding of the current attack as you remember earlier and earlier experiences. You may touch on one of the original incidents of the particular attack, or you may sense how the current attack is a distortion or even a reaction to a feeling or an attack hidden underneath.

> Different realizations begin to arise. I have not been able to stay in touch with my heart in following through on a project; I've needed external motivation to continue. By undermining my focus on the project, the attack is actually trying to protect me from the disappointment of failure or a bad response from others. I notice feelings arising of sensitivity, longing, fear, and sadness. Especially, I feel a helplessness that makes me feel very young. I sense some primal relationship between my excitement and desire for discovery, sharing myself with my mother, and her negative reaction to me. It is hard to focus and stay with the discomfort in my body and mind. And yet I feel intensely in myself in this moment, present with the clearly defined and limited sense

of myself stimulated by the attack. I am not engaging to avoid the discomfort.

In this regressive process, you may also notice that it is not only a feeling you are tracking but a whole cluster of awarenesses, including belief, bodily sensation, movement impulses, perhaps other senses (smell, sound), and maybe a visual image as well. These all fit together to make a complete gestalt provoked by this attack.

> I can feel this young sense of myself as a small boy poised between his own excited, open heart and an anxious concern for his mother. He is frozen with indecision and stands hardly breathing, arms hanging at his side, watching his mother from several feet away. I am aware of how uncomfortable it has been to feel myself this way.

You and Your Self-Image

This gestalt is called a *self-image,* a three-dimensional sense of yourself (with or without visual image) based on a past experience or repeated experiences. Though it is called an image, it seems quite real because you can feel it in your body and emotions, and it has a particular movement and way of experiencing the world. Nevertheless, it is an image because it is a snapshot of the past or, more accurately, a movie of the past. It is fixed and doesn't change, even though it has motion. And it is predictable and lifeless, even though it has emotional energy. When you are attacked, you are affected primarily by becoming identified with a particular self-image from your past. The provoked feelings themselves are not the problem; what limits you and creates self-rejection is the self-image those feelings are associated with.

Every attack you experience provokes a particular self-image in you. This is who you unconsciously take yourself to be in that moment, and your behavior is an expression of that identification. Each self-image can be traced back to some early situation in your childhood that became crystallized as this internal image. Therefore, though you may think and act outwardly as if you were an adult, unconsciously you are acting like the small child you once were. It is no wonder you feel unable to function effectively.

It is also possible to see that as long as you are identified with the small child, any effort to stop the judgment will still leave you engaged with the judge. This is because the experience and desire of the child was to remain engaged in order not to threaten the relationship with the parent. That child is a frozen self-image from the past. The image arose from the experience of being engaged. Therefore, stopping the engagement will mean ceasing to identify with the child, and this means completely severing the relationship with the parent part of you. The voice will stop. You will be alone inside, without child or parent.

Other-Image as Judge

This brings us now to identifying the judge. Just as the early history around that attack reveals who you were at that time, the memories can also disclose the source of that particular attack. In other words, as you experience yourself being attacked and allow the experience to fill you, you may be able to identify who in your past spoke to you in that way (most often someone in your family). It may be she used the same words, or different words with the same implied feeling, or it may be you just knew she felt that way because she attacked others or herself that way. You may also find you were interpreting an early experience as a rejection or an attack when it wasn't. However, at the time, you had no perspective to be able to see that.

What is important is to get a sense of where that particular judging energy came from in your own history—and understand that it didn't originate with you. Just as each attack provokes a specific self-image, each self-image is connected to a specific *other-image* that became internalized as your judge. How freeing it could be to realize that each time you are engaged with a particular attack, you are actually dealing with Uncle Harry. As a child, you were probably helpless with an adult like Uncle Harry: you couldn't defend yourself or express what was true for you. Now you are larger and older and can respond differently.

This kind of exploration of an attack can reveal what is submerged under your familiar depression and rationalizing. It can also open up old and powerful feelings that have long been suppressed, which might subject you to more harsh self-judgment. Awareness is very powerful, and this process of exploration must be undertaken in safety, especially from your judge. In other words, discovering that you are feeling like an angry and humiliated four-year-old is not a reason to attack yourself. It is important that the awareness be held in a space of gentle and respectful kindness.

Because you still believe that you are in some way that child, you cannot treat your child self-image like a photograph you can discard. It feels real to you, and you must respect that fact as truth for you at this moment. Thus, the more you can feel how difficult it was for that child, the more your own loving kindness will be stirred. Feeling compassion for the young part of you that was so affected by the attack is the natural response to being in touch with the truth of the situation. There is nothing to be done but be aware of what happened and remain with your new understanding of why this attack has such an impact on you. The more you see the truth, the more the process of disengaging will be a natural unfolding of what needs to happen.

POINTS TO REMEMBER

- To experience yourself *under attack* rather than lost in *engaging the attack* requires shifting your focus away from the outside and toward the inside: from the judge and its story to yourself and how the judgment affects you.
- When you are attacked, you are affected primarily by becoming identified with a particular self-image from your past. The provoked feelings themselves are not the problem; what limits you and creates self-rejection is the self-image those feelings are associated with.
- Just as each attack provokes a specific self-image, each self-image is connected to a specific *other-image* that became internalized as your judge.
- Feeling compassion for the young part of you that was so affected

by the attack is the natural response to being in touch with the truth of the situation.

EXERCISE: EXPLORING YOUR EXPERIENCE WHILE UNDER ATTACK

Step 1. Choose a familiar self-attack. If a friend is willing to help you, ask her to sit facing you and calmly speak the attack to you as your judge would (no malice in delivery is needed) and then to sit quietly with you as you explore. If you are doing this alone, it is helpful to tape yourself delivering the attack several times and then play back one delivery of the attack and pause while you explore.

Step 2. After listening to the statement, just be with yourself and notice what happens: Did you feel it hook you? How did it affect your body? What feelings were stirred by the attack?

Step 3. Listen to the attack again. Keep noticing. Be aware if you begin to engage, and try to bring yourself back to your feelings only. Notice the tendency to become frozen and keep from being affected. Feel that. You want to learn about what happens to you when you hear this attack. If there are no feelings, notice that. Are you aware of numbness, deadness, emptiness? How does it feel to be that way? If certain feelings or emotions are present, do they remind you of earlier times when you felt the same? Was something similar to this said to you in childhood? Who said it? Are you aware of feeling as though you were in that situation now?

Step 4. Repeat the attack as many times as you need to in order to sense as deeply as possible the effects it has on you.

We still don't understand that our attitudes, ideas, and beliefs are actually responsible for our suffering. We pay lip service to this idea but we don't know it completely and totally. So we continue in our old patterns. The work we do here is simply to see the picture completely, seeing exactly what it is you are doing and how that affects reality.

This is the way that real freedom, actual change, will come about. To live in freedom and absolute fulfillment, we need a complete, radical shift, and such a shift can occur only when there is a complete understanding of what we are actually doing. All the work you do here is based on understanding what you do and how you interfere with the natural process. If you try to do anything other than understand the situation, your effort will be a blockage, a resistance, an interference. You cannot make yourself grow; you can only cease to interfere. You cannot make yourself happy; you can only stop your judgments. Growth and expansion are natural; they are the life force itself. And you cannot predict its direction.

— A. H. Almaas, *Diamond Heart Book 2*, p. 109

Frank looked in Sue's face and saw a very upset young child. She was shaking, and he could feel how much pain she was in, though he had no idea what it was about. He took a deep breath, exhaled, and then, holding her hands, asked, "Can you tell me about what is so painful, Sue?"

She looked down at his hands holding hers and slowly began to speak. "I'm remembering the day I first learned to ride my bike. My parents had guests on the terrace for drinks and hors d'oeuvres. I was practicing and wanted to show Daddy how I could ride. He encouraged me to ride over to where they were sitting. I was a little wobbly but OK until I got near the little tables on the terrace. Then I got nervous. I fell over, knocking down the hors d'oeuvres table. Vegetables, crackers, and dip went flying everywhere.

"As I think of it now, it was probably a pretty funny sight with food everywhere, though, of course, no one laughed. At the time, all I was aware of was the mess I made and everyone's eyes on me. I was scared and bruised and wanted to hide. Then my father came over and dragged me from under the bike by my arm, glaring at me as if I had said a dirty word or something. I can still feel the bruise from his grip and smell the alcohol on his breath. He began to scold me, ☺ 'Look what you've done: hurt your leg, ruined everyone's appetizers, and made a fool of yourself all by pretending to be better than you are. You should be ashamed of yourself!' I did, I felt so ashamed that I had fallen. I just cringed and wept for a long time. ☺ Why am I still so incompetent?"

Frank felt his heart expand and soften, creating a comforting cushion to hold Sue's little girl. Her hands would alternately grip his hands and then relax. Tears welled up in her eyes every few minutes as her body relived the trauma from her father's rebuke and her own shame. Frank gently stroked her hair.

"How confusing to have him encouraging you one minute and blaming you the next. It seems he was more concerned about your impressing his friends than about how you felt. I bet it was pretty scary to fall on the terrace with everyone watching—especially your father. You must have really wanted to feel that he was proud of you." His voice was tender as he verbalized feelings he sensed were there in Sue, and this seemed to help her relax and breathe more deeply.

"You're right. I felt ashamed because I failed to make him proud of me—and all this time, I believed it was because I was too young to control my bike."

15

COMPASSION

THE HEART'S DIRECT ANTIDOTE to judgment is compassion. Because the judge sees only what is wrong and what needs fixing, you know you will get no compassion from it. You will therefore be wary of exposing painful, scary, or negative parts of yourself, for you can be certain the judge will make you wish you hadn't. Everything you think and feel can be used against you. Its job is to maintain the status quo, to protect you by maintaining a restricted sense of self. If you expand or feel too good, the judge will give you a "dose of reality"; if you shrink too much or collapse, it will remind you that things aren't so bad and that you will survive. Its job is not to validate you, acknowledge your courage, or appreciate your pain.

At best, the judge will try to fix your pain, tell you what you did wrong that made you feel hurt, how to take care of it, why it's not worth worrying about, or how you have felt much worse. In this way, the judge mirrors all the ways your pain and hurt were dealt with as a child.

Certainly, when specific actions or events cause physical or emotional pain for a child, it is appropriate for parents to do what they can to remove or minimize the source of the hurt. In this way, many people got help with physical pain and attention to emotional pain. However, the situation was different when the source was not clear or could not be removed, such as a divorce, the death of a family member, a parent's depression, or peer pressure at school. In these situations, few people had their pain accepted and held as natural. Emotional pain in a child was often uncomfortable for the parents because it reflected an element of life they couldn't control or were intolerant of in themselves. This discomfort shifted the parents' focus to getting rid of the pain through denying, avoiding, discounting, or compensating for it. The child learned to feel that something was wrong if she was feeling pain. When the pain was treated as a problem, ultimately, the child came to believe *she* was somehow a problem for having the pain in the first place. As a child, part of you longed to have someone just be there with you in your pain, listen to you, hold you, and show you that pain is a natural part of life. This is what compassion does.

Compassion and Pain

Compassion is a natural response to hurt and pain in yourself or in another. The heart softens and opens. Compassion feels warm and soothing, like a gentle salve. It gives the heart the strength to feel the pain as well as the truth of the situation causing it. Most adult pain cannot be removed by external action, nor is it resolved by logic or cheering up. Frequently, suffering arises from situations you can't or don't want to change, or it remains with you from experiences you had long ago. It takes a large heart to be touched by the reality of such pain and not rush to change or stop it. When you feel the presence of compassion for your own hurt, you know it will be all right and you don't have to do anything, change anything, or fix anything. Yes, the hurt is there, and you can be with it because there is compassion in your heart. Compassion arises from a heartfelt understanding of your own truth, and it supports your willingness to be with that truth.

So hurt naturally brings compassion if the heart is not blocked, and compassion allows you to tolerate more of the hurt feelings. In most cases, you recognize that your hurt originated long ago and is not caused by the present situation. If you can make space to stay with the hurt, you realize that you have felt it many times before. It is familiar to your heart. You remember other times when you felt the hurt, and as you do, the hurt reveals deeper and deeper roots into your past. Feeling it unwinds a thread of suffering back to forgotten wounds in childhood. You may find yourself feeling the original situation of betrayal, rejection, or humiliation that has remained a scar in you all these years. Compassion offers the gentle spaciousness to see and feel these deep gashes in the heart. Simply recognizing what hurt you so long ago begins to heal you and make you whole, for it allows you to be with yourself in that original hurt with a fullness and an understanding not possible at that time.

When your hurt is treated by others as something to be avoided or gotten rid of, the implicit rejection and hostility support a state of disconnection inside you. In contrast, being with someone who has a kind, open, and accepting heart allows you to feel embraced in your hurt. You no longer have to hide the hurt, pretend you feel differently, find a way to fix things, or know what it all means. You can simply be with what is arising and feel supported, seen, and understood.

Feeling your own compassion is like having spaciousness in your chest, room to breathe and be with your feelings. The unconscious holding against the pain in the heart relaxes. You can rest in what is true: there was hurt; that can't be changed. You feel the pain, and you are larger than it. You experience a sense of allowing and support for the truth, without needing to do or be anything. The warmth of tender kindness is mixed with the cool freshness of reality.

Compassion and the Judge

As anger can be the barrier and doorway to true strength, so hurt can be the doorway and barrier to compassion. If you are unwilling to acknowledge or be with your pain, it will be hard to experience compassion for yourself or others. The judge specializes in attacking you for feeling your pain. "What good is it to feel pain? It won't change a thing! . . . You are such a crybaby. . . . Watch out, you might lose it and start crying; then we'd really be in a mess. . . . Feel your pain? Are you some kind of masochist? . . . Your pain is a joke compared to some people's. . . . You want to feel pain, that's your problem. Don't expect me to feel sorry for you. . . . I know it hurts, baby, but cheer up. It could be a lot worse, let me tell you."

Compassion is a direct antidote to the judge's poison. That

poison is neutralized by the soothing warmth of an open heart. Tenderness dissolves the harshness; allowing undoes the rejection. The critical stance loses its grounding and falls away. Where there was structure, now there is spacious holding; where there was belief and knowledge, now there is the truth of the unknown.

But notice how your judge will turn its attention to the compassion and attack it in an effort to create reaction and hardness again. It will try to make kindness seem like weakness, sentimentality, or selfishness: "Compassion is just spiritual pity. Give it up. . . . You accept that pain and you will be asking for more, believe me. . . . Aren't you such a nice person, acting so kind and concerned. . . . Being soft-hearted doesn't get you anywhere in this world; that's for wimps. . . . You can't just sit there looking spiritual; you have to *do* something. . . . Haven't you indulged your hurt child enough?" For the judge simply to allow the compassion without comment would threaten its fundamental perspective—that the world is a dangerous place and you are all alone and require constant and critical attention to survive.

The True Gift of Compassion

Allowing yourself to feel deep hurt is not the same as supporting the identification with the child who is in pain—though it will include recognizing how you have unconsciously identified with that child and been motivated by her feelings. Instead, being with your pain is the path to allowing the fullness of your heart and its truth. It is not a means for justifying helplessness or establishing blame. Neither is it a way to get the attention and comfort you never got as a child.

The compassion and open-heartedness of the soul were not there in the environment at critical times for you as a child, and therefore, those qualities were not recognized or encouraged to arise within you. But open-hearted compassion is the quality that will truly comfort you now. Getting others to hold you and give you attention feels soothing but tends to support your belief that you are still that child. Your hurt child is an inner place of stuckness that prevents you from relaxing and feeling fully. Touching your own suffering can take you beyond the temporary relief of being comforted by others. It will penetrate the stuckness, open your own compassion, and allow your soul to deepen into the spaciousness of the heart.

This openness of the compassionate heart is a doorway to an intimate connection with all of life. Ultimately, compassion goes beyond awareness and empathy to the recognition that you are not separate from everything around you. In the openness of a truthful heart, there are no boundaries, no walls against the flow of life, inside or out. You can know the experience of other people, of flowers, trees, and squirrels, of the wind and rocks, because your heart is completely awake, open, and undefended. At its depth, compassion creates a disarming capacity to touch and be touched—a quality essential for allowing you sensitivity and contact with your experience and your world.

The judge must always keep a distance from you and your situation in order to stay in control. Compassion means no separation between you and the hurt; you feel it with no reactions and hold nothing back. Pity and sympathy, on the other hand, create distance, separation, and often a feeling of superiority. When you have compassion for yourself, you heal the splits perpetuated by the judge— big and strong versus small and weak, superior versus inferior, and me versus you. What remains is the simple truth of where you are.

Compassion is a vital support for contacting the unfamiliar as well as the buried parts of your experience. With it, you have an ally in the heart for being with whatever you discover, whether you like it or not, whether it feels good or not. Without it, you are at the mercy of the judge every time your experience brings you something old or something new.

PRACTICE: BEING WITH PAIN

The next time you are with someone who is feeling pain or hurt, practice opening your heart to this person's experience and notice any impulses to move away or come to the rescue. Are you tempted to explain or analyze the difficulty, offer suggestions, voice anger at the situation, say it will be all right, even offer physical comfort? If you speak, try simply to acknowledge your awareness of the hurt or difficulty. Remember, the practice is to provide support for being with the pain. This may be especially difficult if the person wants to escape the pain, but practice it anyway. Notice what happens.

There is a beautiful kind of cause-and-effect relationship between truth and compassion. They go together. Compassion leads to truth, truth to compassion; and what makes us avoid either or both of them is usually pain. We want to feel good. We want to protect our beliefs, our ideas about who we are. We want to protect ourselves from seeing the truth about others. We all have these cherished beliefs about who we are, who others are, how things are, how things are supposed to be. Seeing through these could bring pain, could bring fear. But that is because we believe the lies. We think the lies are the truth, because we don't trust the truth itself. But the truth itself is the point, regardless of whether it accords with our beliefs.

— A. H. Almaas, *Diamond Heart Book 1*, p. 98

Frank put on the backpack, Sue attached a water bottle to her belt, and they started up the trail away from the parking lot. The sun was bright, and the fresh smell of eucalyptus permeated the afternoon breeze. Two squirrels chattered at them from a nearby tree, and they watched a pair of deer climb up the steep slope into the woods on the right.

Sue seemed fully recovered from her near accident while driving. As she hiked up the old logging road, she hummed to herself. After they were silent for a while, she asked, ✺ "Do you still love me?"

Frank hated this question. It always seemed to come up after some vulnerability on her part and some intimacy between them. ✺ *Why the hell can't she feel it? Haven't I done enough already to show her I love her with holding, caring, and sweetness? Just for that, I feel like saying, "No, I can't stand you!"*

He did his best to sit on his reaction and simply said, "Yes, I do."

✺ "But I don't know if I can trust you. I'm afraid you were only being nice because I was in so much pain. And anyway, I don't think I deserve to be loved."

Frank could feel himself getting more tense. It felt as if she wanted him to judge her. His judge happily obliged her in his mind. ✺ *She sounds like a sniveling, pathetic little kid, whining about how worthless she is. Well, she's right. She doesn't deserve any of what I give her!* It was tempting to say it out loud, but he held his tongue.

✺ "I just can't help it. I am sure you are going to get tired of me one of these days and leave. You only stay 'cause you want to help me, but you must get sick of all my problems. How do you put up with me?"

Frank just walked in silence, but the judge in his mind had an answer: ✺ *I can't stand you, and I am only waiting for the perfect moment to slip out and leave you for someone else to be your good daddy and try to convince you you're not a total jerk. Grow up!* The thought gave him some kind of perverse pleasure, but he was more aware of feeling constricted inside by the interaction with Sue. He didn't like getting sucked into this negativity in himself. Suddenly, he saw that he was being his father in response to his own insecurity as a child. He had felt so unsure of himself and constantly needed reassurance from his parents because he had no siblings to compare himself to, only adults. He remembered feeling his father's impatience and disgust with his helplessness and realized that he had come to identify with his father in relation to his own and others' neediness. Sue was a perfect partner with whom to play that out.

16

DISIDENTIFYING

IN THIS CHAPTER, WE will briefly summarize what we have been learning and then move through the steps of the disidentification process. We have seen that any psychic process that controls you gets much of its power from being unconscious. Therefore, the first phase in regaining control of your own heart and mind is to make the particular process as conscious as possible. By being curious and willing to be in touch with what you are already experiencing, you are becoming more aware of the psychic activity of self-judgment.

Self-judgment is the constant valuation of yourself according to standards learned in the past. It manifests as attacking and engagement. The more you become conscious of the inner activity of attacking and engagement, the more you realize that almost any mental activity used to stop judgment ends up supporting rather than ending it. This is because the effort to stop the attack is initially motivated by the experience of yourself as the victim of the attack—that is, the child. But as you have seen, acting from that self-image of the child-victim always leads to some form of engagement. In other words, real disengagement requires disidentifying from the child self-image so that you can be truly effective in stopping the attack.

Disidentification is implicit in the process of defending against attacks. A true defense does not function in support of any self-image, whether child or judge. It is independent of the mind. But what does this mean? And how do you stop identifying with who you think you are, with the familiar images that define you?

Exploring the following approach to disidentification can help you recognize and support your own movement toward defending yourself—a movement based on your own aliveness and not your identifications.

The Parent-Child Dynamic

Imagine yourself in a department store, looking for some underwear. As you start down one aisle, you overhear in the next a mother arguing with her child. Suddenly, you hear the sound of flesh slapped, and the mother's voice jumps a few decibels: "Didn't I tell you not to touch anything? Why don't you ever listen to me? I ought to have you thrown out on the street to walk home by yourself. If only your father were here, he would give you the kind of spanking you deserve." The child is whimpering and soon breaks down crying. "What's the matter with you!" she screams, "You are such a big crybaby! Just for that we won't go to the movies, and you'll stay in your room the rest of the day." The next thing you know, the mother stomps past, dragging the child by one arm as she heads for the exit.

The whole event is very painful to hear and see. If you don't simply shut it out and numb yourself, what are your natural responses to such a situation? What is your uncensored impulse? Many people would feel so outraged at how the mother is treating her child that they would like to corner the woman and give her a good talking to, even without knowing more details—tell her to shut up and pick on someone her own size, as the saying goes. Others would be more inclined to avoid confronting the mother and simply slip in and pick up the child, carrying him off to a safe place—protecting him from the mother's ire and comforting him. Of course, in real life, neither of these actions is realistic because such an event is part of a long history, and a stranger can't generally intervene without committing to major involvement and unknown consequences.

What is important here in your exploration is the recognition of the basic instinctual movement toward stopping the attack. The preceding example was extreme, but it differs only in degree, not kind, from many other situations where a parent loses a sense of mutual respect with a child and resorts to being bigger and more powerful. Perhaps she says, "No, you don't feel that way!" or "How dare you talk to me that way. You should be ashamed of yourself!" As an outsider to such a situation of parent attacking child, you naturally have feelings of compassion, protective energy, and outrage. This is the basis of defending—stepping in and ending the interaction. You are not saying the child is right and the parent is wrong as much as responding to inhumanity in the interaction, the sense that something basic about human integrity and respect is being violated. Somehow, the underlying truth about human nature has become painfully distorted.

As a child, you could not stop this kind of violation, so you became identified with the distortion as being part of who you are. The result is that you are constantly reliving the various "department store incidents" of your early life. Disengagement in childhood would have required someone's breaking the dynamic and protecting you. Disengagement now, when you are an adult, means not being identified with reliving these childhood dynamics.

In these dynamics, you are identified with either the helplessness and worthlessness of the child or the contempt and hatred of the parent. Either way, what is happening in the attack/engagement cycle seems inevitable and unstoppable. The person identified with the child is feeling defeated: "I feel so small and bad that I deserve to be punished," or "I feel so scared and helpless that I can't even imagine doing anything to change the situation," or "I hate you so much, I would rather die than give you what you want." There is little chance of persuading this person to break free of the cycle.

Similarly, the person identified with the parent/judge is feeling frustration: "This child is so pitiful the only option is to beat him. I have to make him behave or keep him out of sight so he doesn't ruin my life!" or "This child can't take care of herself; she doesn't know what to do, so I have to discipline her till she learns not to get into trouble." Trying to talk this person out of the attack is like trying to tell someone he shouldn't try to kill the ants running across the kitchen counter.

In both cases, what is needed even to bring in the idea of real disengagement is a change in perspective. Ultimately, this means recognizing that the images with which you are identified are just that—images; they are not all of you, and they certainly are not what is most alive in you. However, your investment in these images of yourself is well established and often unconscious. Undoubtedly, there are many good reasons why you continue to hold on to these identifications. Recognizing who you are beyond them can take time. In the meantime, here are some tools to help you.

A Change in Perspective

Visualization is a good tool for encouraging the first step in disidentification. If you have recognized the early childhood dynamic at the root of a self-judgment and it is particularly painful and overwhelming, try the following: First picture that child (you) in front of you as you were at the age and in the situation associated with that dynamic. See your features, your clothing if you can remember it, your facial expression, your behavior. If you see yourself in the midst of an interaction with a parent, fill in the details of the scene. If you are by yourself in your room, picture the room. See and feel how that child is feeling and how you are dealing with those emotions. Watching yourself in a situation in which you are ashamed or helpless may itself be very difficult or painful. The goal is to step outside of that child enough to see yourself as if you were someone else—to observe yourself in your shame or helplessness.

How is it to see this child, and what does it make you feel? As in the department store fantasy, imagine how you would like to respond to that child if you had the opportunity. This might include intervening in a confrontation, kicking out a parent, picking up and holding the child, or talking to the child and telling her you see how much pain she is feeling. Any response that is a movement toward shifting the situation indicates some disidentification from the judgment loop and plants the seeds of disengagement. If you can't feel any desire or capacity for response in yourself, simply imagine what that child needs most at this moment as you see her in front of you. The universal need in such a situation, especially with children, is for someone to see and hear them, for someone to recognize and understand what they are feeling.

In some cases, picturing the situation isn't enough to break your identification with the small child; you cannot move far enough away from the helplessness of the child and the sense of unchallengeable power in the parent. At this point, it can help to bring a third party into the situation. First, consider if there was an adult in or around your family who was a support for you as a child, someone you could trust who valued you as a person and gave you a sense of security and comfort. Now, in this painful dynamic when you are being attacked and can't protect yourself, imagine this supportive adult appearing and imagine what he might have done to support you. Maybe he would have engaged your parent in some way to distract her from attacking you; maybe he would have rescued you in some way. If this works, again you have the seeds of disidentification and defending through someone else's imagined support.

However, some people didn't have any supportive adult in their life as a child, so this option is not available. In this case, imagine someone you feel close to now, who cares about you and supports you, entering that childhood situation and acting on your behalf.

In Session

Judy, a young woman with whom I was working, was in touch with the deep pain and judgment she had felt as a child when her mother turned away whenever she asked for something. She felt trapped, alone, and helpless about this, aware that her judge treated her the same way. I asked if anyone had supported her as a child. Judy said no. "How about now?" I asked. "Yes, my boyfriend." When I suggested that she imagine him entering the situation with her mother, she burst out laughing. "I couldn't help but laugh," she said, "because I was picturing how my boyfriend wouldn't have accepted that bullshit from my mother." That spontaneous release in itself indicated a small shift toward disidentification, giving Judy a sense that she could be supported in that situation, that it was not totally hopeless.

The visualizations just described are based on your identification with the child. What happens when you identify with the parent who sees no recourse but to attack this "bad" child? It is not uncommon to believe you deserved to be punished, abandoned, or ignored when you were young. In this case, you are identified with your own parent against your childhood self. For some reason, you are committed to being loyal to your parent's view of the world and to how you as a child upset that view or went against it. Because of this, you are not able to recognize or allow whatever feelings *you* may have had at the time.

If this is your experience, what is needed is more investigation of your childhood situation to recognize how your expectations and standards for this child are unrealistic. Perhaps you were colicky as a baby and put your parents through great stress having to deal with you, even causing loss of work due to the constant attention needed to care for you. Or maybe you were scared of the dark and took much longer than your siblings to learn to sleep alone. Maybe you wet your bed until you were ten, and so your parents had to get you up night after night to go to the bathroom. In each of these situations, you are probably attacking yourself for not having learned to control yourself better. All these things are beyond the control of a small child, but to be ignored, rejected, or unloved because of these behaviors will be experienced by the child-self as a judgment of who you are.

In Session

Agnes was under recurring attack from her judge about being overly sensitive and emotional. She traced this attitude back to her father. She felt a strong positive connection to him because he was more affectionate and attuned to her than her mother was. However, as a child, she firmly believed it was her fault that she was emotional and scared and couldn't be the happy girl her father wanted. He would become sad, withdrawn, and disappointed in her when she was worried or upset. This would make Agnes more upset and tend to make the situation worse. The result was she believed that her judge's merciless attacks on her for being emotional were deserved. After all, if her father was such a caring and important person for her, it must have been her fault when he was disappointed in her.

Her perspective seemed to imply that her father was the one

who needed support rather than Agnes the child. I asked her how she thought a small child could be responsible for an adult's feelings and explained that it was perfectly natural for a child to have strong emotions, to be frightened at times, and to need to know that her father isn't going to withdraw from her because of those feelings. Agnes said she had ended up believing that some badness in her meant she couldn't be what her father wanted. When I told her that being how she was as a child was completely natural and that her father's response was beyond her control, Agnes burst into tears. Nobody had ever suggested that before. She felt an internal relaxation as she for a moment stopped being negatively identified with her child-self.

You need help to recognize that certain childhood behaviors were beyond your control and, even if you caused your parents trouble, what you needed was compassion and support, not rejection and judgment. When you see this, you will begin to give yourself permission to have your pain and hurt about not being held, loved, and supported. Once you can start to identify with yourself as a child, the visualization process can be used to support the movement toward disidentification.

Disengagement relies on contacting the instinctual energy that wants to preserve the natural life of the soul, the life that was denied and closed down in the child. In the face of parental judgment, the child got cut off from the sense that support to be herself could exist either internally or in the environment. In beginning to disidentify from the child, it is possible to recognize that the energies of both strength and compassion do exist in you now and can be turned to your own soul's benefit.

Two Kinds of Suffering

Judgment causes two different kinds of pain and suffering. One moves you to do something about the judge, to change things. It is what gets people interested in dealing with their critic. Actual freedom from the judgment process, however, requires getting in touch with the second kind of suffering.

The first suffering is the hurt of the child when it is being attacked by the parent. As an adult, you feel this pain when told by your judge that you are stupid or a failure. It is humiliation at feeling small and helpless. It is the shame you feel when you believe you are not as good as the people around you. Your desire to get relief from being attacked pushes you toward dealing with your judge.

However, this motivation usually just results in engagement—trying to defeat the judge. You want to prove it wrong, win its approval, show how it is inconsistent or misinformed, or in the most extreme case, attack and kill it. The problem is, you want to go on being who you feel you are when you are being attacked. You think the problem is all with the judge, your parents. If you could leave home, you would have it made.

But you did that, and it didn't work. Remember, the child also wanted relief from attacks, judgments, and standards, and the way he got relief was to give up parts of himself by engaging with his parents. He learned to behave in particular ways and feel certain things in order to maintain a relationship with them. The desire to change your parents or get rid of them means you want to stay identified with the child. This isn't possible because the child in you exists only in relation to the parents in you. Get rid of one and you have to get rid of the other.

It may seem as if the visualizations in this chapter focus on supporting and protecting the child from the parent. In reality, they are designed to help you find in yourself energy and resources that can respond to that early situation in a more appropriate way than you could in childhood. The child couldn't do anything but what she did. Now you can do something different. You need to disidentify from the child in order to recognize those resources and stop responding out of that self-image.

This brings us to the second kind of suffering in relation to judgment. This is the much deeper pain of how an attack causes you to identify with the child, thereby separating you from who you really are. Only after you have experienced the specific attacks for a long time do you begin to feel that the resulting pain is not as bad as the feeling of once again being caught up in an internal drama that cuts you off from your real life—from your own strength, joy, and compassion. It is not so much that you feel humiliated by what the judge says; it is humiliating that you are instantly taken over by an internal process that forces you to feel small and ashamed. How is it that you are so controlled by this sense of being a child? In taking you over so completely, isn't the child just as powerful as the judge?

This second suffering is the one that fuels the spiritual quest. Spiritual seeking is a recognition that there is more to life than what you are aware of in your familiar daily existence. You sense that you are more than just a physical body and the drama of your personal history. You find yourself questioning the definitions of self that have been given to you because you want to know the deepest truth of who you are and why you are here. You feel deep pain in being separated from the sense of wholeness and aliveness that is your birthright. You long to reconnect with the depths of your soul.

It is the response to the suffering created by this separation that you were tapping into when you imagined yourself in the department store at the beginning of this chapter. It is the movement beyond the child's engagement with the parental judge that you are activating by viewing your child from a distance. In doing so, you can recognize what was missing in the scene—the deep desire to protect your connection with what is most essential in your own humanness: the flow of your soul.

To wake up to the life of your soul, you must feel the way your judge keeps your life small, the way it controls your feelings and behavior, the way it is always waiting to come down on you. This suffering is not that of a small child but that of a *soul* that has remained small, a soul that is stuck moving in circles. You are not a small child doing what it has to in order to survive a difficult childhood; you are a soul condemning yourself to live out an endless pattern of deadening self-images. Only in that recognition is there the possibility of rediscovering the soul's true defense. Are you willing to stand up and be heard? Are you willing to stop the soul betrayal? It's time to say to your judge: "Get the hell out and let me have my life!"

You must discover that the judge and its attacks, and the child and its hurts, are painful, frustrating distractions, but distractions nevertheless. They prevent you from having the space to discover who you are now. You can be involved in the struggle to defend your child forever and miss the truth that will end that struggle: you are no longer that child and have not been for a long time. Forgetting that again and again is what really hurts.

POINTS TO REMEMBER

- Any psychic process that controls you gets much of its power from being unconscious. Therefore, the first phase in regaining control of your own heart and mind is to make the particular process as conscious as possible.
- The more you become conscious of the inner activity of attacking and engagement, the more you realize that almost any *mental* activity used to stop judgment ends up supporting rather than ending it.
- Disengagement relies on contacting the instinctual energy that wants to preserve the natural life of the soul, the life that was denied and closed down in the child.
- Real disengagement requires disidentifying from both the helplessness and worthlessness of the child and the contempt and hatred of the parent so that you can be truly effective in stopping the attack.
- In a visualization process, any response from outside the parent-child interaction that is a movement toward shifting the situation indicates some disidentification from the judgment loop and plants the seeds of disengagement.
- In beginning to disidentify from the child, it is possible to recognize that the energies of both strength and compassion do exist in you now and can be turned to your own soul's benefit.
- Judgment causes two different kinds of pain and suffering. One moves you to do something about the judge, to change things. The second kind of suffering is the much deeper pain of how an attack causes you to identify with the child, thereby separating you from who you really are. This second suffering is the one that fuels the spiritual quest.

- You can be involved in the struggle to defend your child forever and miss the truth that will end that struggle: you are no longer that child and have not been for a long time.

EXERCISE: LOOSENING CHILDHOOD IDENTIFICATION

This exercise will help loosen your identification with your self-image as a child. Make a list of all the ways you made life difficult for your parents when you were young. Even if you were not conscious of doing anything to bother them or make them mad, know that it happened many times. Imagine what those situations might have been.

- What behaviors bugged your parents (bad habits, sneaky activities, special cravings, demanding attention, being silent, needing help)? Did you ever use these to your advantage to bribe or control?
- What kinds of power did you have in your household, and can you think of ways in which you manipulated situations to get what you wanted?
- Can you connect with the enjoyment you may have felt at wielding this power against the adults?
- Can you recognize how your having power may have frustrated them?

If you are identified with being a brat and having gotten your way as a child, or with having been a constant problem for your parents, explore the ways in which you may have enjoyed that role and the power it carried. Then it might be useful to take the opposite tack and make a list of ways in which you were taken advantage of.

"Listening to you, Sue, asking me for reassurance that way and my feeling your neediness, for the first time I can remember how afraid I was of my parents' abandoning me. I was so aware that I didn't know how to do things and was always asking them for help and instruction. Compared to them, I seemed so slow at everything. I could feel my father get impatient, and I was sure that someday he would get fed up and leave me. I was constantly wanting reassurance that he wouldn't go away, but I didn't ask for it very often because I was afraid it would make him more impatient to see me so insecure. I learned to treat myself the way he did because I thought I must be an incredible burden to him. I realize I thought that would make me more like him and less like me." Frank's words seem to break some kind of spell, and he could feel his inner pressure to be like his father relaxing.

At the same time, his awareness, so focused on Sue and his inner state, opened up. Suddenly, he was again in touch with the beautiful afternoon: the trees, the birds, the colors, and the shadows. He was especially aware of Sue and how alive and immediate she looked. He couldn't explain it, but the world felt very spacious, open, and allowing.

Sue also relaxed. "Does that mean you love me?" she asked in a playful tone. "Even if I have to ask you over and over again?"

"Who, me? Well, I don't know. I guess I have to find out who I am first if I'm not my father; then I'll tell you if I love you. In the meantime, you look very lovable and mysterious. In fact, everything looks fresh and new. Reminds me of how you were feeling on the porch this morning. Do you notice it? Things look familiar, but as if they have been washed clean. You look that way, and I feel that way. What a change! One minute I am totally locked up reacting to you, being my impatient father about ready to tie you to a tree and gag you, and the next minute I don't know who I am. Except that I'm feeling spacious, empty, and free of all that stuff."

  ❈ *What is this? Some kind of New Age be-here-now crap? You sound like a space cadet.*

This time, Frank heard his judge as if it were a fascinating new birdsong, meaningless but striking. Sue stood watching him in his new state, then taking his hand, she started them walking up the path. As he walked, Frank was still getting used to how open and receptive he felt—to Sue's hand in his, to the ground under his feet, and to the empty space in his head.

17
SPACIOUSNESS

ONE QUALITY IN YOUR experience that you are much more aware of when it is missing is the sense of spaciousness. When it is there, your life flows easily: you feel relaxed, simple, and free to operate in a straightforward, unrestricted way. Obstacles still confront you externally, but internally life feels natural and relaxed; you do what you want or need to do, speak your mind, respond freely to others, and generally feel a sense of balance and acceptance of what happens. You don't necessarily think, "I am feeling spacious"; things just feel easy.

When the spaciousness is missing, you have a very different sense about living your life. You feel under pressure, hemmed in by the choices you make, tense in your body, or held back in your self-expression. The externals of your life put stress on you: you feel trapped by your schedule, your commitments, the demands of others, and your own limited energy. Your judge is active. It is at these times that you find yourself consciously saying, "I need space!" or perhaps, "I need time to slow down, to relax, to take a vacation and get away from it all."

Inner Space

What is this space? Is it something around you or between objects, such that moving away from things will give you space? Or is it something less physical that arises within you? This spaciousness, the sense of having room to breathe, is in fact a quality of the mind.

When you do not feel confined by mental boundaries—limitations on what you can think, feel, and imagine—you feel spacious. When the mind is not full of thoughts, plans, and worries, it feels like quiet, empty space. When you are not identified with particular beliefs and ideas about yourself, where you are going, what needs to happen, and how to get there, you are full of open space.

Spaciousness is paradoxical. You sense its impact and thrive in its presence. Yet when you first turn your attention to your own spaciousness, the tendency is to experience nothing, and so you look around for something. "I have no thoughts and no feelings. I don't feel anything." You are so used to relating to objects in your awareness—ideas, emotions, sensations, memories—that without them, you feel there is nothing there. This is true, except that nothingness is also space. Empty space. Room to move. Room to be.

The ground of your being—who you are beneath all the history and conditioning and learning and feelings—is spaciousness. Even your experience of your body can be full of space. Remember, according to physics, there is a huge amount of space between every molecule and atom in every cell and organ in your body. What if you could be aware of that space? Your visual and tactile senses report that your body is solid, but that doesn't mean that your inner experience of it has to be, nor that your inner experience of yourself has to be closed, limited, and solid. I am suggesting that you are most relaxed and natural when you feel open in your mind, not bound up or constrained—and you feel this when you are in touch with your own spaciousness.

Self-Images and Space

Attacks are one of the most effective methods of shutting down space. As soon as you become identified with the small, helpless child in you, your experience is dramatically limited. Other people look like your judge; you expect to be attacked; you feel contracted and uncomfortable; your awareness is limited; and you have few options for behavior. Your self-image has completely closed you in, as though you had entered a room with no windows. You feel a lack of inner spaciousness.

A self-image is like a structure that appears in the mind, shutting down the openness. It puts boundaries around the space and limits what can be experienced or perceived. The judge's job is to make sure those structures stay there so you don't get "lost in space." This is why one of the most distinctive characteristics of freedom from the judge and inner attacks is the implicit sense of spaciousness. Ending self-judgment removes a certain contracted self-definition and frees the mind of rigid mental constraints. What remains is unbounded space.

When you disidentify from a self-image, you step out of that windowless room, and your sense of inner space returns. You may notice that you can breathe more easily, relax, and settle in a way that wasn't possible moments before. Now you are not so confined, limited, or tense in whatever situation you find yourself. Sometimes, you are surprised to realize how tight or constricted you felt without being aware of it.

Usually, you consider space simply a by-product of inner change, an indicator that you are free of some previous confinement in yourself. You conclude that space is what is left when the restrictions are removed. And generally, you rest for a few moments and then quickly resume your busy life with more breathing room. What you are unlikely to do is linger with the sense of having space, curious about where the space came from and what it means to feel spacious. If you could begin to recognize the spaciousness as a positive quality in you—as a tangible presence, not just a loss of constriction—you might start to value the openness and not immediately rush to fill it.

The Experience of Space

You can sense space even though it seems nonexistent. However, perceiving the nothingness of inner space in the activity, congestion, and rush of modern life requires a subtle sensitivity. You must slow down or even stop in order not to miss it. Spaciousness is rather like air, with a light, open, fresh quality to it. It is generally empty, meaning it is without thoughts or feelings—a wonderful quiet absence, a relief from all the sense of busyness and inner clutter. You feel expansive because spaciousness itself has no boundaries. A sense of clarity arises because there are no obstructions, no walls, just openness. Space gives you a feeling that there is room for everything. In fact, space is an openness that is necessary for allowing new experience. Without any space, how can something new arise?

On the other hand, spaciousness can come into awareness first as a feeling of emptiness. A sense of emptiness usually indicates you are feeling nothing instead of something, so it can easily become the experience that something is missing or lacking. When you look for what you think is missing, however, you do not experience the space itself. Instead, you experience an unpleasant gnawing sensation associated with the belief that you are missing something. If you can recognize that a belief, not your immediate experience, is making you feel the sense of lack, it is possible to disidentify from the belief. You can then allow the emptiness without trying to fill it. In this way, the negative sense of emptiness can transform into the positive sense of spaciousness.

Space and the Judge

The judge will attack your experience of space from different directions:"So you are feeling emptiness in your head. You numskull, that means you are stupid! . . . If you start losing your sense of boundaries, you are asking for trouble. . . . Quit spacing out and get to work! . . .What do you mean, you don't feel guilty about what happened? . . . Don't bother trying to sense yourself; there's nothing there—and that's your problem!" Until you begin to recognize spaciousness for what it is—the authentic presence of your beingness without any content—your judge will easily distract you from experiences of open emptiness. All it has to do is call up the image of something missing and you will fill up the space with searching and worrying!

Spaciousness has its own particular power in relation to the judge. It is what is in between and around words, objects, and ideas. The more you are aware of space as an experiential quality, the more you are focused on the open field in which everything arises. This is the opposite of content, of the narrow, focused engagement with the judge. The judge's message is seductive compared to other content, but compared to empty space, it is no more powerful than a TV commercial and considerably less pleasant than a nice piece of music. When you are feeling spacious, the judge is not right in your face, even if it is present, so it can't exert its usual degree of pressure. In fact, spacious means space to choose, space to ignore, or space to go around. Feeling spacious brings elements of our experience back into proper proportion, and the judge's significance rapidly diminishes.

Space and the Soul

To experience your own spaciousness is to recognize the true nature of your soul, a felt sense that has nothing to do with personal history, ideas, behavior, or accomplishments. It is always there but easily ignored. It is tangible and powerful yet difficult to focus on and even harder to describe. In fact, the mind has no way to grasp the sense of inner space. There is nothing to hold on to, point to, or think about.

If you are like most people, it is a challenge to hang out with any kind of empty space, whether in your schedule, with another person, or inside yourself. You like the sense of ease and freedom the spaciousness brings, but being in direct contact with the empty space causes uneasiness. This is why you usually feel the spaciousness only when you are glad that something is missing or gone. Then you experience space as just a relief. The rest of the time, it is felt as the lack of something you need—even when you have to search for what is missing.

With time and awareness, it becomes possible to accept and appreciate the experience of spaciousness in your head, your body, or your sense of who you are. This opens the way for the sense of barren or frightening emptiness to become the experience of open space. When you stop looking for something to fill the space, you can begin to see the space where you always are. You can feel and embrace your own spacious nature.

PRACTICE: ATTUNING TO INNER SPACE

Sit quietly and close your eyes. Sense your arms and legs, and notice what you actually feel. For a moment, forget everything you know about what shape and size your body is and even where it is in space. Now sense where the edges of your arms and legs are; feel their surfaces.

Can you feel them all over? Probably there are some surfaces you cannot perceive at this moment. This means that, in those places, you cannot tell where you end and where the air begins. If that is so, does it mean the air is solid or that you are empty space like the air? Does your body actually feel solid? Undoubtedly, some places feel dense or contracted, stiff or thick, but what about other places that might feel hollow or empty, open, or just not there?

Do this exercise periodically until you can begin to feel your own inner spaciousness.

Space brings about expansion in the qualities of our senses, our sensations, and our mental capacities. It deepens our intuition. It expands our awareness into new dimensions of ourselves, some we would never have conceived could exist. It brings new capacities for perception and experience. In addition, space has the surprising and powerful capacity of expanding itself, continuously increasing the openness and dissolution of boundaries, allowing ever-greater understanding of ourselves and our minds.

— A. H. Almaas, *The Void,* pp. 31–32

This was definitely a day to experience Frank going through changes, and Sue was beginning to take it in stride. She had to admit that this Frank was a lot more enjoyable than the rather serious, predictable husband she was used to. She even felt *herself* more flowing. She was always more changeable than he was, but today she found herself going to new places, not limited to the familiar cycle of emotions she usually experienced. Like that joy and curiosity this morning followed by the understanding about her shame . . . even the shift just now from feeling her neediness for reassurance. It was exciting.

Sue found herself wanting to skip, and before she knew it, she had let go of Frank's hand and was skipping along the path. She couldn't remember when she had last skipped. She felt so young and free.

After a few minutes, she stopped to catch her breath and wait for Frank to catch up. Suddenly, out of nowhere, a thought popped into her mind.

> *You didn't take the video back this morning, did you? I knew you'd forget it, and it was due by 11 AM. And what about that CD you were going to return? That reminds me — you have no more cash; when are you going to ask Frank for more? You are still so dependent on him financially because you just can't get your massage practice to work. Sue, the successful failure!*

Sue felt barraged by the voice in her head, and if it weren't for the fact that she was still out of breath and very much aware of her body sensations, she would have been completely deflated by its words. They were so familiar and guaranteed to hit her where she was most vulnerable: issues around money and work. She felt a little nauseous and disoriented as she paced around in a circle while her breathing slowed down. Where normally she would have been paralyzed by this self-attack, she found herself shaking her head and stamping her feet in response to its incessant pressure. In her mind, she was imagining bombs going off, buildings collapsing, and ships sinking.

> *Did you tell Frank that two clients canceled for this coming week and one doesn't want to come back at all? Nobody really wants to work with you, and they won't unless you learn to be a success and believe in yourself.*

That was it! Standing now with her eyes closed and fists clenched, Sue found herself shouting, "Shut up! Do you hear me? SHUT UP! Get the hell out of here and leave me alone!"

Frank appeared behind her and tapped her on the shoulder, asking in a mock serious tone, "Who are you yelling at?"

18
STOPPING SELF-BETRAYAL

ADULTS AND OLDER KIDS used to play a trick on me when I was little: they would distract my attention and take something from me while I was looking in the other direction. Do you remember this being done to you? They loved the joke, but for me, it was deeply humiliating. As they laughed at me, I stood there feeling stupid and foolish. My shame seemed all the more horrible because I was younger and trusted the older people around me. Their response to my pain was always, "You can take a joke, can't you?" They were implying that if I were strong and grown-up, the joke wouldn't have bothered me.

So I tried to "be a good sport," to play along and not be upset. After all, I wanted to be liked and accepted. However, someplace inside, I felt I had betrayed myself, and I didn't know why. Because I believed that my strength was in being able to "take it" and not feel hurt, I decided I must have been betrayed by my curiosity and trust. I figured that these movements of my heart were responsible for my feeling hurt. So my own feelings were the culprit, not the unkind actions of others. I ended up feeling less open, more suspicious, and more sensitive to attack. It was only much later that I recognized that the real self-betrayal was in not speaking up for myself and saying I didn't want to be treated that way.

Engagement as Self-Betrayal

This incident is quite analogous to the attacking process we are exploring. In your adult life, your judge is constantly distracting you with worries about what is wrong with other people, the situation, yourself; or with warnings about what to do, what not to do, what to avoid, what won't work; or reminders of past failures, losses, and disappointments. The judge succeeds at this by turning you into the child who was rightfully worried by these things and believed that your own weakness was the source of the problems. However, the very effort of attending to these concerns brought up by the judge seems to cause some deeper loss—the loss of who you are in the moment before you turn into the child.

When the judge tears you away from contact with yourself in the moment, you are unconsciously reliving an original wounding in the soul—the wound of self-betrayal. Many times in your childhood, you were faced with a choice of whether to stay with your own experience—what you were feeling as true and real—or to turn your back on that reality and adopt the one presented to you by parents and family. To reject the latter would have threatened you with rejection, isolation, abandonment, and possibly even death. Inevitably, you chose to accept and operate within the consensus reality of your familial environment, seeing others and yourself the way outside influences mirrored these things.

You began to see yourself as cute, if that's what your parents kept describing you as, or smart or bad or slow. Maybe you felt curious, but your parents called you nosy; or you felt energetic, but you were called restless; or you felt bright but were called too smart for your own britches. Sometimes, you may even have felt like a shining star or a warm cloud or a solid rock, but you were always treated as just a small human child. Eventually, you stopped recognizing the truth of your own experience and lived more and more out of your adopted reality. The unavoidable self-betrayal was complete.

Self-betrayal is another term for the self-rejection described in chapter 4, which was the result of distancing yourself from your own feelings as a child. At that time, distance was needed for you to survive and later avoid parental attacks that couldn't be stopped. Now you are seeing that by engaging the judge, you are turning away from your present reality, replicating this original self-betrayal. Responding to the judge on its own terms—by discussing, negotiating, placating, arguing, counterattacking—identifies you with the past, with the self-image of the deficient child. Every time you look where the judge is directing your attention, you find some worry, problem, or lack that you believe is important, if not crucial, for dealing with your present situation. But so often, these concerns are only important in relation to the standards the judge created long ago. You are deceived into believing that the judge knows what is really going on now. After all, it knows all of your weaknesses and failures, doesn't it? Meanwhile, by listening and reacting to it, you take on the deficient child self-image and lose touch with something more real inside you.

The more you see this process in action, the more you see that it takes you away from the truth. You are not a helpless child, and all these worries and problems are not important enough to constantly bend you out of shape. You may not know who you are, but you damn well know you're not a fearful toddler, even if the voices in your head make you feel that way! If the judge is pointing to real problems, you can deal with them much more effectively if you are not being treated like a three-year-old! Do you ever find yourself saying, "I can't believe this is still happening! How can I continue to treat myself this way? Who is running this show anyway?" If so, good. Be indignant. This is not unlike what naturally arises in a child who has been tricked or treated disrespectfully: "It's not fair. That hurts. I was just being myself. Leave me alone!" It is time to stand up and speak for yourself and the truth of your experience. It is time to activate your essential strength.

The Soul's True Defense

The energy for active defending is available to you the moment you recognize that your deepest nature is being constricted by the experience of being attacked. This strength springs from a desire to be free of frustrating and limiting identifications. Such a desire stirs profound indignation at the lies, deception, and inhuman behavior. The sense of outrage awakens your essential strength and with it the capacity and clarity to defend your own truth in the face of judgment. Ultimately, this truth is nothing but the integrity and aliveness of the human soul.

Essential strength is felt as red vibrant heat rising up from your belly to destroy the falsehood, the injustice, the repressive activity of the judge, whether it is coming from another person or from inside you. This movement is based in compassion—a felt understanding of the hurt and limitation being suffered—and thus supports a true disengagement that will serve the humanity of all concerned. It will not wreak vengeance or act out of blind rage. This essential quality may begin as anger at the debilitating effect of self-judgment, but it emerges as an assertive strength to be yourself without the need for acceptance, approval, or acknowledgment of anyone else. Most fundamentally, it is the strength to be yourself without a self-image but with a sense of presence that is grounded, clear, and vitally alive.

True strength is the basic instinctual energy of survival and self-protection, which we recognized as missing or blocked in the judgment process in chapter 4. Now it is operating on a level that incorporates intelligence, awareness, and understanding of your true nature and what needs to be defended. Strength is the essential aspect that the judge is most effective at blocking—the part of your essence that was especially undermined by the judgments of powerful adults. You as a child did not have the physical presence and capacity to embody this instinctual energy for your own protection. Even if you could have, it was dangerous to do so because you were still very dependent on adults for survival. That is no longer the case. Now you can begin a vital aspect of your journey: recovering that compassionate, intelligent vitality—the strength essence.

In Session

Paul arrived at a session in a state of agitation after returning home that morning on a plane flight that was two hours late. He had scheduled several of his dental patients in accordance with his planned return time, but because of the major delay, he had missed those appointments. He knew that what had happened was beyond his control, but his stomach was still tied in knots, and he kept flipping between guilt and anger as his mind endlessly devised permutations of what could or should have happened.

When I asked him what was causing him to be so upset, he said it was the fact that he was late: "I have a long history of being late, and it is just not OK for me to screw up that way."

"So your judge is attacking you about something that wasn't your fault?" I asked.

"Maybe," he said, "but I should have known better and flown home last night."

"Well, now you know," I said, "but isn't there enough to do getting things straightened out and going on with your work? Why continue to beat yourself up about it?" Paul looked perplexed as he felt the pain from the knot in his stomach. "What would you like your judge to do?" I asked.

"Give me a break and go away," he replied impulsively. "But I don't know how to get it to do that."

I suggested we do a role play. I would act as his judge and talk to him the way he was doing in his head, and then he would respond to it.

"Paul, you sure blew it this morning. I can't believe you were late again. No matter what happens, you always manage to screw it up. Why didn't you come back last night? How do you expect to get your dentist's office off the ground if you pull stunts like this?"

Paul just sat and listened. "What's going on?" I asked.

"I totally agree with everything you said. It's all true."

"How does it make you feel when you listen to me as your judge?"

"I get really tense and hold my breath."

"That is what's important here. Whether it is true or not doesn't matter at this point; what matters is that you are engaged, drained of your energy, and unable to pay attention to your life. Respond to your bodily experience, not to the words in your mind. Let's try again."

Paul looked at me, took in a deep breath, and said, "OK, here goes. Leave me alone. It's not my fault what happened, and I'm doing the best I can."

I asked him how it felt, and he wasn't sure. "Can you feel how you were rationalizing at the end—trying to justify your position?" He nodded. "It doesn't work to try and convince the judge to leave you alone. Try it once more, and this time keep it short and sweet.

Remember, you want to break the connection with the judge." I began the judge's commentary again.

"Paul, you are a flake. The airline may have been late, but it was your fault, so . . ."

"FUCK OFF!"

After the explosion of energy, Paul was silent. This time, his intention had been clear, and Paul was quite surprised at how relaxed he felt in his stomach and how quiet his mind was. He had defended himself and now felt disengaged.

When strength is present, you feel alive, awake, and prepared to take appropriate action to deal with anything that stands in the way of your living your life. This quality separates you from old self-images that might lure you into engaging with the judge and also gives you the energy and capacity to stop further attacks or attempts of the judge to take control. You feel a decisiveness and a clarity that cut through the judge's efforts to make you feel a particular way.

Disidentification and disengagement are not exclusively results of the strength of your being, but they are most effectively supported when it is present. Active defending is not possible without it. Strength is profoundly cut off by the aggressive control of the judge, so being willing and able to draw on this quality creates one of the most significant shifts in working with self-judgment. Strength is central in the process of being able to stand up and take charge of your own life in a real way.

The ability to defend effectively depends on your *unwillingness* to live with the falseness of what is taking place and your ability to see and directly challenge your habitual self-betrayal of engaging the judge. You as a child did not have the option of staying with your own truth; you were forced into self-betrayal by the need for parental support. Now, that is not the case: if you recognize and value what is real in you, you *can* stay in touch with that reality. Then defending against the deception is much easier. However, the deceptions of the judge are subtle and seductive; they often appear to be addressing matters of survival, masking its true agenda: to seduce you away from what is true in the moment. It can be particularly difficult to recognize the attack as a distraction when your sense of who you are and what you value in yourself is still tied up with either the judge or the threatened child.

All of the exploration we have done so far into the judgment process has been leading to this point: the moment when some part of you stands up and says, "Enough!" Until now, you were willing to keep negotiating, accommodating, and adjusting to try to get around the judge. How many thousands of times have you done that? Have you had enough? You feel the larger circles of repetition that constantly bring you back to the same spot where the judge calls the shots. It is not working, it is not what you want, and it is not the truth. Are you ready? Are you at the end of your rope?

Finally, the weight of the truth is too much. The time has come to do something different, to break out of the loop. Have you tried everything else to manage things? If not, you are probably not ready. True strength does not arise because you want it or because you know you should have it. It only appears when all your attempts to outwit the judge have failed and you realize that even if you outwit the judge, you have failed. Because essential strength undoes the familiar, the cozy, and the comfortable, you will only open to it if you feel you have no choice. One form the feeling takes when it arrives is quite distinctive: if you don't act, you feel you just might explode.

In fact, when that last straw finally descends on the camel's back, the soul's direct response will feel like an explosion. When strength is ignited as the true defender of the soul, its action is not planned, organized, or thought out. It blows the mind with a force that is spontaneous, visceral, expansive, and unapologetic. After all, only a psychic bomb can destroy both the vast and elaborate structures of the judge's home and your habitual rituals within it.

One of the most common discomforts of aggressive direct response to the judge is feeling that it is not nice and is even downright hostile or violent. Yes, it *is* hostile and it's *not* nice—and for good reason: you are defending your life. If you are constrained by the need to be polite and considerate, you will never regain your inner freedom. It is the judge that demands those niceties toward others while disregarding the integrity of your soul. You *must* learn to protect yourself from inner attacks, and perhaps the most difficult step in doing so is confronting your reluctance to use the full force of your instinctual energy in defending. If you don't use it to support your truth, the judge will continue to use it against you.

POINTS TO REMEMBER

- Engaging the judge is a replication of your original self-betrayal as a child, when you gave up your reality for your parents'. By listening and reacting to the judge, you take on the deficient child self-image and lose touch with something more real inside you.
- The energy for active defending is available to you the moment you recognize that your deepest nature is being constricted by the experience of being attacked. The sense of outrage awakens your essential strength and, with it, the capacity and clarity to defend your own truth in the face of judgment.
- Disidentification and disengagement are not exclusively results of the strength of your being, but they are most effectively supported when it is present. Active defending is not possible without it.
- The ability to defend effectively depends on your *unwillingness* to live with the falseness of what is taking place and your ability to see and directly challenge your habitual self-betrayal of engaging the judge.
- True strength does not arise because you want it or because you know you should have it. It only appears when all your attempts to outwit the judge have failed and you realize that even if you outwit the judge, you have failed. Because essential strength undoes the familiar, the cozy, and the comfortable, you will open to it only if you feel you have no choice.
- You *must* learn to protect yourself from inner attacks. Perhaps the most difficult step in doing so is confronting your reluctance to use the full force of your instinctual energy in defending.

EXERCISE: ASSERTING YOUR TRUE STRENGTH

This exercise is practice in reclaiming your own aggressive energy and aliveness from the judge. It is not practice for how to treat other people (though if they are persistent in attacking you, it might be useful to say "ENOUGH!").

Don't be stopped because it feels artificial or fake. Your judge is the one telling you that that's a problem! This is practice. It might not feel real to begin with. If you have never stood up for yourself this way, it will feel unfamiliar and unlike you. It might even feel dangerous—as if you are asking for trouble, asking to be hit yourself, or even asking for God to strike you dead. This will make you aware of how much prohibition you carry against being loud and strong in defending yourself. This is why you practice. Remember, you are contacting the place in you that feels attacked just by hearing the words your judge uses all the time. You are also encouraging the recognition that you have every right to claim the aggressive energy inherent in the attack to support your own aliveness. Go for it!

Step 1. Ask a friend to help you practice.

Step 2. Make up a list of at least ten familiar self-attacks and give it to your friend.

Step 3. Ask your friend to read off the attacks one at a time, allowing you to practice with each one. The delivery should be clear and strong without being vicious or nasty.

Step 4. Respond to each attack with a clear statement designed to stop the attack. Practice using one of the following four responses: "SSSHHHHH," "Enough," "Shut up," or "Fuck off!" These are increasingly strong in content, so use whichever one you can. They are obviously not meant as an engaging response to the attacks. The goal is to stop the attack altogether.

Step 5. Ask your friend to repeat each attack until he is satisfied that you have really made your point—that he has been stopped by your response. Feel free to use as much intensity and volume as you need. Ground your energy in your body, sense your arms and legs, experience the sound coming from your belly if you can, and allow yourself to get bigger with each response. Stamping your foot as you say your statement can also help to ground the energy in your body. This exercise is to challenge any prohibition against being big and loud, but be aware that bigger is not *necessarily* better; the important factor is to connect at a gut level with your words—fully intending that what you say will end the interaction.

Step 6. Pause periodically and just breathe; sense how you feel in your body. Do you feel more tense? more open? bigger? tighter? more alive? more scared? numb? weak? strong? hot? Talk about how you feel. Try not to judge anything you feel (if you find your judge getting involved, say "SHUT UP" to it). Simply notice the experience and be curious about it. What might be making you feel the way you are?

At some point, it will become clear that you are directing this energy at the images of your parents, who are the main power source of your judge. Most people do not want to hurt their parents or are scared to be angry or hostile toward them. Doing this exercise will expose the fundamental conflict between affirming your own life and being subjugated to the inner life you experienced with your parents. You are being aggressive toward an image here, not a real person; therefore, what is being challenged in saying "ENOUGH" or "FUCK OFF" has no real substantial existence. The only thing being destroyed is an image in your mind.

If you were emotionally or physically abused as a child, this exercise may bring up difficult feelings related to those experiences. To directly express aggressive energy may be simply impossible at first. Many people who have suffered abuse find specific healing work necessary to address the trauma before they are ready to defend themselves aggressively. If this is the case for you, honor your own timing and trust your experience to guide you.

So, to have the correct attunement or the correct relationship to the teaching means really to risk being unfaithful to your mother. It is your superego, it is your personality, it is your unconscious that you risk. Remember that Jesus said, "Leave your parents and follow me." That's what he meant, because you are usually listening to your mother, and you try all the time to fight her—you argue, you get angry, all that. But you still listen. That is what you listen to all the time. And, instead of listening to Jesus, people are still listening to their mothers. Jesus had nothing against mothers and fathers. Jesus meant you to listen to the teachings that are present in your essence, rather than listening to your superego.

— A. H. Almaas, *Diamond Heart Book 1*, p. 201

"Who do you *think* I might be yelling at? Not you. Just my friendly, ever-present judge. Would you like to have her?" asked Sue in a remarkably energetic voice.

"No thanks—quite unhappy enough with my own judge, thank you," replied Frank. "You OK? One minute you're skipping out of sight, the next you're raging at some invisible demon."

"I'm fine." She continued talking in a louder-than-usual voice as if she wanted someone to overhear. "In fact, I feel finer than I have in a while. You know my judge is always on my case about how I'm a failure and a loser and not worth anything because I don't measure up to its standards. Well, damn if I didn't just get it that what I am worth hasn't got a fucking thing to do with old judge-face. I think we should call it Hammerhead, 'cause that's the way it feels. What do you think?" She swung her arms around and stamped her feet again for good measure. "It just swings that gavel and pounds on my head!"

"Oooh, I like you when you get hot and alive and fit to be fried! Go kick its butt, honey . . . old Hammerhead!" Frank was fascinated.

Sue swaggered a bit as she took some deep breaths and hissed a few times. At that moment, a bright ray of afternoon sun broke through an opening in the trees and fell on her face, giving her a golden glow as she closed her eyes from the brilliance. She stood still and felt the sun's warmth on her skin. "Mmm, I like that."

After a few moments, the sun moved on, but Sue continued to stand with her eyes closed, sensing herself. She and Frank stood on the path in silence for several minutes, listening to the sounds of the late afternoon.

"You know, I feel as if I am experiencing my own sense of value for the first time," she commented quietly. "It's like a sweet brown molasses in my chest, so delicious, and it's me." Her eyes were closed, and she spoke with the gentlest intimacy, knowing that Frank was there with her. In the most inexplicable way, she felt absolutely clear that she belonged here, that she was home. It was not home in a physical sense but in the awareness that her simple presence in her life at this moment had implicit value and meaning. She was no more and no less than anything else in the universe, but she was herself, and her inherent value was precious.

Sue opened her eyes and looked wide-eyed at Frank, with an unusually intense sense of discovery about her. "I am pure value," she purred.

19
VALUE

VALUE IS A QUALITY that refers to worth or significance. It is the element that determines the degree of meaning or satisfaction in your life and how much importance you give to the people, things, and situations in it. Value is an underlying element in your experience that clearly affects how you live, yet you never consider it an experiential quality in itself. You seldom think about it as separate from what seems to *have* value. You refer to value as a characteristic of certain objects, relationships, events, choices, or concepts. Or else you believe it is an abstraction used to compare the relative importance of different things and experiences: some have more value than others.

Value is an expression of what an object or experience means to you, either by itself or in relation to other things. As a property of an object, value can vary over time or even pass from one object to another (for example, for many people, voice mail has acquired the value once held by the answering machine). As an abstraction, it appears to exist in the mind as a tool for describing and assessing experience. Does value originate in your experience or first arise in your mind? How do *you* take on value at certain times and lose it at others? What does it mean that you can *feel* valuable? Does value have an existence independent of mind and its evaluation and comparison?

The Measure of Value

In Western culture, there is general agreement that value is received, derived, or created through good fortune (talents, looks, inheritance), hard work, schooling, acceptance by others, therapy, meditation, inner work, and on and on. It doesn't matter how it comes. The unshakable belief everyone carries is that you must earn value, be given it, be blessed with it, or in some way receive it. It isn't there as a natural birthright.

This is where your history and the judge come in. Like everyone else, your parents believed in value as an acquired quality, so they did not recognize or mirror your own inherent value. They undoubtedly were aware of it but attributed it to something other than who you were as a human soul. The inability to recognize their own inherent value makes it very difficult for parents to accept its implicit presence in anyone else, even their own children. As a result, you got a clear message that value was achieved in certain ways, by meeting certain standards. If you didn't meet those standards or engage in the prescribed activities, you came to believe you were not as valuable.

From then on, you measured your value according to those standards. The real problem, however, is that you came to see yourself as something other than your soul nature. Value is an essential part of that nature. When you are experiencing yourself as the true nature of the soul, you have value and you *are* value. When you are identified with something other than your soul nature, you do not experience having value, much less being it. So ultimately, it was giving up your recognition of your true nature that cut you off from knowing your own value.

Your judge has developed many different standards and beliefs about the parts of your life that are valuable, but its overriding principle that has dominated your life is that you are not intrinsically valuable. You must get value in ways other than just being who you are. As long as you believe this, the judge will have a strong influence over you. If you don't accept the judge's position, then your task is not to learn how to value yourself but to understand why you don't see your own inherent value. You don't have to make something happen. You simply need to be curious and explore the fact that you value anything but yourself. Each time you turn toward something else as the source of your value in the moment, you must ask why. How did you learn to value something else more than your own being?

Life Lessons

Stephan always had a passion for building things, so it was natural that he would make his living as a cabinetmaker. He loved what he did and preferred working with his tools and his transformations in wood more than almost any other activity. Stephan felt incredibly blessed that people would pay him for doing something that he found so rewarding. His judge agreed: "You are one lucky person, and it sure helps that other people are tuned in to how good you are at this stuff." His value in life felt synonymous with the joy he felt in crafting wood into new living forms.

Stephan was only twenty-four when he won his first major award in a national cabinetmaking competition. His internal judge was happy: "Hot shit, Stephan, it's about time the world caught on to what you do!" His work was featured on the cover of two trade magazines, and his reputation spread across the country. He was now in great demand and soon realized there was no way he could fulfill all the requests for his work. This was a new and unsettling experience. For the first time, he could, and even felt obliged to, charge high prices for his work. "Hey, what's the problem? This is what you've been waiting for," said his judge. "Appreciation and the money to show for it."

But how should he choose which jobs to accept? His judge debated with him every step of the way. Should he select those that were most interesting to him? "Maybe, but let's not be too hasty in making decisions." Stephan had never paid attention to the people who bought his work, much less to where his pieces might end up being placed or seen. Should he consider only those jobs that would make more money or garner more attention? Knowing what was important didn't seem as simple and clear as it used to.

Stephan was intrigued by an offer from Richard Gibson, a hot upcoming Hollywood star, though he was intimidated at the thought of dealing with someone with that much fame and money. But he managed to put in a call to Gibson's agent and arranged to talk to the star himself. After he and Richard hit it off on the phone, Stephan had the courage to make a request: "I would like to come see where my piece would go so I can choose the appropriate wood and style to match your house." Richard was happy to oblige, and the agreement was completed. Stephan felt clearer in himself from this interaction; he hadn't lost his self-worth in the face of fame and wealth, while recognizing the value of his own experience and capacity. His judge tried to put a different spin on what he'd done: "Smart move. You really showed him who's boss. Can't let them know you are intimidated by all that money."

After that, Stephan decided to work only for high-profile customers. This satisfied the part of him that liked recognition and financial rewards; he came to believe these meant his work was of good quality. He hadn't realized before that the approval of important people affected his sense of value. As the years passed, he felt certain that his reputation was established and would carry him through tough times.

Three years later, the fashions of the wealthy took a sudden turn, and handcrafted wood was out. Within weeks, his reputation was more of a hindrance than a help. Stephan's pieces were taking so long to do because of their high-quality craftsmanship that few people were willing to wait for one. Orders were canceled, and Stephan started to get anxious. For a single man, this was bearable, but Stephan had recently married, and his wife, Pam, was pregnant. His judge was not very sympathetic: "Great timing—getting married just when the bucks run out. But, hey, are you going to let the whims of the rich and famous continue to run your life? Let's get real. Enough of these fancy, arty pieces. Start turning out furniture. It's time to make money."

Stephan went into a major depression. For the first time in his life, he was questioning his self-worth: his work and its success had always been what was important to him. Almost overnight, he was no longer a success, the money was drying up, and he wasn't sure whether his work had any real value. His judge tended to agree: "You aren't good for anything except making furniture, and it's just wood, so get down off your high horse, climb out of your hole, and start making money to support your family." Somehow, it didn't feel right to turn his back on his artistic creativity to focus on utilitarian production. But now more than ever, he *had* to work. He had

to put energy into something that felt meaningless, something that made him feel like a failure.

At the same time, Stephan had come to realize that his life was more than his work. Being a husband and becoming a father were important now, more so than making furniture. While his wife and future child felt priceless to him, he wondered if he was of any value to them beyond the money he could make with his hands. He felt worthless, tired, and withdrawn and had a hard time concentrating. Pam had met him at the height of his success, and he feared her disappointment. He found it difficult to face her, as he tried to hide his internal collapse. Stephan was feeling hopeless and despairing of ever finding a true source of value—value that would feel real and lasting.

In this story, Stephan's life went through many changes in relation to value. Initially, he valued the feeling he got from doing his work. Then, as he became more professionally successful, he began to value the rewards of his work: money, reputation, and a sense of worth based on the attention of others. At one point, he affirmed his belief in his own capacities, but that belief was not tested until his fortune turned. The turning coincided with experiencing a shift in value from work to relationship and family. The combination was too much for him to integrate, and his belief in himself dissolved. We left him painfully reconsidering his previous ideas about value and not liking what was exposed.

One dimension of maturing is the continual transformation in what we feel is important in life—changes in value. For Stephan, his sense of value shifted from discovering his own capacities, to the rewards he could achieve, to the power he could exert, and eventually to the family he hoped to create. For most people, the focus in early adulthood on capacity, productivity, and possessions (with a healthy dose of concern for the response of others) tends to shift to an emphasis on more internal qualities such as responsibility, caring, satisfaction, gratitude, and support for others. Sometimes, this shift in values, when not fully understood, contributes to the experience of midlife crisis. However, over time, the natural deepening of what is valued creates a greater sense of stability and centeredness in which one feels less at the mercy of life's changes.

The Judge Controls Self-Esteem

Most people's sense of value and self-esteem lacks this inner center; it fluctuates according to the ups and downs of life. Stephan's sense of personal value was completely subject to changes in external conditions: when things were going well, he valued himself, and when the tide changed, he crashed. During the course of his changing fortunes, the judge played a mercenary role. Rather than being a steadying force to ground him as circumstances changed, it cheered him on during times of success and chided him when things went poorly. By the end of the story, his sense of self-worth had yet to develop any internal stability.

The judge mercilessly dictates standards and ideas about what gives you value and what doesn't. It is more loyal to those standards than it is to you. It is convinced that your self-worth can feel secure only if you measure up—and continue to measure up. The judge believes that all will be lost if you don't, so it motivates you, rewards you, chides you, punishes you, encourages you, rails against you, all in an effort to keep you focused on its set of values. If you don't meet the standards or decide they are not important, it tells you that you are worthless. And there is no worse fate than feeling worthless. Thus, your self-esteem is constantly manipulated by the judge. And you accept its verdict, believing that is the only way to avoid feeling a terrifying sense of no value.

The irony is that, though the feeling of worthlessness is painful and disturbing, it does not have the significance the judge says it does. Feeling you have no value does not mean there is something terribly wrong or that you actually have no value; it simply means you have lost touch with your value. You can't *not* have it: you *are* value. It is part of the substance of your soul. But before you can reconnect with your inherent value, you must feel what it's like to have lost touch with it. This is the state Stephan finds himself in at the end of his story. He must feel the despair and hopelessness, the meaninglessness and emptiness. The question is whether he will be able to stop his judge's attacks so he can open to those feelings. The biggest barriers to allowing the no-value feeling are the vicious attacks of the judge telling you how bad and disgusting you are for feeling worthless. But being willing to experience without judgment how it is to feel that you are without value is the doorway to truly valuing who you are.

The True Source of Value

We are now approaching Stephan's final question: What is the true source of value? We have seen that it can seem to come from certain good feelings (capacity, joy in creating new work); at other times from specific activities, possessions, or accomplishments (quality cabinetmaking, money, national award). Sometimes, value seems to arise as a result of meeting social or personal standards (standing up for what you believe) or taking on certain roles in life (husband, father, cabinetmaker). Most often, value seems given to you through the appreciation and approval of those you love, admire, and depend on.

Clearly, you can feel a sense of value from any of these things—or from none of them. What is striking is how easily these "sources" of value change. Value seems completely relative—always dependent on where you are in your life, what you are doing, and how things are going. It is because of your belief that value lies outside of you that you abandon yourself, turn your back on your own truth, and listen to your judge. This belief is the source of the self-betrayal that is revealed as you pursue your process of self-discovery. From this perspective, the journey of inner unfoldment becomes successful the more you are able to value yourself *regardless of what is going on in your life.* You must learn to value who you *are* more than what you do, whom you know, how you feel, what you think, and how you behave. Only in this way will you find the motivation to be yourself fully and deeply, no matter what.

However, the more you are able to recognize and connect with your true nature, the more you realize that there is no action you can take to value yourself. Value is not something over which you have control nor something you can assign to yourself. It is part of the very nature of who you are. What from one perspective looks like a maturing of personal values toward the deep inner nature of things is, from another perspective, simply an uncovering of the truth about reality. As you clear away the opinions, preferences, and judgments about yourself and make contact with the direct experience of being in the moment, you find that the experience of being yourself is inherently valuable and each moment of living is implicitly meaningful.

Stephan gives value to all the external manifestations he identifies with value, without recognizing that he is the source of value. This is the activity of projection, in which a part of one's own experience is disowned and instead experienced as belonging to someone or something else. But that value he projects outward is naturally present in him no matter what he is or isn't doing because it is inherent in who he *is*. His joy in creating is full of value because Stephan is experiencing that joy, and his value infuses the experience of joy. Similarly, his working for famous people feels valuable, his making money feels valuable, and his standing up for his capacity feels valuable because his own value infuses these experiences.

However, Stephan's experience of value is controlled by what he learned growing up: that value is a result of certain external conditions. Consequently, he experiences it only in the context of particular situations and then attributes the feeling of worth or self-esteem to those situations. His history has determined that only in those contexts can he experience his own value.

Knowing True Value

What is needed is to begin to experience value as a state of being you can feel and know in yourself directly. At some moment, you have encountered the distinct flavor of feeling worthwhile, feeling that you matter, that something in your very existence has value. Though it might become apparent in response to some person, event, or activity, this intimate feeling genuinely expresses your true nature regardless of the situation. It arises in the heart as a sweet, velvet liquid like a luscious, amber nectar. Value has a preciousness and a richness that is both light and substantial at the same time. When experienced, this quality gives you a sense of home and a feeling that you have a right to be here because you are made of the same essential substance as everything else in the universe.

By its nature, that substance is of value and must be recognized, supported, and treasured. You realize that the loss of this self-knowing is what causes you such pain as you get caught up in the judge's beliefs about what is worthwhile. The experience of value is intimate and personal; it affirms your being with a pure knowing that you belong and are welcomed by life. To know yourself this way dissolves much of the motivation for even paying attention to the judge. Why bother?

Value is the experience of you as meaningful presence. The more you taste this heart quality, the more you realize it is at the very center of every moment of your life. It is there waiting to be revealed at the heart of every thought, feeling, action, role, or experience that arises out of you. The value remains no matter what form your life takes. It is the nature of who you are.

PRACTICE: EXPLORING VALUE

As we have seen, experiencing value is more about peeling away layers of belief than actively trying to change anything. Your sense of value permeates how you live, so it is useful to bring more attention to seeing through your beliefs about what is valuable. The practice to support this is brief and simple, and best done whenever possible.

Throughout your day, pause and ask yourself: "What am I doing? What am I valuing that makes me do this? Where did I learn to value this? What relationship does this valuing have to my sense of my own value?" Anything you are doing can be taken on several different levels: as performing a physical activity in the moment, carrying out a course of action over time, playing out a role in a social flow, pursuing an intention to make something happen, or even acting to maintain a particular sense of self. Because value is a factor through all levels of experience, you can do the practice in relation to any level. This practice is particularly useful when you are engaging the judge because the judge's power is based on a particular standard of valuation.

An hour later, as Frank and Sue were heading back to the car in the gathering dusk, they discussed what to do about dinner.

Sue began, ❧ "I feel frustrated because I know you won't want to go out tonight since we ate out on Wednesday."

"So, let's see," Frank responded in an amused tone. "You are telling me you want to go out to eat, but rather than just say it and be a responsible participant here, you are making me out to be your father who won't let you have what you want. I know because you made me feel guilty."

❧ "Well, isn't it true that you don't want to go out?" she repeated aggressively, ignoring what he said.

The amusement left Frank's face as he continued walking. "Sue, I'm feeling manipulated here. I don't like your telling me what I am feeling. I don't want to play this game. If I say yes, you win because I'm the one saying no to what you want. If I say no, you win because you get to go out without having to ask for it. What's going on?" He sounded exasperated.

Sue walked on in silence, watching the clouds on the horizon. Then she turned back to Frank. "You're right. I want to go out, and I feel guilty about spending money. I feel ashamed I'm not making enough to stop worrying about it. I guess I'm trying to deal with my resentment that I don't have money, that I'm not able to make money, and ❧ that I married someone who doesn't make enough money either!"

"Damn, woman, no wonder you're angry. I understand. I'm such a po' boy who barely keeps us fed. Why, just yesterday I felt blessed by heaven 'cause I found a quarter on the street. Here, I surely think it's right that you have it." With that he reached in his pocket, pulled out his wallet, and began fishing inside. "Let's see, was this it?" He pulled a quarter out, looked at it, and put it in her hand. "No, maybe this was it." And he put another in her hand. "But it might have been this one." He added that one. "You know, I really can't remember. I guess I'll just have to give you all of it." And he emptied all of his change into her hand.

With a big smile on his face, he looked at her and said, "Maybe it will be enough to go to Burger King."

Sue's judge could not hold still. ❧ *He's making fun of you. You are a sucker if you buy that crap!*

Sue returned Frank's smile. "You know, I keep smelling a judge around here. It's time we leave. And I accept your gracious offer, but I'd rather have a burrito than a burger. How about it?"

20

DEFENDING AGAINST
JUDGMENT

YOU ARE NOW BEGINNING to defend actively against the judge. You have recognized your identification with self-images of both child and parent in the judgment loop and considered ways of loosening those identifications. You have contacted your deep desire not to betray yourself through engaging with the attacks and explored what it might feel like for your true strength to support you. Now is a decisive moment when you can break the loop of attack and engagement and step away from your long history of self-judgment. This step must be taken over and over again. You must find the strength and clarity to defend yourself in different ways, at different times, with different attacks. Now it is time to look more closely at this basic activity of defending: the immediate active steps you can take to repel an attack in order to go on living, growing, and exploring who you are in your life.

Defending is the practice of active disengaging, which is supported by activating your vital survival strength and intelligence. This was the focus of the exercise at the end of chapter 18. Defending is immediate work, whose aim is to interrupt, in the moment, your engagement with self-attack in order to stop it. You use defending during the day as you work and interact with people. You also use it in your inner exploration when a self-attack is making it difficult to stay with your experience in an open way.

Defending is more than just a new version of your familiar inner dialogue. It requires contact with the vitality of your soul and calls upon all the essential qualities you have been introduced to in this book. These aspects begin to form a kind of fluid structure, a living soul presence, that responds flexibly as needed to support the freedom and truth of who you are. For you to act freshly and without judgmental constriction, you must know yourself in a way not defined by your history. You must know yourself as an organic beingness, a living structure of qualities essential to who you are and free of who you have been or what you have done.

In the work on disidentification, it is important to examine the content of an attack, how it affects you, why you believe it, where it came from, and who it makes you believe you are. However, such mental understanding must be in the service of extracting you from the grips of the attack; it is not merely for self-improvement or to make you a better person. To be of transformative value, that understanding must appear at the moment you feel attacked and incite you to break free of your judgment loop and its history. The work of exploring and understanding clarifies the vital need for defending, and defending creates the space and provides the energy for continuing the work of awareness and understanding.

Defending is a conscious act of confronting head-on the attack you are experiencing by bringing your full awareness to the fact of being judged and acting on that awareness. You are attempting to connect with the deepest awareness of yourself at the moment and speak from that place in order to disengage from the judgment. The deepest awareness of yourself may mean you feel trapped and unable to respond; it might mean you believe what the judge is saying and can't imagine anything but agreeing; it could mean you are feeling very tense in your body with a head that is full of cotton; it could mean you are experiencing yourself as a little kid trying to cope with Dad's anger; it might mean you are feeling viciously stung by the attack as if it were a slap in the face; it could mean you are suddenly aware of the absolute absurdity of this voice from the past trying to tell you who you are; or it might mean you are totally fed up with listening to this voice that says the same thing over and over. Whatever the awareness of yourself, you accept the challenge of speaking from that place with the intention of stopping this pattern

of self-attack. There is no right answer or response, except one that
works.

Here are some guidelines, however:

You must be willing to act on your own behalf. This means that
you must do more than simply observe, watch, think about, or
detach from the attack. Even if you create space from the judge by
withdrawal, you can operate freely only within that limited space of
avoiding the judge. This results in a passive, contained, protective life.
There is no freedom for the soul to expand, flow, and unfold spontaneously. You must summon enough energy to step out of the judgment loop *consciously*. The judge has taken over your own inherent
aggressive energy. You must begin to reclaim this energy in order to
take the initiative and act forcefully when needed. And that strength
is most needed when speaking in an active way on your own behalf.

This strength can take different forms, but the underlying sense
is of aliveness and a focused energy. It may manifest as the clarity to
distinguish between self-attack and seeing the truth, the courage to
say what is true for you, the expansiveness to agree with the judge
without feeling wrong or guilty, the burning desire to stand your
ground, the intensity to stare the judge down, the indignation at its
condescension and disrespect, or the power to cut through the bullshit with humor and a sword!

**The statement should be short (no more than ten words), direct,
and conclusive. Speak as though you expect to say nothing more.**
In other words, you are speaking in order to end the interaction—
that is, the engagement with this inner voice (even if another person
said the words that set off your self-judgment). The form the statement takes is not important: it could be a question, a statement, an
exclamation, or even a sound. The one exception on length is the
exaggeration disengagement described later in the chapter and used
by Frank in this chapter's episode; extended talking can be a way to
hijack the judge's momentum and stop the attack.

**If you attempt to reason with the attack, it is almost guaran-
teed that you will remain engaged.** In other words, if you respond

by arguing, denying, justifying, challenging, explaining, or compromising, you are engaging the judge. You have implicitly accepted its right to judge you, and you are simply looking for a favorable verdict: you are hoping to win. In defending, you do not try to win, you simply intend to stop and then let it be known you have stopped. In fact, the desire to beat the judge is one of the hardest motivations to overcome in order to truly disengage. You have to be willing to give up the game of win or lose with your judge and get on with being you. In defending, the content is largely irrelevant; what is important is the fact of being attacked. You recognize that it *is* an attack and that what you want most at the moment is to be free of it.

Planning a response almost never works. What works is being in the moment and responding spontaneously—ideally, surprising yourself. Don't think about it too much; the worst that can happen is it won't work and you'll still be where you were before and you can try something else. Often, you will find the judge saying, "Oh, you can't say that; that's _____ [stupid, attacking, inappropriate, off the wall, dumb, and so on]." That inner response is another attack trying to keep you engaged and is often an indicator that what you were about to say *will* work—in fact, is exactly what is needed. Remember, a good defense is not a reasonable response to the attack but a break from what is expected, something that catches the judge off guard by not playing its game. This will often mean speaking out of character for you, as your normal pattern is to be engaged.

With these four guidelines in mind, let's look at a simple example of defending.

> Roger has a fortieth birthday party for himself and invites a number of good friends. At the party, he gathers everyone together to tell them the amazing things that have happened in his life recently, how scared and excited and alive he has felt. After the party, he hears his mother's voice in his head saying, "You'll be sorry you did that because no one likes to listen to someone talk about himself and make himself important. You made yourself

look very self-centered." This is a familiar refrain, after which he normally feels depressed and guilty for days and avoids seeing or talking to any of those friends for fear they are judging him. This time, however, he stops what he is doing, feels the collapse happening inside, the tight chest and held breath. He feels the joy and excitement he felt during the party draining away as if it were a dream from which he is waking up. Roger feels an ache in his chest and anger in his belly. Before he knows it, he says to the voice, "How dare you shame me. Shut up!"

Recognizing the Shift

This brings us to the shift that occurs when active defending works. The shift *is* the disengagement, and it's internal. You may notice it as it occurs or only afterward when you become aware of feeling different. What does it feel like? Common experiences are of a sense of release (the holding, tension, or pressure is gone), space (more room to breathe, look around, or move), quiet (the multitude of voices in the head is gone), energy or lightness (the depression, heaviness, or deadness has lifted), or presence (being extended into the past or future stops, and you feel right here now). On an emotional level, it may be experienced as feeling self-assured, separate, disoriented, or not caring about the voice even if it's still there. Be aware that not all experiences of the shift are necessarily pleasant, such as feeling alone, expanded, disoriented, or empty.

This shift in your sense of yourself is the actual experience of disengagement. Just as it has been important to feel and understand the depth of engagement with the judge in order to truly want to disengage, so it is vital to learn to recognize and value the disengagement when it has happened. This may seem obvious, but it is not. When you are strongly oriented toward seeking a change in the judge or the content of its attacks, you may not initially value the shift of disengagement. This is because it may make no change in the judge or the content of the attack. On the other hand, the judge and the attack may disappear in the moment. Regardless of what happens with the judge, *you* are where the action is. The shift changes your sense of yourself and your relationship to the judgment so the attack is no longer effective. You are no longer susceptible to being judged. That is what is important, but only experience will help you actually believe it.

Life Lessons

Hannah had been working for some time on her ability to support herself in her relationships with men. She wanted so much to have a committed relationship that she found it very difficult not to become compliant and passive in the face of anything a man might do or say to her, in the hope that he would like her and keep calling. Recently, she had met someone new whom she enjoyed a lot. They spent one afternoon together at his place and afterward made tentative plans to have the next date at her place a week later, on a Monday holiday. She checked in with him midweek, and he confirmed his desire to connect but said he couldn't make a definite time because he was trying to schedule something else first. That was fine with her, and they made a phone appointment for Monday morning to finalize the plans.

He didn't call as he had said he would, so she finally called him and asked what was up. He sounded surprised and replied that because she hadn't wanted to make definite plans, he figured she wasn't really interested, and he had made other arrangements. Hannah was shocked and normally would have collapsed at that outright attack, giving in to her own judge declaring *that* it was her fault for (1) not getting him to commit earlier, (2) not having seen what a jerk he was sooner, or (3) acting so self-protective that he lost interest (her judge's catchall complaint!). She could feel the momentum of this familiar self-attack that would overwhelm her and allow her to avoid how hurt she actually felt by his heartless behavior. This time, however, she was not going to engage her judge. Instead, she pulled herself together and said simply that she was quite upset at his statement and very hurt by his disregard for what had actually happened. She made it clear that she did not appreciate his actions at all. He began to justify himself, so she told him she had nothing further to say and hung up. She still felt hurt but noticed she did not feel in the hole of self-attack that was so familiar after an incident like this. Because she did not get hooked by her judge, Hannah felt grounded in herself and experienced a surprising clarity in her own state of being.

One other thing to be aware of about the shift: You may recall that your internal attacks developed as a protective mechanism to keep you away from powerful, painful, or overwhelming feelings (rejection, hurt, betrayal, weakness, helplessness, hopelessness, grief, even joy or passion). By engaging the judge, you stopped moving toward those specific feelings. Now, as you learn to disengage, be aware that you are not necessarily going to feel great even if you are no longer under attack. What may arise is the original feeling that your judge was protecting you from. For example, guilt provoked by an attack may be protecting you from the hopelessness that will arise if you stop feeling guilty.

This is often the biggest challenge in truly defending: you must honestly want the truth of your own experience more than you want to avoid pain or feel pleasure. These will always lead to the familiarity of engagement. The truth supports who you actually are, but it is often difficult to be with as you peel away the layers of your inner life. With care, guidance, and the support of the various qualities of your essential nature, you have the capacity as an adult to be with your own truths one step at a time in a way you could not be as a child. This is what is necessary in order to be truly yourself.

Methods of Defending

What follows are some forms that defending could take, followed by an example of each. The judge's activity is aimed at blocking contact with the freedom and expansiveness of the living soul. So each form points to a way of tapping into the dynamism and aliveness of who you are now, unconnected to your history. All are possible as defenses against self-attack as well as external attack. Only one or two disengagement forms would be appropriate in any given situation. Which one depends on the context and nature of the attack and on your tendencies in terms of engagement. If the attack is serious and rational, humor might be a good defense. But if you normally engage with the judge by sarcastic counterattack, then humor is probably not a good choice because it is too close to your familiar engagement patterns.

1. **Aggression:** Fuck off! Shut up! Stop! Leave me alone! Because attacks are aggressive acts, reclaiming that aggressive strength is vital. As indicated earlier in the chapter, the mobilization of aggression is a fundamental, difficult, and highly effective defense for stopping a self-attack. *Strength* is the particular soul quality that fuels this defense. (Chapter 11: Frank; chapter 18: Sue, Paul, exercise; chapter 20: Mary.)

2. **Indignation:** *How dare you speak to me that way!* A close cousin to direct assertion, indignation is righteous anger with the additional feeling of outrage at the judge's lack of respect for your dignity or anyone else's. (Chapter 20: Roger.)

3. **Truth**: *That hurts me* or *It scares me when you talk that way. Stop it!* Simply speaking your own truth in the moment may break the engagement, and it works well combined with the assertion disengagement. The point here is that your awareness becomes focused on your own experience rather than on the content of the attack or the presence of the judge (either of which means engagement). Your soul is in contact with *truth,* and your words support that, giving life to this defense. (Chapter 20: Hannah, Mary; chapter 22: Sue.)

4. **Humor:** *I only let bullies say that to me.* This approach is not to accept the seriousness of this judgment business. The power of humor is in its ability to break through the expectations and assumptions inherent in engagement with judgment. Mental functioning cannot maintain its established pattern when aliveness is activated through the experience of spontaneous laughter. Humor draws on the soul's *joy* and *strength* to fuel its challenge to self-attack. (Chapter 13: Frank; chapter 20: Mary.)

5. **Agreement:** *You're right. I don't know what I'm doing.* This may sound like getting involved with the content. And it is if you are hooked by it—if you accept the statement as a judgment.

The defense, however, is simply to defuse the attack by acknowledging the content without accepting the negative valuation. In fact, this can be a very effective defense because the judge's power depends on your feeling judged or bad about how it describes you. If you have enough *strength* and *acceptance* to allow what is true, or even what might be true, in the content of the attack, this defense can be a simple acceptance of the judge's observations without taking on any blame. (Chapter 20: Jeff, Mary; chapter 6: Frank's dish washing.)

6. **Exaggeration:** *Yes, I'm the dumbest* (use an adjective appropriate to the attack) *person in the whole country.* Defending with exaggeration is a more energetic form of agreement: claiming the negative quality as something you are strange enough to enjoy, and so the attack ends up giving you energy. Remember, your attacks get most of their power from causing you to reject yourself. So this disengagement relies on *acceptance* and *joy* as a ground for its effectiveness. (Chapter 20: Frank.)

7. **Exposing the judge:** *Who cares what you think?* or *Who are you to judge me?* This is basically calling a spade a spade and not accepting the authority of the judge or its right to make any kind of pronouncement about you. The more you have a sense of your own *value* and the *strength* to align with it, the more conviction this defense will have. (Chapter 20: Mary; chapter 22: Sue.)

8. **Surrender:** *Now you've made me feel guilty.* This response is basically an acknowledgment that the judge has made you feel exactly what it wanted to. You are surrendering any effort to change that and at the same time describing the activity of the judge rather than believing that it means there is something wrong with you. This defense draws on *personal will* and *strength* in accepting the power of the attack without becoming identified with the feelings. (Chapter 20: Frank.)

9. **Disinterest:** *Thanks for the advice. I'll have to think about it.* Here, as with number five, you don't fight the content but consciously stay neutral and actively end the interaction.

Again, *personal will* and *strength* provide the groundedness needed to stay connected to your intention of not engaging. (Chapter 23: Frank.)

10. **Changing the subject:** *Have you ever seen such a great shirt?* With this response, you are not engaging *and* you are actively placing your attention elsewhere. By connecting with your own *spaciousness* and *strength* to shift your attention away from the attack, this defense refuses to allow your awareness to be controlled. (Chapter 8: Frank.)

11. **Compassion:** *If I'm really acting that way, it must be painful for you.* This is focusing on where the other is coming from rather than on yourself, as the judge wants you to. This response generally requires considerable disidentification and *strength* not only to avoid getting hooked by the attack but also to put yourself empathically in the judge's shoes and feel the discomfort or concern underneath the judgment. To act from *compassion* can bring healing to an inner battleground, and it is the approach most likely to transform a relationship filled with judgment into one characterized by openness and communication. (Chapter 20: Jeff; chapter 24: Sue.)

12. **Breathe and sense:** *Breathe but do not support the attack internally or externally.* Practice sensing your arms, legs, and belly to keep yourself grounded as you experience the attack. This defense activates *awareness* and *personal will* as supports for its effectiveness. (Chapter 5: Frank; chapter 9: Sue.)

13. **Active visualization:** *Picture in your mind taking some action that halts the attack.* This strategy uses *strength* energy without needing to externalize it. For this to work, you must let yourself feel the effects of your imaginary action such as explosion, dismemberment, or machine gun blast. The object is to reclaim your sense of power and control over your process. Anything goes, but don't let the judge make you feel guilty for seemingly violent behavior. You're only destroying images! The goal is not to get caught up in revenge but to free your own energy and feel the freedom. If macabre acts do that, fine! (Chapter 18: Sue.)

In all of these means of defending, the words themselves only provide a sense of what the defense is. The actual disengagement occurs
inside you on a gut level. If you feel this shift, the particular words and
form of response will often take care of themselves. If you don't feel
it, saying the words won't necessarily get you there, but they can help.
This skill doesn't develop overnight; it takes practice. The most
important thing is to start doing it, even if it doesn't always work.

Disengaging Rather Than Engaging

Let's now look at a couple of examples of someone being attacked.
The first scenario demonstrates staying engaged, the second successfully defending against the attack.

> Jeff was at his desk paying bills when his wife, Louise, called from
> the bathroom, "Why can't you ever clean the bathtub after you
> take a bath? It looks like a pig had a field day in here. You never
> consider the fact that someone else lives here!"
> "How do you know I was the last one to use the tub?" Jeff
> barked back.
> "How do I know? Well, you did take a bath last night,
> didn't you? And I've been at work all day. Who else would it be?"
> Jeff tried a different comeback: "Yeah, so what! How many
> times do I have to clean your hairs out of the drain so I can take
> a shower without having to stand in warm water up to my
> ankles!"
> "You know, you are an asshole!" came the disgusted reply
> from the other room.

As he listens to Louise, Jeff is hearing his own judge's internal
attack that he blew it, proof that he is a slob and selfish. He starts by
rationalizing that maybe he is being falsely accused and then shifts
to counterattacking her. He stays engaged, and so does she.

Now the same interaction with Jeff defending:

> Jeff was at his desk paying bills when his wife, Louise, called from
> the bathroom, "Why can't you ever clean the bathtub after you
> take a bath? It looks like a pig had a field day in here. You never
> consider the fact that someone else lives here!"

"I did enjoy my bath. Sorry I left a mess. I'll clean it up as soon as I'm done here," Jeff replied.

"Never mind, I'm already doing it." Louise was not to be denied her suffering. "How come I'm the only one who takes responsibility for having a clean house?"

Jeff sat feeling the angry pain in her comment before asking, "Would you like any help?"

"No. I work best alone," came the swift reply. There was a pause, then Louise said, "But thanks anyway."

This time, Jeff focuses on the problem Louise brings up rather than the veiled accusation behind it, thus avoiding getting engaged with the judgment. He defends by agreeing with his wife's assessment of the problem but not the implication that he is at fault. Louise, though, does not give up easily and attacks again, taking on the victim role and pulling for Jeff to feel guilty. Again, he defends himself by avoiding challenging her blanket generalization (this would be the obvious rationalizing engagement) and by avoiding taking on the guilt. He basically exposes her ploy by offering to help, a compassionate response. This makes it clear he will not get involved with her self-righteous suffering but will respond if she is truly in need. She gets the message.

Next, we have Mary dealing with a self-attack:

Mary had recently stood up for herself in a new way in an intimate relationship. After nine months of putting up with complaints and dissatisfaction from her partner, she finally came out and told Joyce to leave if she found the relationship so disappointing. "I do not have to listen to your attacks on me any longer. This is who I am, and if I'm not what you want, take responsibility and get out." Joyce felt attacked and hurt and refused to talk to her for several weeks. At first, Mary felt strong, centered, and proud of herself for taking a stand, but after a week with no word from Joyce, she began to feel lost. About that time, the unmerciful attacks from her judge started.

"It was about time you stood up for yourself. But how could you have been so blind to have not seen what was happening earlier? You should have done this the first month! How come you put up with her whining for so long?" Her judge harped on her every spare moment.

Mary would try and reason with it. "Look, I've never been able to say anything like this before. I think I deserve a little credit, don't I?"

"For what? For finally having the guts to act halfway like an adult? How old are you, and how many years have you put up with this kind of treatment from partners? And don't forget six years of therapy!"

"Well, I kept hoping if I tried hard enough to please her, she would start appreciating me and not complain all the time," pleaded Mary.

Her judge was not impressed. "Why should people appreciate you when you act like a child? You didn't deserve anything better because you thought it was your fault. You make me sick."

"You're right. I can't believe how bad I am. I have been a total wimp to put up with this kind of treatment from others. I think I deserved every bit of it. I hate myself."

Mary has expanded into new and unfamiliar territory by defending herself against Joyce's attacks. But separating from Joyce does not separate her from the attacks of her own judge. The judge is putting her back in the familiar territory of self-loathing to distract her from the feeling of loneliness. At first, she rationalizes in an attempt to get some sympathy from the judge. She wants her judge's support for what she has done. When this doesn't work, she finally absorbs the attack and collapses into self-hatred. Whatever expansion had happened in her interaction with Joyce has been completely lost.

Now, let's see what happens if Mary disengages.

. . . At first, Mary felt strong, centered, and proud of herself for taking a stand, but after a week with no word from Joyce, she began to feel lost. About that time, the unmerciful attacks from her judge started.

"It was about time you stood up for yourself. But how could you have been so blind to have not seen what was happening earlier? You should have done this the first month! How come you put up with her whining for so long?" Her judge would harp on her every spare moment.

After trying to ignore its relentless badgering, Mary responded with frustration, "Hey! I don't need your complaining at me any more than I needed Joyce's. So leave me alone."

"You want me to leave you alone? You are alone enough already. And it's all your fault. You always pick losers to be in relationship with."

"I do. You're right."

"Well, what's your problem?"

"I'm slow."

"You're slow? . . . Of course, you are. That's why decent men are never interested in you."

"Boy, you are boring. You sound just like my mother. Go talk to her. I'm busy." Mary laughed as she felt herself being prodded with a broom the way her mother used to do when she thought Mary was making fun of her.

"You are getting way out of hand, young lady. You better watch your step or you will really get into hot water. You need me. Nobody likes an independent bitch!" Her judge was on the defensive and fighting for its life.

"Shut the fuck up!" roared Mary in her mind. There was silence as she felt the heat and intensity of her own strength. She felt space inside and around her and once again was aware of feeling lost and lonely without Joyce around. But the strength felt nourishing. Feeling strong and lonely was a new combination and definitely preferable to being attacked.

This time, Mary does not buy into the content of what her judge is saying to her. After passively not engaging doesn't work, she defends herself by exposing the judge as doing the same thing Joyce did. She speaks the truth about how annoying and unhelpful its comments are. This only stirs it up more. Next, she defends with agreement, upsetting the judge's timing—and still it persists. Humor is next, as she recognizes the way her mother talked and acted toward her. When her judge viciously attacks again, she summons her own aggressive energy to silence it. This brings her back to being centered in herself, which means feeling the loss of the relationship with Joyce. Now, though, she has space from her judge so she can feel lonely without feeling bad about it.

Remember, inner and outer judges are often persistent: they won't give up easily. If you defend yourself, they may attack again. If they do, defend again. Sometimes, you may find that no matter how often you say the words, or how many different approaches you try, disengagement will not happen. This may mean you are not yet ready to separate from the self-image (you feel too identified with the hurt or angry child to let it go). Nevertheless, practice is valuable for observing your process and seeing what keeps that attack active in your life.

Your ability to defend actively and immediately against an attack—stopping yourself from engaging the judge—directly supports bringing peace and quiet into your inner life. Inner stillness will never arise without a commitment to disengaging.

POINTS TO REMEMBER

- Defending is the practice of active disengaging, which is supported by activating your vital survival strength and intelligence. Its aim is to interrupt, in the moment, your engagement with the attack in order to stop it.
- It is important to examine the content of an attack, how it affects you, why you believe it, where it came from, and who it makes you believe you are. However, such mental understanding must be in the service of extracting you from the grips of the attack; it is not merely for self-improvement or to make you a better person.
- Defending is a conscious act of confronting head-on the attack you are experiencing by bringing your full awareness to the fact of being judged and acting on that awareness.
- Just as it has been important to feel and understand the depth of engagement with the judge in order to truly want to disengage, so it is vital to learn to recognize and value the disengagement when it has happened. When you are strongly oriented toward seeking a change in the judge or the content of its attacks, you may not initially value the shift of disengagement.
- The shift changes your sense of yourself and your relationship to the judgment so the attack is no longer effective.
- As you learn to disengage, be aware that you are not necessarily going to feel great even if you are no longer under attack. What may arise is the original feeling that your judge was protecting you from.

- This is often the biggest challenge in truly defending: you must honestly want the truth of your own experience more than you want the comfort or familiarity of the engagement.
- Sometimes, no matter what you try, disengagement will not happen. This may mean you are not yet ready to separate from the self-image (you feel too identified with the child or the judge to let it go). Nevertheless, practicing is valuable for observing your process and seeing what keeps the attack active in your life.

GUIDELINES FOR DEFENDING

- You must be willing to act on your own behalf.
- The statement should be short (no more than ten words), direct, and conclusive. Speak as though you expect to say nothing more.
- If you respond to the content of the attack, it is almost guaranteed that you will remain engaged.
- Planning a response almost never works.

EXERCISE: THE PRACTICE OF DEFENDING

Defending is a practice. You must *practice* it. Unfortunately, it is difficult to do this by yourself except when real-life opportunities arise. The following exercise is a start at developing a sense of what it feels like to defend effectively. It is best done with a friend who is willing to help. You could also try it with a tape recorder. The exercise is similar to the one at the end of chapter 18, but it will take you beyond simply accessing your strength in the face of an attack with generic statements. You can now develop the capacity to respond specifically and to be aware of the shift of disengagement.

Choose a familiar self-attack and give the statement to your friend to deliver to you as if he or she were your judge. That person's task is to support you by simply and clearly delivering the statement to you as if he or she meant it but without exaggerated malice or negativity. The words of the attack will do the work needed. There are four simple steps in working with this attack:

Step 1. *Hear and feel the statement.* Notice your engagement on an experiential as well as a content level.

Step 2. *Take a breath.* This step is probably the most important, as it will help you connect with yourself in the moment. If you have been practicing sensing your body, that can be an additional part of this step. Experience yourself breathing and being in your body at that moment.

Step 3. *Respond.* Follow the guidelines listed above: short, direct, spontaneous. Remember, what defends you is as much the energy and commitment in your response as the content of your words.

Step 4. *Check yourself and see if you are aware of a shift from how you felt at step 1.* Remember that a shift will manifest as some kind of change in how you are feeling—physically (less tension, easier breathing, more energy), emotionally (feeling lighter, less depressed, more determined), or mentally (thoughts disappear, the judgment becomes silly, the attack loses relevance for you). If you felt a shift, perhaps you disengaged. You can check this by seeing whether you still feel involved with or affected by the attack. If you do, try again. The shift might not immediately feel as if it deals with the attack because it doesn't provide an answer, but if it shifts your relationship to the attack, this is at least a first step in defending.

If your response worked, you can try a different attack. If your response didn't work (which is common in practicing), have your partner deliver the attack again and go through the steps again. Keep practicing until you find a response that truly defends you. Be aware that you may not be ready to separate from some deep attacks on your own. This is normal.

If you are using a tape recorder, tape yourself delivering one of your attacks. Repeat it several times in a row with pauses in between. That way, you can pause the recorder after each delivery and practice responding.

Frank and Sue sat on the porch with their burritos and beers as the evening sky filled with colors from the setting sun. The neighborhood was quiet now, and the air was still surprisingly warm. They ate their food in silence, enjoying the chance to rest and be engaged in a simple, satisfying activity like eating. They both felt a sense of relaxation and plenty of time. No rush. And what was particularly unusual was that they didn't need to talk. They were clearly aware of each other as they were aware of everything from their food to the flowers on the porch, from the first crickets chirping to the reds and golds in the western sky.

As they sat, the sky gradually darkened until all the flaming color was gone and a rich dark blue band arched over the horizon where the sun had set. It was harder to see their food, but neither Frank nor Sue felt any need to see.

Frank was amazed at how incredibly sensual it felt to wash his mouth with a swig of beer and feel the subtle burning of the carbonation and the slight bitterness of the brew as it slid down his throat. It felt like such a rich complement to the textures and flavors of the burrito. He found himself savoring even the feeling of chewing itself—the way the muscles in his jaw worked and his tongue pushed the food around in his mouth.

Sue looked at Frank and caught his eye. They gazed at each other without any feeling of needing to communicate and without any discomfort. It was satisfying just to be there with each other and the summer evening.

Frank noticed that he felt very peaceful and still inside as he continued eating. He was aware that the darkness seemed to bring a similar quiet to the air around them. He found he was totally contented with this slow, relaxed, and very attentive process of having dinner. There was none of his usual rushing to down his food or the need to talk, think, or read to fill up the space. In fact, he was amazed that he could hardly remember ever really experiencing eating before. It was not about the kind or even the quality of the food or how it was cooked; it was about the actual experiencing of eating. Or was it really about the stillness inside him? That stillness seemed to outline every movement, every sound, every sensation with a hissing quiet. The inner quiet felt like a blanket that absorbed any familiar sense of himself, leaving only awareness and the activity of eating.

21
PEACE

ONE CHARACTERISTIC OF DAILY life that increases and decreases in intensity but never seems to disappear is a sense of busyness or constant activity. It is common to experience the nonstop quality of external activity, but equally pressing is the activity of the mind—the agitation, restlessness, preoccupation, dialogue, and busyness of one's inner world. In fact, the possibility of a truly quiet mind seems like a dream for a future vacation, retirement, or enlightenment. It is hard to imagine having no thoughts, no concerns, no worries, no plans, no regrets—just stillness inside like the quiet in the desert or the mountains. Some people would question why one would want such a state; others spend much of their life searching for a taste of that inner stillness.

There *is* such an aspect of your true nature—a sense of inner peace—but you seldom have a conscious experience of it. Your inner busyness is obviously a major obstacle to your ever encountering such an inner quiet. And as you might guess, a primary player in maintaining inner activity is the judge. How often do you find the judge appearing with some comment or concern just as your mind is beginning to settle and rest? And how often is the content of your mind an ongoing engagement with the judge in one of those endless loops of attack and defend?

When Everything Stops

Inner peace is a sense of total stillness, with no activity, no movement, no sound. But more than that, there is no desire or need for activity, movement, or sound. The stillness is like a thick blanket of total quiet. Have you ever been engrossed in an activity and suddenly been interrupted by a loud noise? Or in a conversation on a cloudy day when the sun suddenly broke through and shone onto the table in front of you? In either case, the interruption of sound or light may have broken your busyness and created a space, a pause, a moment of suspended time. Everything stopped, and suddenly you were aware of subtle sounds: breathing, the clock ticking, electrical hums, birdsongs, your own heartbeat.

At those times, you usually pause only briefly before plunging back into your conversation or activity. However, if you were to stay in that suspended moment, you might notice a deep stillness that envelops everything. It is as if your familiar focus and involvement vanished and all that remains is your awareness of exactly where you are and what is happening. You become aware that you are not thinking, not planning, not remembering, not worrying, not imagining: none of your familiar mental activity is occurring. Because your usual sense of self-recognition depends on familiar inner dialogue, when it stops, *you* seem to disappear. The world continues to be there, but without your doingness, will you continue to be? Everything seems very quiet, though you notice that sounds are there as usual. In fact, your hearing seems more acute, and the sounds are distinct and clear-cut against the background stillness.

At this point, the mind generally kicks in again as you metaphorically shake your head to get the familiar thinking engine going. You feel compelled to reestablish where and who you are, what you were doing, and what needs to be done, in an effort to pick up where you left off. The stillness is gone, and you are back to "normal."

Stillness is a close cousin to the quality of spaciousness we explored in chapter 17. They are the two sides of the coin of natural mind. The mind feels free and alive and awake when filled with space; when peace comes, the mind becomes so still it almost disappears. Spaciousness is light, airy, open, and empty. Peace is open, still, quiet, and full of a palpable presence. Space feels as if everything were gone, no barriers remain, and you could see forever. Peace feels like a smooth, dense blackness that descends and dissolves everything, leaving only the serenity of complete darkness. Spaciousness is daylight in the mind, and peace is night.

Stillness and Judgment

The judge is not at all interested in this kind of stillness in which the mind stops. The judge only exists in the mind and its activity. No mind means that the judge loses all its control, so it attacks such experiences as dangerous if they last for more than a moment.

"You will get nothing done if your mind stops because you will forget what you are doing. . . . You will look and sound like a fool when there are no thoughts. . . . A blank mind means you are stupid and dumb. Besides, if you were to stop completely, you might never get started again. . . . You will wander around like an idiot and be taken advantage of and humiliated by everyone. . . . Vigilance is required at all times. You cannot afford to really relax your guard ever. . . . Peace is an illusion—and a dangerous one."

The judge gets much of its power from your early experiences of being expected to think and produce words. It is not uncommon for a child to have an empty mind when he is absorbed in playing and interacting with his world. But too often your *awareness* of having no thoughts came at very unpleasant times, such as when you were expected to answer an adult's question, or you needed to remember something important, or you were so scared or upset you couldn't talk. In those situations, you may have been looked at disapprovingly, accused of hiding something, blamed for not learning, or reprimanded for being disrespectful of elders. Seldom would anyone recognize or appreciate the experience of an empty mind with no answers to what seemed like irrelevant questions.

A blank mind thus became associated with being stupid, feeling lost and alone, or experiencing fear and humiliation. So as an adult, the moment when your thoughts stop becomes a dreaded experience. It is at least embarrassing and at worst potentially damaging if it happens in situations in which you are expected to produce. Because of this, it is easy for the judge to keep you away from such moments of no-thought. The consequence is that your negative associations with empty mind cause you to reject a basic element in the experience of inner peace.

However, if you challenge the judge's position—and allow yourself to stay in the quiet—you begin to feel the stillness as peacefulness that permeates everything. Time seems to stop even though things like breathing, looking, and listening continue to happen. It is like the timeless feeling when you step outside late at night and look up at a star-filled sky and feel the overwhelming, expansive quiet. You find a sense of palpable mystery everywhere, as if everything has been soaked in the color of midnight. How mysterious that everything is still here and operating as usual, but without thoughts directing, connecting, and obscuring the silence.

The Mystery of Peace

Is it possible to talk when you are not thinking? Can you recognize objects without thinking about them or labeling them? How can things move when the world seems full of stillness? These are the mysteries of essential peace. It is as if all the mental compartments for reality were stripped away and the world is washed clean. Everything looks simple and immediate—no different than before but somehow more naked, more mysterious, each thing unique in its own beingness. The sense of being here in the present moment is palpable, and it becomes clear that remembering, labeling, comparing, and defining are activities of your mind, not aspects of reality itself.

One of my first experiences of the power of stillness occurred while I was driving across the deserts of Nevada. I remember sitting inside my car, with the windows rolled up and the familiar sound of the engine and the radio, watching the dramatic, barren landscape. I was not prepared for what happened when I stopped the car and got out. The silence was overwhelming. I could hear the sounds of insects and occasional birds, but the predominant sense was of a thick silence that I could almost feel on my skin. I had previously thought of silence as simply a lack of sound, but in the desert, it was clear that silence is actually audible. It affects the eardrums and perhaps the whole body. In fact, it was so powerful in erasing my previous familiar car world that I almost jumped right back into the car. The intensity of stillness was so unfamiliar to me, it was a bit spooky when I first encountered it in such a dramatic form. Only after several minutes of standing in that world of open space, bright light, and silence did I relax and begin to feel affected very deeply by the stillness and peace.

Inner stillness is felt as true peace, so deep and restful that you feel as if you can breathe fully for the first time. At last, you can just be present without reservation, with no agitation inside—no judge evaluating, comparing, criticizing, or analyzing. This peace has power—the power to erase inner agitation and dissolve your familiar mental preoccupations, including identifications with the judgment process. Inner peace leaves nothing behind—nothing but simple being. Not being *someone* or *something,* just being. You are that being, that stillness—alone in a deep, refreshing quiet.

PRACTICE: BEING WITH THE STILLNESS OF THE NIGHT

Find an opportunity to experience the quiet of nighttime. This could be either late in the evening after your house and/or neighborhood has gone to bed and the only activity is the refrigerator, the clock, and the electric lights or very early in the morning before the human world and even the sun are awake. Find a comfortable place in your house or outside on a porch or in the yard where you can simply sit and listen and feel the stillness of the night. Notice how you feel and what you are thinking. Especially notice if you feel affected or touched internally by the sense of quiet and aloneness.

Sue finished eating and went inside to see what was on TV. She wasn't sure if she wanted to veg out in front of the tube, but she had a hard time imagining doing anything else. Now that she was relaxed and quiet, she felt the need to be entertained. She hoped maybe Frank would join her so she would feel less guilty.

After finding that a movie neither of them had seen was about to start, she went to find Frank. Standing in the doorway, she watched him sitting peacefully in the dark, finishing his beer. He looked as if he could stay there forever, and she began to get a little anxious. "*What About Bob?* is on TV soon. We never saw it. You wanna watch it with me?"

"Watch TV? What's that?" Frank was shifting gears. ✆ "Oh, come on, Sue, I can't believe you would even suggest something like that when we have been so real here. TV is so fake and passive; it's for those who can't tolerate real life." His voice felt like a knife coming out of the dark, and Sue felt stabbed by his judge's condescension.

"You're one to talk about the TV! You get so righteous when it comes to what's 'real' and what's 'shit.' I feel like shit right now because of the way you look down on me; so shut up!" Sue could feel herself on the verge of tears but was determined to hold herself together.

"Wait a minute," said Frank. "I wasn't trying to attack you. ✆ It just feels like you're trying to run away from something real here and lose yourself in the tube. What else could it be?" The righteous tone in his voice was still there.

Sue felt weak in the knees but committed to not caving in. As she took a breath, she began to feel some of the inner strength and heat she had felt in confronting her own judge on the hike that afternoon. This time, she didn't yell. Her voice was calm and controlled when it came out but carried a distinct sense of power: "It seems you think you are my judge. Well, you're not. No one gave you the right to judge me, so shut up!"

Silence. Sue felt very alone as she stood rooted in her own truth. Between her and Frank, a vast empty space had opened up. She couldn't feel where he was or what he was thinking. But at that moment, she didn't care, and she began to feel a little sad. As she remembered to breathe, Sue was able to relax inside and realize she was still here and the world hadn't ended. She spoke into the dark before turning to go back in, "I'll be in the living room watching if you want to join me."

22

AFTER THE JUDGMENT IS GONE

❧

YOU HAVE NOW LOOKED in detail at the judgment process: how you feel attacked by the judge, how you betray yourself through engaging the attacks, and how you can actively defend yourself against those attacks. Your goal throughout has been disengagement—the experience of stepping out of the judgment loop altogether. This is a natural movement that results from disidentification with the inner experience of judgment—no longer identifying yourself with the particular self-image that hooks you into the attack.

We spoke in the last chapter of the internal shift that occurs with disengagement, but we haven't considered all the implications of the shift. Generally, the experience of the shift is pleasurable because it brings a release from the limiting self-image—as if you were finally taking off a tight suit you had been wearing all day. This release is often accompanied by a sense of spaciousness, energy, or inner quiet. However, other, more unsettling aspects of the experience of disengagement arise as you practice defending yourself. In particular, disengaging brings the experience of feeling alone.

Separation and Aloneness

To disengage actually means to create a sense of separation. We have been talking about the judgment loop as an internal dynamic focused on maintaining an inner relationship with the other (judge, adult, parent). So to break out of the loop means first and foremost stopping that relationship—not modifying it or changing its emotional tone but actually stopping it. Disengaging separates you from the other and, more important, from the experience of being in relationship. This can be dramatic and unexpected. With no inner relationship, you are alone.

Such aloneness may be painful or frightening because you associate it with isolation, abandonment, helplessness, or loss. These are the feelings you originally had as a child when you felt the loss of relationship to your parents. It will be uncomfortable to stay with this aloneness because it means having to tolerate difficult feelings. The tendency is to do something to make the feelings go away—a desire that has the same motivation as the original impulse toward engagement. This undermines the disengagement and draws you into the loop again because engagement seems preferable to the aloneness and its painful associations.

On the other hand, aloneness can feel intimate and quiet without feeling lonely. With no pressure or demands from anyone, you can be at ease—fresh, open, and spacious. Just you inside, being simple and uncluttered in your experience. You are aware of yourself, and you are not concerned with anyone else. No one is in your psychic space. You are alone, so you can relax your constant attention and guardedness.

It is a great relief finally not to have to worry about what anyone else is thinking or feeling about you—about what you do, how you behave, or what you feel. Throughout your life, consciously or unconsciously, this has been a predominant concern. You grew up learning to put a great deal of energy into tracking the judge in others for signs of disapproval, rejection, discomfort, anxiety, or disappointment. Even when others are not around, the same process goes on internally with your own judge. This is your familiar reality.

The inner state of aloneness is, in fact, so unfamiliar that, in general, people find it uncomfortable to stay with. To have the feeling of no inner dialogue and no internal sense of expecting or seeking another's response may feel like too much freedom, too much quiet, too many possibilities. Real aloneness like this is closely related to inner spaciousness and essential peace. In reaction, judgments such as "What about your mother or your lover? Don't you care about what they think?" or "Now what are you going to do with no one around to help you?" may arise. These effectively end the solitude through the reappearance of the judge. To maintain the aloneness thus requires repeated disengaging.

Aloneness with Another

We have been speaking of the internal aloneness that arises when the judgment process is only in relation to yourself. However, if you are interacting with someone when you feel attacked (especially if you feel attacked by that person), upon disengaging, it will feel as though you were separating from that person—perhaps even ending the relationship. Yes, you wanted it to end in its limiting, judgmental form, but you may not have anticipated what it would feel like if the disengagement were successful.

If the judgmental behavior of the other person is an unusual occurrence and you are successfully confronting it through defending yourself, the disengagement will separate you from that specific attack without damaging the ongoing relationship with that person. Defending yourself in this case will tend to clear the air and allow the relationship to return to a more familiar ease and openness. However, when you disengage from a long-term pattern in a relationship, you are separating from the ongoing relationship as it has been defined. If you are successful in defending, you have stepped out of the assumptions that have defined how you and this person relate. Suddenly, you are there and the other person is there, but the relationship is no longer there: there is nothing in between. No conversation, no words, no images—as if an empty space suddenly appeared between you.

Remarkably, you are now simply present with another human being with no images clouding the air, no familiar patterns of engagement interfering with direct and immediate contact with this other being. This may be a moment of delight and freshness, enjoyment and relaxation. Or it may be an acute encounter with the unknown. Who is this person when you don't have a relationship with him or her? Who are you when you don't know what your relationship is based on? At this moment of disengagement, the opportunity exists for contact without relationship, not unlike what you feel when first meeting someone. If you have a history with this person, the challenge is to relate without returning to and getting lost in the "relationship." Is it possible simply to be present, open, and in touch with the reality of each moment?

Reengaging

Staying with a connection that is this immediate and undefined is often intolerable either for the other person (who may take the disengagement as rejection) or for you. It is not easy to have empty space in a relationship, especially if it was not mutually desired. The first reaction after defending yourself is most often a desire to fill up the space, to "repair" the gap that just opened up between the two of you. This usually manifests as wanting to back down from the disengagement you just achieved in order to "reconnect"—in other words, to reengage. This can happen even before you stop talking, by adding a rationalization or counterattack at the end. For example: "I don't like it when you say that to me. Stop it! . . . But I don't want you to take it personally; I'm kind of upset today." The trailer after saying, "Stop it!" is a rationalization that reengages you with the attacker. Or, "You have made some good points about the way I do things . . . but you always act so self-righteous I don't know why I should take you seriously." This time, the use of agreement as a method of disengaging is followed by a counterattack for a successful reengagement!

Because defending is difficult to execute and disengagement is hard to maintain, reengaging is common initially and not to be considered a sign of failure. It is merely a stage in learning. Again, the task is to recognize what you are doing and have compassion for your own process. Even without verbal reengagement, you may be reengaging internally to avoid feeling the separation caused by the disengagement. Notice that. If you find yourself still thinking about an interaction you disengaged from—how you could have done it differently or better, how well you did, how you can't tell if it worked, how you still feel angry, and so on—the likelihood is that you have reengaged. Recognizing that, you have the possibility of stopping the reengagement activity and experiencing the space, the discomfort, or the aloneness you were avoiding.

Self-Evaluation

You may be wondering how you can assess your progress *without* reengaging: when you want to know how you have done, it's easy to fall back into the old belief that the judge is best equipped to assess you. What other inner resources do you have to turn to for accurate feedback? Answering this question requires distinguishing self-evaluation from self-judgment.

Let's look at self-judgment. How do you end up feeling when you consult with the judge? You either feel good about yourself or bad about yourself. Instead of asking the judge its opinion, a more helpful question to ask yourself is: "Do I feel more open to the truth of my situation?" Remember, a judgment is a statement of evaluation that implies an assessment of your value or worth and is felt as a rejection of your present state. What else can you get from the judge except more judgment?

What you are looking for is help in knowing whether the disengagement worked and how it could work better, not an assessment of your worth or value. This means keeping the sense of your personal value separate from the evaluation of your functioning. This the judge cannot do because it believes that your value is always conditional. Furthermore, it is not interested in the truth.

To evaluate your progress objectively, you must wean yourself from the judge by learning to draw on your own direct experience. What did you feel after disengaging? How did that feel in relation to how you felt before? Did the disengagement work for you? To answer these questions without activating self-judgment is not easy. For instance, one of the most common responses to such questions is "I don't know." This is a perfectly appropriate response. If you have been depending on your judge to evaluate your performance, your feelings, and your learning, to wean yourself will require tolerating the unknown. You will need to gradually learn to rely on a source you have had difficulty trusting—your ability to discern truth in your own uncensored experience.

There is nothing wrong with not knowing. It is necessary to allow not knowing so a true letting go of the judge can occur. To reject your experience of "I don't know" will only send you back to the judge. This movement of rejecting uncertainty and not knowing is often experienced as self-doubt. Be careful; this is often another form of reengagement. You must learn to trust that you can hang out with not knowing long enough to begin to recognize the elements of your own experience. This becomes your personal source for determining where the truth lies and discovering for yourself what works and what doesn't.

Not Knowing Yourself

Having examined the aspects of aloneness and not knowing, we return to the fact that true disengagement means separation. Initially, you experience this as separation from another if that person was experienced as the attacker (and often this will be a close friend or intimate from whom you do not want to be separated). Eventually, you realize that the separation is, in fact, from your judge, which you have projected onto the other person, and from your own self-image. In other words, it is separation from who you have taken yourself to be. Either way, it can be scary and uncomfortable.

What is it like to let go of your self-image of being a helpless or deficient child? Or to let go of your sense of being in control and knowing what's going to happen? If you let go of your *idea* of who you are, who are you? And who is the person you are with, if not the judging or critical adult you are seeking to please and have like you? How will you relate if you are not depending on certain ideas and images of what is taking place? All of these questions are important, and you must answer them from the truth of your own experience.

In Session

Meghan was feeling a strong contraction in her solar plexus that blocked her ability to take a deep breath and ground herself. She kept forcing a large inhalation and shifting her position in an effort to make her upper belly relax. When I asked her why she was struggling, she realized she didn't like the contraction, and her judge told her it meant there was something wrong with her: "You're cutting yourself off, and you must be trying to hide something. You should be ashamed." Meghan realized she *was* feeling ashamed, and that was why she was trying to force the relaxation. It didn't work.

I encouraged her simply to allow the contraction and go with it, breathing as shallowly as her body seemed to want to. (This is a physical variant of the exaggeration disengagement, in which you claim as valuable a quality the judge considers negative and wants you to reject.) As she did so, she felt as if she wanted to stop breathing, to squeeze herself into a very small space and disappear. She felt like a young child in pain. The contraction spread to her arms and legs and was very uncomfortable. However, after a few minutes, she felt her whole body beginning to relax as if melting. There was no effort involved this time since the body itself was ready to release. Meghan began to feel quite settled in herself and after several minutes said, "I feel like not talking at all." I encouraged her to go with that feeling.

As time passed, she became quite visually focused on me, though she kept looking away. She seemed uneasy. At one point, Meghan closed her eyes but soon opened them again as if to see what was happening with me. When I asked her what her experience was, she said she was finding herself preoccupied with visual contact, even though it wasn't comfortable to look directly at me. As we explored the situation more, it became clear that after disengaging from her self-judgment, allowing the contraction to release itself, and then feeling the silence of her own presence, Meghan felt the lack of familiar self-image/judge relationships inside. Unconsciously, she projected this sense of separateness on our relationship and became concerned about having no connection with me. This meant that it was too uncomfortable to stay with her own experience of presence and silence because it seemed to threaten our connection—hence, her desire to make eye contact. As she recognized this, Meghan was able to settle into her own stillness once more and trust that we were still in contact.

Remember, when you acknowledge the truth that underlies the engagement being acted out—that you are not a child and the other is not your judge—you allow contact with yourself minus those images and ideas. Only through such contact is it possible to discover your true knowing of who you are. At the same time, you open up the possibility of authentic contact with (and for) the other person. The other person might or might not join you in that more truthful place.

Opening to the Truth

Disengaging from self-judgment is done specifically so that you can be in a place of greater self-truth. Having defended against your judge, you have the space and safety to be present with your experience, free of rejection, prejudice, or blame. This may mean being with either the content that was embedded in the attack or an experience the attack was keeping you away from. For instance, in the first case, if you have attacked yourself for hurting someone, defending against the attack will allow you to consider your hurtful actions in a more open, compassionate way. Such safety is necessary to explore the truth of why you acted the way you did, which leads to understanding rather than guilt. In an example of the second situation, disengaging from a self-attack about not planning an outing perfectly may lead to an unfamiliar feeling of joy and enthusiasm about the experience you are embarking on. This reveals that the attack arose to keep you from feeling such expansion. Either way, disengaging can bring more contact with the truth and greater self-understanding.

Disengagement is not a knife for cutting the judge out of your life, though the impact of the judge on you will likely diminish. It is not a method of changing the way others treat you, though this could be a by-product. It is a process of recognizing the truth of what is occurring inside you as you go about your life. You feel pain and disconnection from yourself because you have identified with ideas of who you are, constructs based on past experiences, and self-images that limit your ability to be present and act from your full humanity. To see and experience this, and then act from your deeper humanity, is to disidentify from those images and disengage from the self-deception and suffering they cause. Disengagement is a vital element in freeing you for the adventure of discovering the truth of who you are.

POINTS TO REMEMBER

- The release that occurs after disengagement is often accompanied by a sense of spaciousness, energy, or inner quiet. However, other, more unsettling aspects of the experience of disengagement arise as you practice defending yourself. In particular, disengaging brings the experience of feeling alone.
- Such aloneness may be painful or frightening because you associate it with isolation, abandonment, helplessness, or loss. These are the feelings you originally had as a child when you felt the loss of relationship to your parents.
- The tendency is to do something to make the feelings go away. This undermines the disengagement and draws you into the loop again because engagement seems preferable to the aloneness and its painful associations.
- If the judgmental behavior of the other person is an unusual occurrence and you are successfully confronting it through defending yourself, the disengagement will separate you only from that specific attack without damaging the ongoing relationship with that person. However, when you disengage from a long-term pattern in a relationship, you are separating from the ongoing relationship as it has been defined.
- The first reaction after defending yourself is most often a desire to fill up the space, to "repair" the gap that just opened up between the two of you. This usually manifests as wanting to back down from the disengagement you just achieved in order to "reconnect"—in other words, to reengage.
- Because defending is difficult to execute and disengagement is hard to maintain, reengaging is common initially and not to be considered a sign of failure. It is merely a stage in learning. Again, the task is to recognize what you are doing and have compassion for your own process.

- To evaluate your progress objectively, you must wean yourself from the judge. This means keeping the sense of your personal value separate from the evaluation of your functioning.
- Weaning yourself from the judge will also require tolerating the unknown. You will need to gradually learn to rely on your ability to discern truth in your own uncensored experience.
- To reject your experience of "I don't know" will only send you back to the judge. This movement of rejecting uncertainty and not knowing is often experienced as self-doubt. Be careful; this is often another form of reengagement.
- True disengagement means separation. Initially, you experience this as separation from another if that person was experienced as the attacker. Eventually, you realize that the separation is, in fact, from your judge, which you have projected onto the other person, and from your own self-image. In other words, it is separation from who you have taken yourself to be.
- When you acknowledge the truth that underlies the engagement being acted out—that you are not a child and the other is not your judge—you allow contact with yourself without those images and ideas. Only through such contact is it possible to discover your true knowing of who you are.

EXERCISE: EXPLORING INTERNAL SEPARATION

Sometime when you are hanging out with a friend, watch the internal pressures you feel to be a certain way. Notice your expectations of the other and of yourself. Do you feel a need to respond to everything your friend says? Do you feel it's important to support the other person in certain ways? Are you looking for the other person to support you in certain ways? Notice moments of feeling pressure to talk when you would rather be silent. These subtle pressures, which we accept as a necessary part of acceptable social behavior, are often maintained by subtle attacks. For instance, your judge may attack you for being unsupportive if you remain silent when your friend makes a self-deprecating remark.

After the time together is over, take a few minutes to write down specific moments of pressure or self-attack that kept you in familiar yet inauthentic territory in the relationship. What prevents you from separating from your own internal standards and judgments?

The wonderful peacefulness was shattered, and familiar Frank was back, all tense and knotted up inside.

   ⧖   *You sure made a fool of yourself. You'd better go and apologize.*
        Oh, shut up!
        Now, now. Just because you're upset, no need to take it out on me.
        You know, you are a pain in the neck.

He hated ending up in this place. It was uncomfortable as hell, and trying to think his way out got him nowhere.

   ⧖   *Yes, I blew it.*
        Well, why did you do that?
        I don't know. I was feeling so real and easy, and then—pow—I'm right back in this goddamn ego stuff!
        You're pretty touchy, aren't you? Was she your mother or something?
        Oh, fuck you. I don't want to talk about it.

Frank tried to breathe deeper, but all he could feel was tension. Nothing to do but let himself be tense and stew in his own juices. He did realize that trying to get or be somewhere else wasn't working. The tension felt like a refusal to be budged: "No. You can't move me. I won't go." Just allowing that realization to come out immediately softened him.

With the softening came the feeling of being a small boy. He could sense there had been fear in the tension. The boy had been scared. Without having to think, Frank could sense that the fear was in reaction to Sue's anger and perhaps even to his own attack of her.

   ⧖   *Well, her anger was justified, and you deserved it.*
        Yes, but so what? I'm more interested in what is going on with my little boy.

The child sense in him was less constricted now but still seemed uneasy. The boy had feelings but seemed reluctant or unable to talk. In fact, Frank had a distinct sense that he didn't know how to say what he wanted. *That sure feels familiar. I just never recognized that the feeling came from such a young place in me.* As he continued to sit and listen, a new feeling arose: the child wanted to go to Sue and be held. As he felt that, it was suddenly crystal clear why he had attacked her. He was uncomfortable with this childish need for contact—his own neediness—so his judge had taken over to make sure it didn't happen.

23
TRUTH

TRUTH HAS BEEN REFERRED to often in this book. What do I mean when I use this word? *True,* when used in contrast to *false,* indicates that a statement corresponds with some verifiable fact or reality. To tell the truth means to speak in accordance with what you know or believe to be real and correct. In this book, truth is the reflection of a direct awareness of your own experience: specifically, truth is a knowing based on immediate contact with reality through your experience. If someone asks me how I'm doing and I say, "OK," very little truth is in this statement because I have said it to complete a social ritual. However, if I were to connect with what I am actually feeling in the moment, I might say, "I don't know" or "Sad and lost." These responses would be more likely to introduce some level of truth into the conversation. From this perspective, social communication is often not about truth telling.

Truth as discussed in these chapters is the direct recognition of realness in the present moment rather than the identification of physical, verifiable facts. The more you are attuned to the truth in your experience, the more you are in touch with and grounded in reality.

How do you know what is true in your own experience? After all, there are many different ways to look at what you are experiencing at any given time. You could look at the physical details of your experience, your motivation and purpose for what you did, the story in your mind about what occurred, how you felt about what happened, and what you believe the experience means, to name a few. Which of these express the truth? Suppose you have a major miscommunication with your partner. The two of you might spend an hour arguing about who said what and in what order, and miss completely the truth of how you felt afterward. Perhaps the most important truth was what you each believed the miscommunication signified about yourselves and the relationship. Either way, the truth of the event is not in the exact order of what occurred, though that may help reveal how the misunderstanding took place.

Many people, philosophers included, would argue that there is no single truth about experience, only a multitude of perspectives, each with its own truth. Furthermore, they would say that it is impossible to determine if one perspective has ultimate truth, because each has its own inherent logic. Certainly, much of your inner dialogue involves expounding on different points of view about what is really true in a given situation. Have you ever noticed that often, just when you have settled on one perspective about what is true, a different voice will pop up saying, "On the other hand, maybe it's really like this . . ." or "But aren't you forgetting such and such?" At these times, you may doubt the likelihood of finding one approach more true than another.

The notion of reality presented in this book is based on the assumption that reality can be known, which means you have the ability to know what is true in your experience. Truth is not something to believe; it is a direct experience of knowing that "Yes, this feels true, feels accurate, feels right." You know truth through a felt sense: a settledness, a solid certainty, or perhaps a shifting or releasing inside you. You relax a little, you breathe deeper or feel clearer, even if you don't like the truth you are experiencing.

This is why you can appreciate someone's telling you how sad you look, even if you weren't feeling it consciously, because a truth you were avoiding is recognized. You instinctively relax the way you were holding yourself and may even find your eyes full of tears. When you experience something as true, it is as if something that was stuck inside is released and begins to move again. You feel a natural opening that allows you to be a little more at home in yourself. You are, for the moment, no longer pretending or hiding or avoiding; you are simply being with what is so. Truth is therefore an indication that you are moving closer to your true nature by being more in contact with your reality. Any given truth has no meaning if it is not seen in that context.

Recognizing Truth

You have within you a capacity to recognize truth. When you consider several possible motivations for why you did something, you usually know which, if any, of the possibilities has more truth in it. This is not a knowing through deduction or accumulation of information but a felt knowing, which you recognize through paying attention to your experience in the moment. The mind can come up with an endless series of explanations or interpretations of your experience, but if you are open to your inner response, you will know which one brings you closest to understanding what is truly happening.

This truth sense is innate but not necessarily recognized or developed. Often, you put more stock in logic, the opinion of experts, or what you read in books than you do in a nonverbal sense of what is true in yourself. "Who are you to know what is really true? You're not an expert. . . . If you guess, you might be wrong. Why not find someone who really knows the answer?" says your judge. But the sense of truth I am pointing to relates directly to your own experience. No one else has better access to your experience than you—if you are willing to be directly in touch with it. This truth sense is not necessarily an ability to know what is true in matters unrelated to you personally. It is not clairvoyance or some psychic power. Its main function is to guide you in being more real with yourself and more in touch with what is real in your life.

This sense of truth can conflict with social consensus or what your partner feels or what your parents believed or even what you felt an hour ago. Because of this, pursuing your truth can threaten relationships and structures you have come to depend on. Truth brings insight, but it is not a means of arriving at rules or standards about life. Neither is it a matter of consensus. Therefore, some people do not find truth useful or interesting even if they are aware of it. You may recognize a clear truth about yourself in the moment ("I need to speak about how much you hurt me"), but if you set that up as an ongoing truth about who you are or what you need, you will cut yourself off from a continuously changing sense of what is true.

Life Lessons

Tony's father died suddenly. A month after attending the funeral, Tony received a copy of the will in the mail from his brother, the executor, asking him to sign off on it if he was not planning to contest it. Tony was stunned to find he had been left a paltry sum compared to his brother, his only sibling. After the first moment of shock, he felt a familiar numbness filling his body, heart, and mind. Once again, he had received only meager recognition from his father, as if he had been merely an attendant in the family long ago, someone passing through who was barely remembered. His judge's voice was almost comforting: "It's always been this way; what else could you expect? Don't forget, you never liked him either."

Not until a friend told him he might be able to do something about the will did Tony recognize his habitual submissiveness in relation to his father. This shifted something, and long-held resentment began to smolder in his belly. During the ensuing hours and days, the anger became a raging fire inside him. He felt furious at his father, his family, and the years of injustice he had borne in silence. His friend's response had exposed the truth of his deeper emotional state, buried under years of rationalized passivity. Scenario after scenario passed through his mind: revenge strategies, lawsuits, scathing letters, hate-filled phone calls, even hiring a detective to spy on his brother. He could scarcely sleep; his obsessive thinking kept pumping adrenaline through his tired veins. It was as if all the hostility locked up inside him since he was a child were now let loose, threatening to drown him in its bilious outpouring. Several times, Tony felt as if he might lose it and become violent; yet something kept him from acting rashly as it simultaneously condemned him to stew in his own juices.

Finally, Tony's practice of inquiry came into play as he found himself asking, "What does it mean for me that this event is happening now in my life?" This question allowed him to experience that what was happening to him now was more important than the memory of what had happened long ago. The truth of his present exhaustion and stress forced Tony to face the overamped state of his body and heart. He realized he felt powerless, weak, and scared underneath the compulsive planning of his grandiose schemes. Unable to fight the helplessness any longer, he gave in. The knot in his belly let go, and suddenly he found himself painfully present.

His body ached, and his heart was sore, but Tony also felt alive and alert. The stories were gone from his mind, and in their place arose a strong desire to take care of business *now*. He felt a willingness and courage to face reality and a dynamic sense of capacity to get the job done. Essential strength infused his soul. Tony had a clear and direct knowing that his powerlessness had been related to the past; he knew this was true because he couldn't change what had happened. His obsessing had been an attempt to deny the weakness but instead had perpetuated it. The moment Tony surrendered to the truth of the feeling, his power to deal with his present situation revealed itself.

He immediately got on the phone to a lawyer who could advise him on the potential for legally challenging the will. The next day, he called his brother and his mother to get their sides of the story. Regardless of the outcome with the will, Tony was clear that he had already won the war in discovering the truth of who he was now in his life.

One of the main reasons you do not recognize or pursue your ability to know the truth (and thereby be in touch with reality) is that knowing the truth in your experience often contradicts your need to maintain certain beliefs about yourself. Sensing the truth can only be a guide for bringing you into closer relationship to reality in the moment. At any moment, if you do not like what you find to be true and you prefer to hold on to a familiar or more acceptable experience of yourself, you will stop paying attention to the truth.

This does not mean your sense of truth is infallible. As you begin to pay attention to your inner reality compass, you will find it affected by your desires, preferences, hopes, and fears. For instance, you may feel that it is true you want an ice cream cone right now.

What you may not recognize is that a deeper truth may be hidden within the truth of that desire. Perhaps you really long for something sweet to soothe an aching heart. If you don't look beyond the surface truth of wanting the ice cream cone because being in touch with the deeper truth would be uncomfortable, then your desire for pleasure will be distorting your truth sense. Through attuning to your sense of truth and being willing to question and remain open to what you discover, you can strengthen your truth-seeking capacity.

This capacity is in fact an aspect of your true nature. Truth is a quality of who you are, separate from any particular content. The more you practice sensing what is true in your experience, the more you can begin to perceive truth as a flavor on its own. It has a very special sense usually experienced as an element of something else: an understanding, a recognition, an insight. This special sense makes you know that the understanding or insight is true. You are in touch with the content of the insight *and* the sense of trueness. This brings a feeling of expansion, of intimacy, of sweetness—a breath of freedom through being more in touch with yourself. To know a fact as true dispels a falsehood that was keeping you distant from yourself. The facts themselves are only the stepping-stones toward experiencing the truth of who you are. That truth is a golden sweet release in the heart, a relaxation into your authenticity.

Truth and the Judge

The judge is not interested in learning the truth; it believes that it already knows enough from the past to run your life. For the judge, the important issues are knowing what to do, how to do it, what might go wrong, and how to keep things from going wrong. The truth is only useful if it will help answer those questions. "You sure feel terrible. Why don't you sit down and explore what's really going on. Maybe if you can figure that out, we can make some change here." The judge's orientation to the truth is to provide you with limited access to it or, if possible, bypass it completely. "The truth might relieve the pain, change something, or help get us back to familiar territory—but a vacation might do just as well, so why go to all that trouble and discomfort?" The judge is aware that it can't control the truth. "The problem with the truth is it often brings up all kinds of stuff you don't want to have to deal with, so better to leave well enough alone."

Truth is your ultimate ally in confronting the judge. Your sense of knowing what is true for you will support your ability to exist free of the judge's influence. The judge can speak through your parents, your teachers, your books, and even your friends. The only thing it cannot speak through is the direct knowingness of your life. The more you know the true nature of your own experience, the more you recognize that it is nothing but truth. The hopes, fears, beliefs, and judgments about your experience are the falsehoods.

The judge itself is nothing but a misunderstanding of what is real. The moment you see your own truth, the judge disappears.

PRACTICE: UNCOVERING THE THREAD OF TRUTH

At least once a day, take a few moments to do an exploration of truth. Ask yourself, "What is the truth of my experience right now?" Remember, the content is less important than recognizing the key element in your experience: the deepest, most fundamental thread of what is happening for you. It might be an emotion that underlies your words and actions but is not being expressed directly. It might be a particular attitude toward what is happening that you are determined to hold on to. It might be an experience in your body that you are trying to avoid feeling. Whatever it is, the recognition will bring some felt response of acknowledgment as you open to more of the truth. Notice how that feels and be curious about how your experience changes in relation to your awareness of what is true.

Sue was twenty minutes into the movie when she heard Frank come into the house. Moments later, he came into the living room and proceeded to settle himself on the couch, with his head on her lap so he could see the TV. She put her hands on his head and stroked his hair while they watched. When the commercials began, he picked up the remote and muted the sound.

"I'm sorry about those comments back there on the porch. They were pretty out of line. It turns out that a young needy child in me was emerging after that quiet time over dinner together. When you asked about the movie, he wanted your attention and to be held by you, but I was not aware of it. My judge protected me from that young feeling by attacking your desire for contact. It blamed you for making me feel vulnerable and so drove you away. Pretty interesting, don't you think?"

"I suppose. It certainly didn't make me feel wanted."

"I know," acknowledged Frank, "but my judge managed to terrify my child as well. My comments were directed at you, but they ended up feeling like attacks on him for feeling vulnerable and needy. Ugghh, that is such an old attitude; it feels almost instinctual."

"I bet that's true for most men," remarked Sue.

The movie had started again, so she turned up the sound. She was more interested in being entertained than carrying on a psychological conversation. In particular, she was interested in snuggling with Frank on the sofa. Sue wrapped her arms around him and settled in to enjoy Richard Dreyfuss and Bill Murray.

After the movie was over, Sue went into the bathroom to brush her teeth while Frank disappeared into the kitchen to do the dishes. ❧ *Well, Sue, it seems like you're back into your before-bed blobbiness. Will any of this day rub off on you?*

Electric toothbrush droning, she looked at herself in the mirror, considering her middle-aged features. It was very familiar to see herself as her judge did: dumpy, uninteresting, aging, and a failure. But at this moment, something shifted, and she clearly felt that that viewpoint was someone else's. In the mirror, she saw a stranger's face.

❧ *You get really disappointed in me, don't you judge? Time for you to go to bed. . . . And please sleep outside.*

Frank finished in the kitchen at that moment, and Sue heard him turn off the light. She had just begun washing her new face when he opened the door to the bathroom and entered.

24
RECAPPING THE JOURNEY

IT IS NOW TIME to review the entire process of disengaging you have been learning. Your work so far has been to see and understand your identification with the judgment process and practice different techniques to help you disidentify from it. Primary among these is actively defending yourself against the judge's attack. However, fully disidentifying from a self-image evoked in an attack may take years of gradually revealing all the ways you are attached to that self-image. When you completely disidentify, the attack stops having any effect on you. You may still be aware of it arising in your mind, but it does not distract you, engage you, or stop you from living your life at the moment. This is the goal of inner critic work—to deconstruct an attack so it is no longer a threat. The ultimate goal is to go beyond defusing specific attacks and dissolve your engagement with the judge and its standards. However, this goal can be reached only through defending against specific attacks, which will allow you to see the larger pattern of self-judgment.

The Structure of Judgment

In review: Three fundamental components are necessary for judgment to take place. You have explored each one as part of the overall process of understanding self-judgment. Undoing the power of the judge ultimately depends upon dismantling each component through understanding the truth about how it operates in you.

First, the judge relies on standards and rules to judge you. These standards are the accepted ground from which the judge operates and gets its power over you. These ideals of behavior are most effective when they are unconscious because you will automatically base your functioning on them without question. When you begin to be aware of these judgmental standards, you find you identify with them as necessary to support your beliefs about yourself. Personal truth seeking over time will reveal that these standards are either false or irrelevant.

Second, the judge attacks you for not meeting its standards. This is the guts of the judgment process—the attacks. Hostile, devaluing statements are the judge's most direct and painful tool for making you conform to its (your own) ideals and standards. More subtle ways include reminders, advice, suggestions, warnings, hints, corrections, praise, flattery, and approval—all based on the assumption that your worth needs to be justified. Actively defending against these attacks is a vital skill rooted in knowing the truth: your value is implicit and not subject to judgment.

Third, the attacks evoke a state of engagement, characterized by rejection or approval. Diminishment, guilt, shame, and rejection are the debilitating effects of negative attacks. Even positive feelings of recognition and approval are the result of an "attack" because they are based on the judge's standards of how you should be. Either way, attacks engender engagement, the judgment loop that locks you into your relationship with the judge. Becoming aware of your attachment to the child and parent self-images in the loop and gradually disidentifying from them are the methods of breaking you out of engagement activity.

The process of judgment is disrupted by undoing any one of these three components. What is most important in the beginning is to stop the attacks. Defending activates strength in you and, over time, many of the other aspects of your true nature. Without defending, you have no room for awareness and understanding to operate. When you do defend against attacks and create space for yourself, it is easier to examine and question the standards you have accepted as necessary until now. Similarly, defending opens up space for contacting the aspects of your true nature, which will support you in looking at your identifications more deeply and without judgment. This will gradually free you from the emotional effects of being attacked.

Later, when you have some grounding in your true nature, the judgment can be stopped at any level: by not accepting standards and rules of self-evaluation, actively defending against the specific attack, or not engaging the attack (in other words, not reacting to the way it makes you feel). When you recognize true nature as your real identity, you no longer identify with judge or child self-images, and the components of judgment disappear.

Disidentification

Disengagement must include actively defending yourself through methods such as those presented in chapter 20, and it must be supported by the long-term work of disidentification. The work of disidentification is based on the practice of being present with the truth of your experience. You don't actually *do* anything to disidentify; you *stop* doing something. You stop identifying with an image of yourself, with anything other than the living true nature of your soul. Of course, this can only happen when you have recognized what you are doing when you identify. And learning to recognize that is exactly what you have been working on: gradually understanding more and more about how and why you identify until you fully understand in your mind, your heart, and your belly that identification with a small, deficient child is a complete misunderstanding. When this happens, you will stop identifying, and the judgment will no longer control you.

Long-term work on disidentification is necessary to bring the deepest transformation in your relationship to your judge and yourself; it takes time to develop a comprehensive understanding of who you are versus who you sometimes take yourself to be. This understanding is much more than mental analysis or recognition; it involves your whole organism, your total being. This complete

understanding is the transformation itself, as identification with anything but the truth of who you are gradually drops away.

The Steps of Disengaging

The process of plunging deeper into your experience requires moving beyond the realm of thoughts and beliefs, which is the world of
the judge. The process you have been working with has been presented sequentially, but it is not a linear process; it does not occur in
neat steps, and it takes place only as more and more of you awakens
to your experience. The following is a summary of the steps involved
in disengaging. You can use it to review what you have learned about
this process. Let it serve as a guide to help the mind participate as
best it can.

1. *Recognize the attack.* Clarify what statement, reference, or implication carried the attack and explore what the judge was saying
   in its most direct ("you" statement) form.
2. *See/feel the effects of the attack.* Are you experiencing loss of energy,
   weakness, numbness, tiredness, contraction, tension, obsessive
   thinking, anxiety, sadness, fear, guilt, anger?
3. *Identify how the judge intends for you to feel through that attack.* Be
   aware of the emotional reaction provoked by the attack—sadness, fear, guilt, shame, hurt, hopelessness, worthlessness—and
   the inevitability of this reaction.
4. *Consider the standard you are being measured against through the judgment.* How do you feel about that standard? Do you believe it is
   true or necessary for you now?
5. *Notice how you are engaging with the attack through absorbing, rationalizing, or counterattacking.* Can you see how that activity keeps
   you away from feeling the true effect of the attack on your soul?
6. *Explore what self-image is evoked by the feelings generated by the attack.*
   How does it limit you? Who was the original judge? Can you
   recognize the person who is speaking to you through this self-
   judgment? How does that image of yourself negate, diminish, or
   limit who you are?
7. *Take definite active steps to defend yourself against the attack.* This is

the aggressive movement toward the freedom and truth of who you are. When your judge attacks you, let it know you don't want its presence or input. If someone else attacks you, speak or do something to clearly separate yourself from the judgment.

8. *Follow what arises after disengaging.* Be aware of reengaging and your concerns about separation, aloneness, and not knowing. Now is the time to attend to any useful information contained in the attack.

Let's look at an example to see how these steps might occur.

In Session

Lois wanted to explore something that had left her feeling disturbed and deflated. Earlier that week, she had opened her mail and found a check for five thousand dollars from her father. She had previously told him that she was looking for a new car but had not asked him for money. The gift came with a note saying, "We knew it would be hard for you to afford the car you wanted, so we are glad to help out. Enjoy!"

Instead of feeling happy as she thought she should, Lois felt uneasy, hurt, and if she was honest with herself, somewhat angry. It didn't make sense, but she felt as if she had gotten bad news instead of good. As Lois paid attention to how she felt, she realized she felt attacked.

The next step was to find out why. When I asked if something in the note bothered her, she said, "Yes, the reference to how hard it would be for me to get what I wanted. That feels like such a familiar dig from my dad: 'You are only a girl. You can't be expected to provide for yourself. You can't make it in a man's world.' He always talked that way and continues to treat me as if it were true."

"So when you read this note, you heard your father's voice through your own judge saying what?" I asked.

"It said, 'You are a helpless, incapable woman.' And that makes me feel like a failure: weak, stupid, ashamed, and dependent on him. It's as if he wants to keep me in my place by sending this money, and then he expects me to feel grateful because he rescued me from my own financial helplessness." Lois's anger was palpable. She paused, and the anger gave way to pain. "You know, what's really sad is that I have internalized that image of myself. I engage with the attack by buying it, believing it's true. Even though I can and do make money and take care of myself in the world, I often think of myself as a dilettante: incompetent, pretending, and ultimately needing a daddy to approve of me, back me up, and take care of me when I get overwhelmed by the big world. I think that is why I have felt deflated since the check arrived. It bears out my worst fear about myself—that I can't be an independent adult."

"Is that how you experience yourself these days, as a helpless child? Or is this feeling something stirred up by this incident?"

Lois considered the question as she recalled how she had felt about herself in recent months. "You know, I have actually been feeling the opposite: more assertive, more sure of myself, and more aware of my own capacity to get things done. But this incident has thrown me back into an old pattern, and that sense of being capable feels far away at the moment."

Many avenues of exploration were open to Lois, but I directed her back to the feeling of being attacked by her father's note. "How could you defend yourself against the statement that you are a helpless, incompetent woman?"

"Just go away! It's not true!" The muscles in her jaw tightened, and Lois looked a little like a pouty child.

I asked her if that worked. She said maybe, but she still felt tense and noticed she was holding her breath. I suggested that instead of trying to contradict the judge, she could let it have its way and ignore the implication of shame and failure. Lois looked puzzled, as if she had no idea what that might be like. I asked her to play her judge and deliver the attack while I played her.

"You are nothing but a helpless, stupid girl who is dependent on me to take care of you."

I grinned at her. "You know, it's so true. I can't do a thing myself. And why should I when I have a father like you who gives me all the money I need?"

Lois looked at me in amazement. My response had stopped her

judge cold. "But that doesn't make any sense. How could you say that? You're just agreeing with the attack."

"Yes, but I am not agreeing with the idea that it means something bad. Who cares what the judge says? The point is to get it off my back. Did that defense stop you as the judge?"

"It sure did. I didn't know what to say. You stole all of my ammunition."

"That's exactly the point. Do you think you could do that?"

"I don't know. I never imagined you could say such a thing. But I like it. I feel all this energy just thinking about it. Go ahead and try me."

"Lois, face it, you will always be an incompetent, stupid girl in need of my help."

"Isn't it great—never having to grow up and always having you there with money in hand? By the way, could I have some more?" Lois couldn't help but laugh as she enjoyed her little joke. Her energy, lightness, and boldness indicated she was out from under the attack.

Lois has been working with her judgmental process for some time, so she is able to bring into consciousness its various components with some ease. Her experience provides a concise example of working through the steps of disengaging outlined earlier in the chapter. As you uncover this process in yourself, you will probably move through the eight steps over an extended period, with only one or a few taking place at a time. For instance, step 7, the active defending, might follow directly on the heels of steps 1 and 2, with the other steps occurring before or after in continuing exploration.

Lois and the Eight Steps

Let's look in more detail at what happened to Lois in this process. In this example, the steps unfold easily for her. She begins with step 2, by noticing how she was feeling and recognizing that her inner experience was of feeling attacked. This was without knowing what the attack was or why she felt attacked by something that her mind said was a great thing: receiving five thousand dollars in the mail! By looking at the specifics of what happened—in this case, the content of the note—Lois quickly uncovers the implicit statement of judgment. She puts it in the judge's words, as "you" statements. This is step 1.

Here, it is combined with an element of step 6, the recognition of the original source of the attack. This recognition was obvious because the self-attack came in an interaction with the person she originally felt judged by, her father. Sometimes, clarifying the attacking statement will immediately bring with it the awareness of whom you heard it from as a child; at other times, you cannot recognize the source, and more inquiry will be needed to reveal it. These first two steps were covered in chapter 4, "Recognizing Judgment."

Stating the attack takes Lois right into step 3, as she feels the judgment's intention to keep her dependent and "in her place" by making her feel weak, stupid, and ashamed. She interprets these feelings to mean she is a failure. This explains why she earlier felt uneasy, hurt, and angry—the reactions to the unconscious experience of failure and dependence. Step 3 is generally a natural result of putting the first two steps together by linking in your awareness the emotional effect of the attack to its actual content. How you are made to feel becomes the basis of the self-rejection provoked by most attacks. This you looked at in chapter 4 as you saw the relationship between judgment and attack.

These first three steps can happen in a few moments of focused attention and investigation, as they did for Lois, or they could take days or weeks to clarify in your daily life. Remember, the judge operates in you unconsciously most of the time—the standards, the attacks themselves, and the way they make you feel. It takes time to uncover the judgment process, just as it took years in childhood to completely submerge it into your unconscious.

Staying with her feelings leads Lois into a recognition of her absorbing engagement with the attack, step 5. This is the material covered in chapter 8, "Engaging the Judge." Later, when I ask her about her relationship to the judgmental beliefs, she sees how engaging with the attack has cut her off from an opposite quality that had been arising in her recently.

Step 4 is touched on only briefly by Lois in relation to her father's judgment that women are incompetent. The implicit standard for her is her father's notion of how smart men are. In response to my question, she becomes conscious that she has been seeing herself recently without this standard and appreciating what she sees. Standards are a central theme in chapter 6, "What Is Judged?"

The self-image the attack evokes in Lois arises next; this is the primary element in step 6. Though, in this session, she does not look at the childhood experience on which the self-image is based, she senses how this belief about herself has colored her perspective on her life in the world. It has kept her from acting with confidence and assertiveness. Chapters 12, 14, and 16 explore the various elements of this step.

Asking Lois whether the child self-image matches her recent experience opens the way for her to shift from being caught up in the "kernel of truth" of the attack's content (her feeling of incompetence) to the deeper effect it is having on her. When her judge speaks through the note, it is psychically sending her back to an early age. She may be attempting to act as an adult, but unconsciously she is experiencing herself as a weak and helpless child who is not smart enough. It is this image of herself—which is continuing unconsciously despite recent changes—that allows the judge's statements to find their mark at the present time.

After Lois remembers some sense of her own truth, I ask her to confront her dynamic with the judge actively through defending, step 7. Remember, all the understanding you gain will have little effect unless you act on it. Everything you have learned about judgment, attacks, engagement, and identification must combine with your own awareness, grounding, allowing, curiosity, strength, compassion, and aliveness to bring about active defending as you practiced in chapter 20. Recognizing that you are being attacked is not enough; knowing how it makes you feel is not enough; knowing the history behind the attack is not enough. You must step out of the judgment loop. This is the real soul work. This is when you actively identify with yourself as other than child or parent. This is when you assert your fundamental aliveness and freedom. This is when you align yourself with the deep longing to be real and present in your life against the self-defeating experience of judgment.

Lois begins with an aggressive defense, but it is too similar to her lifelong strategy of trying to deny her father's assessment of her. The desire to disengage is there, but the method does not free up any of her constricted energy. I suggest using exaggeration as an expansive, nonconflictual defense. This is a much more effective approach for her in breaking up the fixed pattern around this familiar attack. This defense would not work for someone who is still strongly identified with the content of the attack. However, Lois had already explored this issue of dependence many times before and was beginning to feel her own inner support. So with my modeling, she was able to break the spell and embrace the words that had always meant shame and failure to her.

Whether she was conscious of it or not, through this defense, Lois was confronting her deep belief that it is appropriate to be judged for her feelings. She unquestioningly accepted that feeling weakness, helplessness, and stupidity means there is something bad and shameful about her. This is the most fundamental standard exposed in her work.

Step 8 is the only one not represented in this example. It is covered in chapter 22, "After the Judgment Is Gone."

Unraveling Engagement

Active disengagement brings deeper recognition of what is occurring in the judgment loop (who you have taken yourself to be and why and how that affects you). As this happens, you naturally see your own experience in a different light. This affects how you feel about your life and who you are. Deeper self-awareness often stirs feelings of sadness and loss at having been so out of touch with reality. Or it might bring desire and determination to see more clearly in the future. Or it might ignite feelings of indignation and outrage at being made to feel so diminished and deficient in order to maintain some childhood sense of safety.

On the other hand, the greater understanding may also bring clarity, acceptance, and appreciation that you were doing the best you could all your life given how ignorant of the truth you were. When this appreciation for the movement of your own soul arises, more internal space opens up. You will find yourself acting more realistically and being less influenced by childhood beliefs, attitudes, and fears.

The best way to integrate the understanding you develop through observation and exploration is to actively challenge the control of your judge. The direct action of saying no to the judgment loop causes a shift in your internal response to attacks. You will draw upon your own deeper soul resources and in the process integrate those qualities into the sense of who you are.

To fully defuse a specific attack will often take months or years as you live with each new bit of understanding and discover how you can act differently because of it. One of the greatest challenges to this slow unraveling is impatience fueled by the judge itself. The judge will focus on what hasn't changed: "Nothing seems to be different. You will never really change. . . . Nothing is happening, so what good will it do to try? It's hopeless." It is important to know that this process is gradual and cannot be planned out or controlled. Some shifts and changes will be recognizable only after the fact. So be wary of the judge's efforts to discourage you.

This long-term process of disengaging from an attack requires unraveling the identifications that spawned the judgment. This means noticing that the judgment does not reflect reality, understanding how it arose, identifying the beliefs that support it, feeling the emotions involved, and recognizing the impact of having lived according to those beliefs for so long. If you keep at it, the true understanding of your situation will unfold. And as you become more grounded in reality, the whole structure of beliefs, feelings, and behaviors around the specific attack will naturally dissolve.

The final resolution of an attack is usually unremarkable. As you work on a judgment, the attack continues to operate in you, but gradually, its power diminishes, taking less and less of your attention and energy as your capacity for staying present grows, until one day you happen to notice that particular attack has no effect on you anymore. It is irrelevant. You are no longer someone who cares about such a comment. You are free of that attack. It may even seem surprising that it ever controlled you the way it once did. What *is* remarkable is the sense of simple presence in the soul when you are freed from engagement with the judge.

Frank stood and watched Sue as she applied her evening cleansers.

🌸 *You're so good, washing the dishes, cleaning the countertop, and now wait-*
ing for her to finish. But just wait, she'll find something to complain about.
Why do you even bother trying to please her?

Rather than respond to his judge, Frank found himself speaking to Sue. "You should hear the voice in my head. It is so repetitive. I used to think it's me who's boring and mechanical, but I think my judge is the real source of why my behavior so often feels empty and repetitive. That judge is just a lifeless machine. I am here enjoying a simple activity like watching you, and it is determined to make me look at things and react to them in a boring old way. Life is much more interesting if I just ignore that voice."

Sue looked at Frank in the mirror. "It's nice that you want to look at me. I feel a little shy, but I like it." She turned and smiled at Frank, drying her face and looking very open and sweet. "It makes me feel alive and new, not stale and useless like I usually do." She dried her face and then stood in front of him as he was looking at her.

"You know, I felt very alone after telling you to shut up. I really meant it, but it was hard to have all that empty space. I felt lost because I had banished the known part, and what was left between us felt unknown. It's funny, I still sense that empty space, but now it feels more fresh and intimate. It's as if I know you but I don't know you. I know me but I don't know me. That's exciting, and it makes me shy, too—not just because you want to look at me but because I have no idea what you will see or who you are. But it's not scary." Then after a pause she added, "Thanks for watching the movie with me."

Frank took her in his arms and felt her aliveness and his own. It was like a subtle current flowing through both their bodies. He felt them both at a point where the mystery of the universe crossed over into the ordinariness of everyday life. He could think of no better word to describe the feeling than "presence." The room was filled with presence—and so were they. Everything around them, including their own bodies, looked familiar, but at the same time, the familiarity felt like a transparent skin over an amazing unknown mystery. Something rich and subtle and alive seemed to fill everything, and as he hugged Sue, he felt a deep sense of gratitude pouring out of his heart.

25
PRESENCE

❧

IT IS APPROPRIATE TO end this book with the essential quality of presence, for it is the most direct doorway to discovering your true nature. Presence is the experiential quality that makes your soul something more than a gestalt of emotions, thoughts, and sensations. A common element in all the soul aspects described here, presence is available to you at each moment.

Presence is more difficult to define than the other qualities we have touched on because there is no emotional component, no obvious sensation, and no story line associated with it. Presence is the aspect of your experience that cannot be remembered. It can be known only in the moment of experiencing it, for when the moment has passed, your mind recalls only thoughts, images, feelings, or sensations; the presence is gone. Presence is a part of other essential qualities such as compassion and strength, but when you remember experiencing these qualities, you can never reproduce the sense of presence in them. If you could, it would no longer be a memory—a past experience—but a present experience of that quality, an experience with presence.

So this is the paradox: You know presence only when you are experiencing it, and you can only experience it as an aspect of the present moment—hence, the name *presence*. Throughout this book, I have encouraged this awareness by inviting you to be in touch with your experience here and now—to be aware of the present moment. But what does it actually mean to be in the present, to be present, to have presence?

People with Presence

At one time or another, you've probably experienced someone as having "a strong presence." (Presence need not be "strong," but when it is "quiet," it often goes unnoticed.) Perhaps it was a speaker who held you and everyone else in the audience spellbound. Or a guest at a party who drew people's attention and held it just by walking through the room. It is hard to define what "a strong presence" means, but it refers to a quality you can sense. You may sense an intensity in the person's energy or a charisma that draws people or a solidness and substance that underlie surface appearance. In general, this quality is felt regardless of anything the individual may be doing to command attention. In other words, presence is something more than an expression of his conscious intention. It is separate from the glitter and entertainment of appearance. In fact, without presence, all the craft and showmanship in the world are merely show and of little sustaining interest.

If an individual has presence, it means that her *presence* in a situation, simply her being there, has impact. Without doing or saying anything, she affects you. You might not like what she says, be uncomfortable with her tone, or find her clothing distracting, but she has some quality that makes you notice her and stirs something in you. You may have your attention drawn by her striking appearance, her pointed remarks, or her dramatic gestures, but if you are aware of the person herself, it is because of her presence. You don't feel manipulated by her surface appearance to stay interested; your attention is effortlessly drawn to her and not easily distracted. Awareness will naturally rest where there is presence.

The Experience of Presence

Presence in you is the direct, immediate experience of your own existence. It is knowing—with certainty and not indirectly through memory or deduction—that "I am here." Not "I am here because I am aware of what is going on around me" or "I am here because I feel self-conscious" or "I am here because I remember walking into the room." It is not even "I am here because I sense the floor against the bottoms of my feet." You can approximate presence when you are sensing your body—feeling your physical existence in this moment—but even this is indirect. When you sense a part of your body, you are still separate from it. You are sensing *it,* not sensing yourself directly. This is so unless you have the direct recognition that you are sensing *yourself* as you sense your body, that you are "present" in your body as you sense it.

So presence is an experience of the soul beyond thinking, feeling, or sensing. It is direct knowing through being: "I am here because I experience myself actually being here at this moment." It is so simple, so basic, and yet so unfamiliar because you were not taught to recognize or value this way of knowing.

Presence is awareness and hereness as well as knowing. It is actually all three condensed into one inseparable experience of being. The fact that you are here is not different from your awareness of yourself, which is not different from your knowing that you are here. This may sound like wordplay until you experience it and realize that knowing, awareness, and hereness are so obviously one thing (presence) that you forget they are usually experienced separately.

If you know yourself as a person reading this book, without being directly aware of yourself as you read, you are not experiencing presence. If you are aware of the sensations that reading creates in your body but are removed from how that experience *is you,* you are not experiencing presence. If you know you are here reading this book and have no awareness of how that is happening, you are not experiencing presence. Presence is your experience when you are knowing yourself at this moment in the experience of reading.

The experience of presence can happen spontaneously without your recognition. What you notice instead are certain sensations or qualities arising in the field of your awareness. During vigorous physical activity, for example, or after a strong outpouring of emotion, you feel your whole body wide awake with intense aliveness. Or one afternoon, you are captivated by the unrestrained spontaneity of small children playing. Or perhaps you find yourself absorbed in conversation, engaged in a challenging task, or simply resting after a long day, and your awareness is concentrated in the present moment with no sense of past or future. These are moments of presence. Many people are drawn to being in nature because it elicits these moments for them. Nature lovers may not be aware of experiencing presence; they only know that something fundamental in their nature is touched and nourished by the presence of the natural world. The vibrancy and immediacy of a living environment evoke the living presence of the human soul.

These random occurrences of presence are sometimes recognized as special moments and other times seem quite ordinary. Either way, you usually notice the quality of immediacy less than the affect involved (excitement, relief, fascination, concentration, stillness, fear). You have learned to attribute the presence in your experience to the emotional conditions or historical causes of your situation. You have not been taught to recognize yourself as the immediate source of aliveness and realness. All the judge's activity conspires to maintain this outward focus. Cultivating an appreciation of presence means tuning in to *what you are* in these moments of heightened aliveness.

Presence Is an Endangered State

Why is it that something so basic as presence seems to be such a rare quality? One reason is that you were not brought up to recognize or appreciate it. Presence, by itself, often doesn't attract attention; it is simple, ordinary, and unpretentious. Often lost in the rapid-fire barrage of stimulation in modern life, presence is a much subtler quality than hype or drama and does not translate through video or pictures. You really have to open to your inner sensing to recognize it. You must let go your focus on where you are going so you can notice where you are. Sometimes, in situations such as a party, a public event, or waiting in line, you have more opportunity to slow down, relax your goal orientation, and appreciate the power of simple presence in others. As you do this, remember that their presence has absolutely nothing to do with their value or usefulness for you. It does not cause anything or result from anything; it just is.

The second reason why presence seems so unusual is because there is so little of it to be perceived. It is a rare person who has real appreciation for the essential quality of presence, and fewer still know how to cultivate it. This is an interesting fact, given that everyone is born with presence. As an infant, you are little else but presence. Spend a few moments with a baby and you feel it. Whether energetic or quiet, solid or sweet, that presence is palpable. Gradually, you lose that unmistakable quality as you and those around you become more focused on what you look like, how you behave, and what you say and do than on the fact of your being.

The less you appreciate presence, the less it stays with you. Furthermore, if you associated it with feeling unseen, you will unconsciously tend to *avoid* feeling your own presence. The result is that most people are cut off from presence by the time they reach adulthood. Adults who still have a strong presence are often not aware of it or see it as simply part of some personal talent or attribute—such as charm, intelligence, sense of humor, or passion—rather than as a quality in itself. Presence is more than any characteristic of your personality: it is the nowness of true nature, the immediacy that is you, and the life at the center of every experience you have.

Presence and the Judge

The more present *you* are, the more your awareness will rest and flow naturally with your *own* experience. As you have seen, your judge is actively directing your attention away from being here now, into the future and back to the past. Its task is to maintain the familiarity of knowing yourself as you always have, so it resists the freshness and mystery of simply being in the present. When great effort is needed to hold your attention on what you are doing or feeling at the moment, you are knowing yourself through memory; you are not experiencing your own presence. If you were, then your awareness would naturally rest here in the present moment and flow with your experience. To be aware of your immediate experience requires disengaging from the activity of the judge and habitual patterns of attention (such as focusing on how others feel about you) while simultaneously cultivating the experience of your own presence.

Presence is your ultimate ground for confronting the judge because presence includes the knowledge that you exist without reference to any outside source. As long as you believe you need an image of yourself, a belief, an idea, or some information in your mind in order to exist, you will be at the mercy of the judge because it lives on ideas, beliefs, and images. However, the moment you recognize your own existence independent of any mental concept, the judge becomes simply words in your mind, no more significant than the label on your shirt or the length of your toenails. Labels and long toenails can be useful at certain moments and cause problems at others, but they have little relationship to or impact on who you are and what it means to live your life.

Cultivating Presence

Presence is the state of being directly aware of your true nature, that which is not affected by history, learning, or environment. You do not need to know in words who or what you are in order to experience presence. You just need to know *that* you are. Presence is not something you do, nor can you do something to be present. Rather, you learn to recognize what is not presence and what prevents you from being present.

Your work with the judge has been a practice of cultivating both these recognitions. Expanding your awareness develops the ground for experiencing presence. It enhances presence by increasing your perception of your present experience—not only of *what* you are experiencing but also of yourself *as* you are experiencing. As your contact with presence develops, your awareness can expand, flow, and rest with your immediate experience. Awareness and presence work together, deepening your experience of your life and your soul nature. Living from this place of direct contact with your own truth gradually replaces the need for the judge as constant companion.

Everything in this book has been designed to evoke indirectly the quality of presence—through increasing awareness of yourself in daily life and through practices that cultivate your sense of your true nature and its essential qualities. Each practice invokes or encourages contact with a particular aspect of your essence. Because presence is part of every aspect, each practice also cultivates presence. For this reason, there is no further practice for presence itself. Simply continue to deepen your knowing of who you are in your life and what it means to be alive, to be here, and to be you.

FINAL THOUGHTS

YOU HAVE EMBARKED ON a journey of confrontation and self-discovery that will free your soul to unfold its potential. Remember, this book is only a map, a way of orienting to the terrain. It is not the truth in itself but simply a way of speaking about the truth. You bring truth to this material by working with it and making it come alive in your own experience. I encourage you to make use of teachers and therapists to support your process. The perspective and presence of an experienced guide are invaluable in helping you stay on track.

Much more could be said and written about working with judgment. Many aspects become apparent only after years of travel and unraveling your experiences along the way. Two such complex issues have been touched on here only briefly: approval as the positive side of judgment and self-hatred as the primal energetic force that drives self-attack. These concerns lie in the territory of further maps.

As the journey continues, judgment appears in shifting guises. Sometimes, the judge becomes subtle and seductive as it turns you against yourself. Other times, it is a vicious demon: brutal, raw, and totally without disguise. Then again, judgment can seem formless and pervasive, a background fog of wrongness or energy-sapping anxiety. Or it may live completely inside and without words, more alive in your cells than as content in your mind. Instances of feeling so merged with negativity that you are unable to separate yourself are especially disconcerting when you have long been clear about the distinction between you and the one who stirs such self-attack.

But do not be discouraged. However the judge shows up, your

true nature can support you on the journey. The real map is ready to reveal itself inside you. Your soul has a greater intelligence than you can imagine, presenting you with experience you can work with and understand. It is your true support, your true guide, your true nature.

And the ultimate fuel for the soul's unfoldment is love of truth and the mystery of reality. The more this love is felt, the more it generates in the soul a profound sense of self-respect, an appreciation for and valuing of all manifestations of who you are. Self-respect gradually deepens into a personal integrity and dignity, as you recognize that each manifestation is a potential revelation of deeper truth. And each truth can only bring you closer to your true nature, the experience of simply Being. From this place, the judge itself appears as a complex and mysterious expression of the soul, a figure to be unveiled, a door to be opened and passed through as you learn to live without shame in the heart of life.

LIST OF PRACTICES
AND EXERCISES

FURTHER RESOURCES

The approach to working with the judge described in this book is based on a path of self-realization and spiritual development called the Diamond Approach. The work was discovered and developed by A. H. Almaas and is taught through the Ridhwan School. The central practice of this path is inquiry into your own experience to discover the truth of who you are. If you are interested in knowing more about this particular path, you can write to the Ridhwan Foundation, at P.O. Box 10114, Berkeley, CA 94709. The following books and article by A. H. Almaas may be of interest in reference to the judge (superego), the development of the personality, the soul, and essential aspects of our true nature:

Diamond Heart. Books 1, 2, 3, and 4. Berkeley, Calif.: Diamond Books, 1987, 1989, 1990, 1997.

Essence. York Beach, Maine: Samuel Weiser, 1986.

Facets of Unity. Berkeley, Calif.: Diamond Books, 1998.

The Pearl Beyond Price. Berkeley, Calif.: Diamond Books, 1988.

The Point of Existence. Berkeley, Calif.: Diamond Books, 1996.

"The Work on the Superego." Berkeley, Calif.: Diamond Books, 1977.

The Void. Berkeley, Calif.: Diamond Books, 1986.

Other approaches to the judge or inner critic that you might find of interest:

Hal Stone and Sidra Stone. *Embracing Your Inner Critic: Turning Self-Criticism into a Creative Asset*. San Francisco: HarperCollins, 1993.

Richard Carson. *Taming Your Gremlin: A Guide to Enjoying Yourself*. New York: Harper & Row, 1983.

Cheri Huber. *There's Nothing Wrong with You: Going Beyond Self-Hate*. Mountain View, Calif.: Keep It Simple Books, 1993.

Robert Firestone. *Voice Therapy: A Psychotherapeutic Approach to Self-Destructive Behavior*. New York: Human Sciences Press, 1988.

INDEX

control
acceptance and, 91–92
functioning of being and, 91–92
regained by making psychic processes
conscious, 206
counterattack, 100–102, 105–6, 108–9,
113
frustration during, 110
curiosity
brought by joy, 173–74
perceived as bad, 161
practice to encourage, 176

defending against judgment, 59, 112,
239–41, 248. *See also* disengaging
from the judge; self-attacks,
defending against
as active disengaging, 239, 253
exercise for practicing, 254–55
guidelines for, 241–43, 254
methods of, 245–48
recognizing the shift in successfully,
243–44
requirements for, 240–43, 253
defense, 58–59
true, 197
deficiency, experience of
as sign of attack from judge, 61
disengaging from the judge, 206, 222, 248,
270–71, 283. *See also* defending
against judgment; judgment loop,
transforming the aftermath of
aloneness, 263–66, 271
following what arises in, 287
need to fill up space, 271
not knowing oneself, 268
reengaging, 266–67, 271
release, feeling of, 271
self-evaluation, 267–68
tolerating the unknown, 272
vs. engaging with, 249–52
recognizing the shift in successfully,
243–44
requires unraveling underlying
identifications, 293
as separation, 263, 272
soul and, 206
steps toward, 59, 112, 117, 149, 157, 167,
203, 253, 254, 286–87
unraveling engagement, 292–93
weaning from judge, 267, 272
disidentification, 197–98, 222, 240,
285–86, 293

change in perspective and, 200–201
exercise for, 207
parent-child dynamic and, 198–200
visualization and, 200, 203
dynamism, 6

emotions
feeling *vs.* expressing, 162–63
positive, 160–61. *See also* expansion; joy
considered unacceptable, 161–62
suppression of, 163
empathy, capacity for, 6–7
emptiness, feeling of, 212, 213
engagements
avoid effects of attacks, 99–100
in social situations, exercise for
observing, 114
engaging the judge, 103, 112. *See also*
judgment loop
in daily life, 111–12
depression felt when, 110
dissociation and, 53
feeling of, 109–11
frustration felt when, 110
inner engagement, 107–9
modes of, 100, 103, 109, 113
absorbing/collapse, 101–2, 106–7,
113
body centers and, 105–7
counterattack, 100–102, 105–6,
108–9, 113
rationalization, 101, 106, 108, 113
survival of child and, 102–3
perpetuates relationship with past,
103
recognizing, 105, 111, 112, 131–33, 286.
See also judgment recognition
requires person's support, 103–4
as self-betrayal, 217–19, 224
existence, elements of human, 5
expansion, experiences of, 136. *See also*
emotions, positive; joy
exercise for observing self-attacks on,
86
stopped by judge, 84
expectations. *See* standards
experience
acceptance of, 96
judgment of, 13–14
learning from, 83
recognizing the truth of, 35
suppression of, 93, 96
by judge, 83